THE MAGNIFICENT MONTEZ

Lola Montez, Countess of Landsfeld
(*From a lithograph by Prosper-Guillaume Dartiguenave*)

THE MAGNIFICENT MONTEZ

FROM COURTESAN TO CONVERT

By

HORACE WYNDHAM

"When you met Lola Montez, her reputation made
you automatically think of bedrooms."
ALDOUS HUXLEY.

WITH 24 ILLUSTRATIONS

BENJAMIN BLOM   New York/London

First Published 1935
Reissued 1969 by
Benjamin Blom, Inc., Bronx, New York 10452
and 56 Doughty Street, London, W.C. 1

Library of Congress Catalog Card Number 70-91592

Printed in U.S.A. by
NOBLE OFFSET PRINTERS, INC.
NEW YORK 3, N. Y.

FOREWORD

SWEEP a drag-net across the pages of contemporary drama, and it is unquestionable that in her heyday no name on the list stood out, in respect of adventure and romance, with greater prominence than did that of Lola Montez. Everything she did (or was credited with doing) filled columns upon columns in the press of Europe and America ; and, from first to last, she was as much " news " as any Hollywood heroine of our own time. Yet, although she made history in two hemispheres, it has proved extremely difficult to discover and unravel the real facts of her glamorous career. This is because round few (if any) women has been built up such a honeycomb of fable and fantasy and imagination as has been built up round this one.

Even where the basic points are concerned there is disagreement. Thus, according to various chroniclers, the Sultan of Turkey, an " Indian Rajah " (unspecified), Lord Byron, the King of the Cannibal Islands, and a " wealthy merchant," each figure as her father, with a " beautiful Creole," a " Scotch washerwoman," and a " Dublin actress " for her mother ; and Calcutta, Geneva, Limerick, Montrose, and Seville—and a dozen other cities scattered about the world—for her birthplace. This sort of thing is—to say the least of it—confusing.

But Lola Montez was something of an anachronism, and had as lofty a disregard for convention as had the ladies thronging the Court of Merlin. Nor, it must be admitted, was she herself any pronounced stickler for exactitude. Thus, she lopped half a dozen years off her age, allotted her father (whom she dubbed a " Spanish officer of distinction ") a

5

couple of brevet steps in rank, and insisted on an ancestry to which she was never entitled.

Still, if Lola Montez deceived the public about herself, others have deceived the public about Lola Montez. Thus, in one of his books, George Augustus Sala solemnly announced that she was a sister of Adah Isaacs Menken ; and a more modern writer, unable to distinguish between Ludwig I and his grandson Ludwig II, tells us that she was " intimate with the mad King of Bavaria." To anybody (and there still are such people) who accepts the printed word as gospel, slips of this sort destroy faith.

As a fount of information on the subject, the *Autobiography* (alleged) of Lola Montez, first published in 1859, is worthless. The bulk of it was written for her by a clerical " ghost " in America, the Rev. Chauncey Burr, and merely serves up a tissue of picturesque and easily disproved falsehoods. A number of these, by the way, together with some additional embroideries, are set out at greater length in other volumes by Ferdinand Bac (who confounds Ludwig I with Maximilian II) and the equally unreliable Eugène de Mirecourt and Auguste Papon. German writers, on the other hand, have, if apt to be long-winded, at least avoided the more obvious pitfalls. Among the books and pamphlets (many of them anonymous) of Teutonic origin, the following will repay research : *Die Gräfin Landsfeld* (Gustav Bernhard) ; *Lola Montez, Gräfin von Landsfeld* (Johann Deschler) ; *Lola Montez und andere Novellen* (Rudolf Ziegler) ; *Lola Montez und die Jesuiten* (Dr. Paul Erdmann) ; *Die spanische Tänzerin und die deutsche Freiheit* (J. Beneden) ; *Die Deutsche Revolution, 1848–1849* (Hans Blum) ; *Ein vormarzliches Tanzidyll* (Eduard Fuchs) ; *Abenteur der beruhmten Tänzerin ; Anfang und Ende der Lola Montez in Bayern ; Die Munchener Vergange ; Unter den vier ersten Königen Bayerns* (Luise von Kobell) ; and, in particular, the monumental *Histeriche* of Heinrich von Treitschke. But one has to milk a hundred cows to get even a pint of Lola Montez cream.

With a view to gathering at first hand reliable and hitherto unrecorded details, visits have recently been made by myself to Berlin, Brussels, Dresden, Leningrad, Munich, Paris, and Warsaw, etc., in each of which capitals some portion of colourful drama of Lola Montez was unfolded. In a number of directions, however, the result of such investigations proved disappointing.

" Lola Montez—h'm—what sort of man was he ? " was the response of a prominent actor, recommended to me as a " leading authority on anything to do with the stage " ; and the secretary of a theatrical club, anxious to be of help, wrote : " Sorry, but none of our members have any personal reminiscences of the lady." As she had then been in her grave for more than seventy years, it did not occur to me that even the senior *jeune premier* among them would have retained any very vivid recollections of her. Still, many of them were quite old enough to have heard something of her from their predecessors.

But valuable assistance in eliciting the real facts connected with the career of this remarkable woman, and disentangling them from the network of lies and fables in which they have long been enmeshed, has come from other sources. Among those to whom a special debt must be acknowledged are Edmund d'Auvergne (author of a carefully documented study), *Lola Montez (an Adventuress of the 'Forties)* ; Gertrude Aretz (author of *The Elegant Woman*) ; Bernard Falk (author of *The Naked Lady*) ; Arthur Hornblow (author of *A History of the Theatre in America*) ; Harry Price (Hon. Sec. University of London Council for Psychical Investigation) ; Philip Richardson (editor of *The Dancing Times*) ; and Constance Rourke (author of *Troupers of the Gold Coast*) ; and further information has been forthcoming from Mrs. Charles Baker (Ruislip), and John Wade (Acton).

Much help in supplying me with important letters and documents and hitherto unpublished particulars relating to the trail blazed by Lola Montez in America has been furnished me by the following : Miss Mabel R. Gillis (State Librarian,

Californian State Library, Sacramento); Mrs. Lillian Hall
(Curator, Harvard Theatre Collection); Miss Ida M. Mellen
(New York); Mrs. Helen Putnam van Sicklen (Library of the
Society of Californian Pioneers); Mrs. Annette Tyree (New
York); Mr. John Stapleton Cowley-Brown (New York);
Mr. Lewis Chase (Hendersonville); Professor Kenneth L.
Daughrity (Delta State Teachers' College, Cleveland); Mr.
Frank Fenton (Stanford University, California); Mr. Harold
E. Gillingham (Librarian, Historical Society of Pennsylvania);
Mr. W. Sprague Holden (Associate-Editor, Argonaut Pub-
lishing Company, San Francisco); and Mr. Milton Lord
(Director, Public Library, Boston).

In addition to these experts, I am also indebted to Monsieur
Pierre Tugal (Conservateur, Archives de la Danse, Paris); and
to the directors and staffs of the Bibliothèque d'Arsenal, Paris,
and of the Theatrical Museum, Munich, who have generously
placed their records at my disposal.

Unlike his American and Continental colleagues, a public
librarian in England said (on a postcard) that he was " too busy
to answer questions."

H. W.

CONTENTS

LIST OF ILLUSTRATIONS

THE MAGNIFICENT MONTEZ

CHAPTER I

PRELUDE TO ADVENTURE

I

IN a tearful column, headed " Necrology of the Year," a mid-Victorian obituarist wrote thus of a woman figuring therein :

This was one who, notwithstanding her evil ways, had a share in some public transactions too remarkable to allow her name to be omitted from the list of celebrated persons deceased in the year 1861.

Born of an English or Irish family of respectable rank, at a very early age the unhappy girl was found to be possessed of the fatal gift of beauty. She appeared for a short time on the stage as a dancer (for which degradation her sorrowing relatives put on mourning, and issued undertakers' cards to signify that she was now dead to them) and then blazed forth as the most notorious Paphian in Europe.

Were this all, these columns would not have included her name. But she exhibited some very remarkable qualities. The natural powers of her mind were considerable. She had a strong will, and a certain grasp of circumstances. Her disposition was generous, and her sympathies very large. These qualities raised the courtesan to a singular position. She became a political influence ; and exercised a fascination over sovereigns and ministers more widely extended than has perhaps been possessed by any other member of the *demi-monde*. She ruled a kingdom ; and ruled it, moreover, with dignity and wisdom and ability. The political Hypatia, however, was sacrificed to the rabble. Her power was gone, and she could hope no more from the flattery of statesmen. She became an adventuress of an inferior class. Her intrigues, her duels, and her horse-whippings made her for a time a notoriety in London, Paris, and America.

Like other celebrated favourites who, with all her personal charms, but without her glimpses of a better human nature, have sacrificed the dignity of womanhood to a profligate ambition, this one upbraided herself in her last moments on her wasted life ; and then, when all her ambition and vanity had turned to ashes, she understood what it was to have been the toy of men and the scorn of women.

Altogether a somewhat guarded suggestion of disapproval about the subject of this particular memoir.

II

Three years after the thunderous echoes of Waterloo had died away, and " Boney," behind a fringe of British bayonets, was safely interned on the island of St. Helena, there was born in barracks at Limerick a little girl. On the same day, in distant Bavaria, a sovereign was celebrating his thirty-fifth birthday. Twenty-seven years later the two were to meet ; and from that meeting much history was to be written.

The little girl who first came on the scene at Limerick was the daughter of one Ensign Edward Gilbert, a young officer of good Irish family who had married a Señorita Oliverres de Montalva, " of Castle Oliver, Madrid." At any rate, she claimed to be such, and also that she was directly descended from Francisco Montez, a famous toreador of Seville.

There is a strong presumption, however, that here she was drawing on her imagination ; and, as for the " Castle Oliver " in Sunny Spain, well, that country has never lacked " castles."

The Oliver family, as pointed out by E. B. d'Auvergne in his carefully documented *Adventuresses and Adventurous Ladies*, was really of Irish extraction, and had been settled in Limerick since the year 1645. " The family pedigree," he says, " reveals no trace of Spanish or Moorish blood." Further, by the beginning of the last century, the main line had, so far as the union of its members was blessed by the Church, expired, and no legitimate offspring were left. Gilbert's spouse, accordingly, must, if a genuine Oliverres, have come into the world with a considerable blot on her 'scutcheon.

Still, if there were no hidalgos perched on her family tree, Mrs. Gilbert probably had some good blood in her veins. As a matter of fact, there is some evidence adduced by a distant relative, Miss D. M. Hodgson, that she was really an illegitimate daughter of an Irishman, Charles Oliver, of Castle Oliver (now Cloghnafoy), Co. Limerick, and a peasant girl on his estate. This is possible enough, for the period was one when squires exercised " seigneurial rights," and when colleens were complacent. If they were not, they had very short shrift.

Mrs. Gilbert's wedding had been a hasty one. Still, not a bit too hasty, since the doctor and monthly nurse had to be summoned almost before the ink was dry on the register. As a matter of fact, Mrs. Gilbert must have gone to church in the condition of ladies who love their lords, for this " pledge of mutual affection " was born in Limerick barracks while the honeymoon was still in full swing, and within a couple of months of the nuptial knot being tied. She was christened Marie Dolores Eliza Rosanna, but was at first called by the second of these names. This, however, being a bit of a mouthful for a small child, she herself soon clipped it to the diminutive Lola. The name suited her, and it stuck.

While these facts are supported by documentary evidence, they have not been " romantic " enough to fit in with the views of certain foreign biographers. Accordingly, they have given the child's birthplace as in, among other cities, Madrid, Lucerne, Constantinople, and Calcutta ; and one of them has even been sufficiently daring to make her a daughter of Lord Byron. Larousse, too, not to be behindhand, says that she was " born in Seville, of a Spanish father " ; and, alternatively, " in Scotland, of an English father." Both accounts, however, are emphatic that her mother was " a young Creole of astonishing loveliness, who had married two officers, a Spaniard and an Englishman."

It was to Edward Gilbert's credit that he had not joined the Army with the King's commission in his pocket, but in a more humble capacity, that of a private soldier. Gallant service in the field had won him advancement ; and in 1817 he was selected for an ensigncy in the 25th Foot, thus exchanging his musket and knapsack for the sword and sash of an officer. From the 25th Foot he was, five years later, transferred to the 44th Foot, commanded by Colonel Morrison. In 1822, its turn coming round for a spell of foreign service, the regiment moved from Dublin to Chatham and embarked for India. Sailing with his wife and child, the young officer, after a voyage that lasted the best (or worst) part of six months, landed at Calcutta and went into barracks at Fort William. On arrival there, " the newcomers," says an account that has been preserved, " were entertained with lavish hospitality and in a fashion to be compared only with the festivities pictured in the novels of Charles Lever." But all ranks had strong heads, and were none the worse for it.

During the ensuing summer the regiment got " the route," and was ordered up country to Dinapore, a cantonment near Patna, on the Ganges, that had been founded by Warren Hastings. It was an unhealthy station, especially for youngsters fresh from England. A burning sun by day ; hot stifling nights ; and no breath of wind sweeping across the parched

" John Company " troops on the march in India

Her Majesty's Theatre, Haymarket, where Lola Montez made her début

ghats. Within a few weeks the dreaded cholera made its appearance ; the melancholy roll of muffled drums was heard every evening at sunset ; and Ensign Gilbert was one of the first victims.

The widow, it is recorded, was " left to the care and protection of Mrs. General Brown," the wife of the brigadier. But events were already marching to their appointed end ; and, as a result, this charitable lady was soon relieved of her charge.

Left a young widow (not yet twenty-five) with a child of five to bring up, and very little money on which to do it (for her husband had only drawn 108 rupees a month), the position in which Mrs. Gilbert found herself was a difficult one. " You can," wrote Lola, years afterwards, " have but a faint conception of the responsibility." Warm hearts, however, were at hand to befriend her. The warmest among them was that of a brother officer of her late husband, Lieutenant Patrick Craigie, of the 38th Native Infantry, then quartered at Dacca. A bachelor and possessed of considerable private means, he invited her to share his bungalow. The invitation was accepted. As a result, there was a certain amount of gossip. This, however, was promptly silenced by a second invitation, also accepted, to share his name ; and, in August, 1824, Mrs. Gilbert, renouncing her mourning and her widowhood, blossomed afresh as Mrs. Craigie. It is said that the ceremony was performed by Bishop Heber, Metropolitan of Calcutta, who happened to be visiting Dacca at the time. Very soon afterwards the benedict received a staff appointment as deputy-adjutant-general at Simla, combined with that of deputy-postmaster at Headquarters. This sent him a step up the ladder to the rank of captain and brought a welcome addition to his pay. In the opinion of the station " gup," some of it not too charitable, the widow " had done well for herself."

Captain Craigie, who appears to have been a somewhat Dobbin-like individual, proved an affectionate husband and

step-father. The little girl's prettiness and precocity appealed
to him strongly. He could not do enough for her ; and he
spoiled her by refusing to check her wayward disposition and
encouraging her mischievous pranks. It was not a good
upbringing ; and, as dress and " society " filled the thoughts
of her mother, the " Miss Baba " was left very much to the
care of the swarms of native servants attached to the bungalow.
She was petted by all with whom she came into contact, from
the gilded staff of Government House down to the humblest
sepoy and bearer. Lord Hastings, the Commander-in-Chief
—a rigid disciplinarian who had reintroduced the " cat " when
Lord Minto, his predecessor in office, had abolished it—
smiled affably on her. She sat on the laps of be-medalled
generals, veterans of Assaye and Bhurtpore, and pulled their
whiskers unchecked ; and she ran wild in the compounds of
the civilian big-wigs and mercantile nabobs who, as was the
custom in the days of " John Company," had shaken the
pagoda tree to their own considerable profit. After all, as
they said, when any protest filtered through to Leadenhall
Street, what were the natives for, except to be exploited ; and
busybodies who took them to task were talking nonsense.
Worse, they were " disloyal."

As, however, there were adequate reasons why children
could not stop in the country indefinitely, Lola's step-father,
after much anxious consideration, decided that, since she was
running wild and getting into mischief, the best thing to do
with her would be to have her brought up by his relatives in
Scotland. A suitable escort having been found and a passage
engaged, in the autumn of 1826 she was sent to Montrose,
where his own father, a " venerable man occupying the position of provost, and sisters were living."

From India to Scotland was a considerable change. Not
a change for the better, in the opinion of the new arrival there.
The Montrose household, ruled by Captain Craigie's elderly
sisters, was a dour and strict one, informed by an atmosphere
of bleak and chill Calvinism. All enjoyment was frowned

upon ; pleasure was " worldly " and had to be severely suppressed. No more petting and spoiling for the little girl. Instead, a regime of porridge and prayers and unending lessons. As a result the child was so wretched that, convinced her mother would prove unsympathetic, she wrote to her step-father, begging to be sent back to him. This, of course, was impossible. Still, when the letter, blotted with tears, reached him in Calcutta, Captain Craigie's heart was touched. If she was unhappy among his kinsfolk at Montrose, he would send her somewhere else. But where ? That was the question.

As luck would have it, by the same mail a second letter, offering a solution of the problem, arrived from an Anglo-Indian friend. This was Sir Jasper Nicolls, K.C.B., a veteran of Assaye and Bhurtpore, who had settled down in England and wanted a young girl as companion for, and to be brought up with, his own motherless daughter. The two got into correspondence ; and, the necessary arrangements having been completed, little Lola Gilbert, beside herself with delight, was in the summer of 1830 packed off to Sir Jasper's house at Bath.

" Are you sorry to leave us ? " enquired the eldest Miss Craigie.

" Not a bit," was the candid response.

" Mark my words, Miss, you'll come to a bad ending," predicted the other sourly.

III

But if Bath was to be a " bad ending," it was certainly to be a good beginning. There, instead of bleakness and constant reproof, Lola found herself wrapped in an atmosphere of warmth and friendliness. Sir Jasper was kindness itself ; and his daughter Fanny made the newcomer welcome. The two girls took to one another from the first, sharing each other's pleasures as they shared each other's studies. Thus, they blushed and gushed when required ; sewed samplers and copied texts ; learned a little French and drawing ;

grappled with Miss Mangnall's *Questions for the Use of Young People*; practised duets and ballads; touched the strings of the harp; wept over the poems of " L.E.L."; read Byron surreptitiously, and the newly published *Sketches by Boz* openly; admired the " Books of Beauty " and sumptuously bound " Keepsake Annuals," edited by the Countess of Blessington and the Hon. Mrs. Norton; laughed demurely at the antics of that elderly figure-of-fun, " Romeo " Coates, when he took the air in the Quadrant; wondered why that distinguished veteran, Sir Charles Napier, made a point of cutting Sir Jasper Nicolls; curtsied to the little Princess Victoria, then staying at the York Hotel, and turned discreetly aside when the Duchess de Berri happened to pass; and (since they were not entirely cloistered) attended, under the watchful eye of a governess, " select " concerts in the Assembly Rooms (with Catalini and Garsia in the programmes) and an occasional play at the Theatre Royal, where from time to time they had a glimpse of Fanny Kemble and Kean and Macready; and, in short, followed the approved curriculum of young ladies of their position in the far off-days when William IV was King.

Although Sir Jasper had a hearty and John Bullish contempt for foreigners—and especially for the " Froggies " he had helped to drub at Waterloo—he felt that they, none the less, had their points; and that they were born on the wrong side of the Channel was their misfortune, rather than their fault. Accordingly, there was an interval in Paris, where the two girls were sent to learn French. There, in addition to a knowledge of the language, Lola acquired a technique that was afterwards to prove valuable amid other and very different surroundings. If de Mirecourt (a far from reliable authority) is to be believed, she was also, during this period, presented to King Charles X by the British Ambassador. On the evidence of dates, however, this could not have been the case, for Charles had relinquished his sceptre and fled to England long before Lola arrived in the country.

After an interval, Sir Jasper felt that he ought to slip across to Paris himself, if only to make sure that his daughter and ward were " not getting into mischief, or having their heads filled with ideas." No sooner said than done and, posting to Dover, he took the packet. Having relieved his mind as to the welfare of the two girls, he turned his attention to other matters. As he had anticipated, a number of his old comrades who had settled in Paris gave him a warm welcome and readily undertook to " show him round." He enjoyed the experience. Life was pleasant there, and the theatres and cafés were attractive and a change from the austerities of Bath. The ladies, too, whom he encountered when he smoked his cheroot in the Palais Royal gardens, smiled affably on the " English Milord." Some of them, with very little encouragement, did more. " No nonsense about waiting for introductions."

But, despite its amenities, Paris in the early 'thirties was not altogether a suitable resort for British visitors. The political atmosphere was distinctly ruffled. Revolution was in the air. Sir Jasper sniffed the coming changes ; and was tactician enough to avoid being engulfed in the threatened maelstrom by slipping back to England with his young charges in the nick of time. Others of his compatriots, not so fortunate or so discreet, found themselves clapped into French prisons.

Returning to the tranquillity of Bath, things resumed their normal course. Sir Jasper nursed his gout (changing his opinion of French cooking, to which he attributed a fresh attack) and the girls picked up the threads they had temporarily dropped.

Always responsive to her environment, Lola expanded quickly in the sympathetic atmosphere of the Nicolls household. Before long, Montrose, with its " blue Scotch Calvinism," was but a memory. Instead of being snubbed and scolded, she was petted and encouraged. As a result, she grew cheerful and vivacious, full of high spirits and laughter.

Perhaps because of her mother's Spanish blood, she matured early. At sixteen she was a woman. A remarkably attractive one, too, giving—with her raven tresses, long-lashed violet eyes, and graceful figure—promise of the ripe beauty for which she was afterwards to be distinguished throughout two hemispheres. Of a romantic disposition, she, naturally enough, had her *affaires*. Several of them, as it happened. One of them was with an usher, who had slipped amorous missives into her prayer-book. Greatly daring, he followed this up by bearding Sir Jasper in his den and asking permission to " pay his addresses " to his ward. The warrior's response was unconciliatory. Still, he could not be angry when, on being challenged, the girl laughed at him.

" Egad ! " he declared. " But, before long, Miss, you'll be setting all the men by the ears."

Prophetic words.

IV

During the interval that elapsed since they last met, Mrs. Craigie had troubled herself very little about the child she had sent to England. When, however, she received her portrait from Sir Jasper, together with a glowing description of her attractiveness and charm, the situation assumed a fresh aspect. Lola, she felt, had become an asset, instead of an anxiety ; and, as such, must make a " good " marriage. Bath swarmed with detrimentals, and there was a risk of a pretty girl, bereft of a mother's watchful care, being snapped up by one of them. Possibly, a younger son, without a penny with which to bless himself. A shuddering prospect for an ambitious mother. Obviously, therefore, the thing to do was to get her daughter out to India and marry her off to a rich husband. The richer, the better.

Mrs. Craigie went to work in business-like fashion, and cast a maternal eye over the " eligibles " she met at Government House. The one among them she ultimately selected as a really desirable son-in-law was a Calcutta judge, Sir Abraham Lumley. It was true he was more than old enough to be the girl's father, and was distinctly liverish.   But this, she felt, was beside the point, since he had accumulated a vast number of rupees, and would, before long, retire on a snug pension.

Sir Abraham was accordingly sounded.   Hardened bachelor as he was, a single glance at Lola's portrait was enough to send his blood-pressure up to fever heat.   In positive rapture at the idea of such fresh young loveliness becoming his, he declared himself ready to change his condition, and discussed handsome settlements.

With everything thus cut and dried, as she considered, Mrs. Craigie took the next step in her programme.   This was to leave India for England, during the autumn of 1836, and tell Lola of the " good news " in store for her.   She was then to bring her back to Calcutta and the expectant arms of Sir Abraham.

Honest Captain Craigie looked a little dubious when he was consulted.

" Perhaps she won't care about him," he suggested.

" Fiddlesticks ! " retorted his wife.   " Any girl would jump at the chance of being Lady Lumley.   Think of the position."

" I'm thinking of Lola," he said.

CHAPTER II

"MARRIED IN HASTE"

I

AMONG the passengers accompanying Mrs. Craigie on the long voyage to Southampton was a Lieutenant Thomas James, a debonair young officer of the Bengal Infantry, who made himself very agreeable to her and with whom he exchanged many confidences. He was going home on a year's sick leave ; and at the suggeston of his ship-board acquaintance he decided to spend the first month of it in Bath.

"It's time I settled down," he said. "Who knows, but I might pick up a wife in Bath and take her back to India with me."

"Who knows," agreed Mrs. Craigie, her match-making instincts aroused. "Bath is full of pretty girls."

The meeting between mother and daughter developed very differently from the lines on which she had planned it. Contrary to what she had expected, Lola did not evince any marked readiness to fall in with them. Quite undazzled by the prospects of becoming Lady Lumley, and reclining on Sir Abraham's elderly bosom, she even went so far as to dub the learned judge a "gouty old rascal," and declared that nothing would induce her to marry him. Neither reproaches nor arguments had any effect. Nor would she exhibit the smallest interest in the trousseau for which (but without her knowledge) lavish orders had been given.

Poor Mrs. Craigie could scarcely believe her ears. For a daughter to run counter to the wishes of her mother, and to

snap her fingers at the chance of marrying a " title," was
something she had considered impossible. What on earth
were girls coming to, she wondered. Either the Paris " finish-
ing school " or the Bath air had gone to her head. The times
were out of joint, and the theory that daughters did what
they were told was being rudely upset. It was all very
disturbing.

In her astonishment and annoyance, Mrs. Craigie took to
her bed. However, she did not stop there long, for prompt
measures had to be adopted. As it was useless to tackle Sir
Jasper Nicolls (whom she held responsible for the upset to her
plans) she sought counsel of somebody else. This was her
military friend, who, as luck would have it, was still lingering
in Bath, where he had evidently discovered some special
attraction. After all, he was a " man of the world " and would
know what to do. Accordingly, she summoned him to a consultation, and unburdened her mind on the subject of Lola's
" oddness."

" Of course, the girl's mad," she declared. " Nothing else
would account for it. Can you imagine any girl in her senses
turning up her nose at such a match ? I never heard such
rubbish. I'm sure I don't know what Sir Abraham will say.
He expects her to join him in Calcutta by the end of the year.
As a matter of fact, I've already booked her passage. The
wedding is to be from our house there. Something will have
to be done. The question is, what ? "

" Leave it to me," was the airy response. " I'll talk to her."

Thomas James did " talk." He talked to some effect, but
not at all in the fashion Mrs. Craigie had intended. Express-
ing sympathy with Lola, he declared himself entirely on her
side. She was much too young and pretty and attractive, he
said, to dream for an instant of marrying a man who was old
enough to be her grandfather, and bury herself in India. The
idea was ridiculous. He had a much better plan to offer.
When Lola, smiling through her tears, asked him what it was,
he said that she must run away with him and they would get

married. Thus the problem of her future would be solved automatically.

The luxuriant whiskers and dashing air of Lieutenant Thomas James did their work. Further, the suggestion was just the sort of thing that happened to heroines in novels. Lola Gilbert, young and romantic and inexperienced, succumbed. Watching her opportunity, she slipped out of the house early the next morning. Her lover had a post-chaise in readiness, and they set off in it for Bristol. There they took the packet and crossed over to Ireland, where James had relatives, who, he promised, would look after her until their marriage should be accomplished.

" Elopement in High Life ! " A tit-bit of gossip for the tea-tables and for the bucks at the clubs. No longer a sleepy hollow. Bath was in the " news."

It was not until they were gone that Mrs. Craigie discovered what had happened. Her first reaction was one of furious indignation. This, however, was natural, for not only had her ambitious project gone astray, but she had been deceived by the very man she had trusted. It was more than enough to upset anybody, especially as she was also confronted with the unpleasant task of writing to Sir Abraham Lumley, and telling him what had happened. As a result, she announced that she would " wash her hands " of the pair of them.

While it was one thing to run away, it was, as Lola soon discovered, another thing to get married. An unexpected difficulty presented itself, as the parish priest whom they consulted refused to perform the ceremony for so young a girl without being first assured of her mother's consent. Mrs. Craigie, erupting tears and threats, declined to give it. Thereupon, James's married sister, Mrs. Watson, sprang into the breach and pointed out that " things have gone so far that it is now too late to draw back, if scandal is to be avoided." The argument was effective ; and, a reluctant consent having been secured, on July 23, 1837, the " position was regularised " by the bridegroom's brother, the Rev. John James, vicar of Rathbiggon, County Meath. " Thomas James, bachelor, Lieutenant, 21st Bengal Native Infantry, and Rose Anna Gilbert, condition, spinster," was the entry on the certificate.

After a short honeymoon in Dublin, first at the Shamrock Hotel, and then in rather squalid lodgings (for cash was not plentiful), Lola was taken back to her husband's relatives. They lived in a dull Irish village on the edge of a peat bog, where the young bride found existence very boring. Then, too, when the glamour of the elopement had dimmed, it was obvious that her action in running away from Bath had been precipitate. Thomas, for all his luxuriant whiskers and dash, was, she reflected sadly, " nothing but the outside shell of a man, with neither a brain that she could respect nor a heart she could love." A sorry awakening from the dreams in which she had indulged. As a matter of fact, they had nothing in common. The husband, who was sixteen years his wife's senior, cared for little but hunting and drinking, and Lola's tastes were mainly for dancing and flirting.

It was in Dublin, where, much to her satisfaction, her spouse was ordered on temporary duty, that she discovered a ready outlet for these activities.

" Dear dirty Dublin " was, to Lola's way of thinking, a vast improvement on Rathbiggon. At any rate, there was " society," smart young officers and rising politicians, instead of clodhopping squireens and village boors, to talk to, and shops where the new fashions could be examined, and theatres with real London actors and actresses. If only she had had a little money to spend, she would have been perfectly happy. But Tom James had nothing beyond his pay, which scarcely kept him in cheroots and car fares. Still, this did not prevent him running up debts.

The Lord Lieutenant of Ireland at that period was the Earl of Mulgrave (" the Elegant Mulgrave "), afterwards Marquess of Normanby. A great admirer of pretty women, and fond of exercising the Viceregal privilege of kissing attractive débutantes, the drawing-rooms at the Castle were popular functions under his regime. He showed young Mrs. James much attention. The aides-de-camp, prominent among whom were Bernal Osborne and Francis Sheridan, followed the example thus set them by their chief ; and tickets for balls and concerts and dinner-parties and drums and routs were showered upon her.

Thinking that these compliments and attentions were being overdone, Lieutenant James took them amiss and elected to become jealous. He talked darkly of " calling out " one of his wife's admirers. But before there could be any early morning pistol-play in the Phœnix Park, an unexpected solution offered itself. Trouble was suddenly threatened on the Afghan frontier ; and, in the summer of 1837, all officers on leave from India were ordered to rejoin their regiments. Welcoming the prospect of thus renewing her acquaintance with a country of which she still had pleasant memories, Lola set to work to pack her trunks.

If she had followed the advice of a certain " travellers' handbook," written by Miss Emma Roberts, that was then very popular, she must have had a considerable amount of baggage. Thus, according to this authority, the " List of Necessaries for a Lady on a Voyage from England to India " included, among other items, the following articles : " 72 chemises ; 36 nightcaps ; 70 pocket-handkerchiefs ; 30 pairs of drawers (or combinations, at choice) ; 15 petticoats ; 60 pairs of stockings ; 45 pairs of gloves ; at least 20 dresses of different texture ; 12 shawls and parasols ; and 3 bonnets and 15 morning caps, together with biscuits and preserves at discretion, and a dozen boxes of aperient pills." Nothing omitted. Provision for all contingencies.

Officers were also required to provide themselves with an elaborate outfit. Thus, the list recommended in the *East India Voyage* gives, among other necessary items, " 72 calico shirts ; 60 pairs of stockings ; 18 pairs of drawers ; 24 pairs of gloves; and 20 pairs of trousers "; together with uniform,

saddlery, and camp equipment ; and such odds and ends as
" 60 lbs. of wax candles and several bottles of ink." Nothing,
however, about red-tape.

A helpful hint furnished by Miss Roberts was that " A
lady on shipboard, spruced up for the Park or the Opera,
would only be an object of ridicule to her experienced companions. Frippery which would be discarded in England is
often useful in India. Members of my sex," she adds, " who
have to study economy, can always secure bargains by acquir-
ing at small cost items of fashion which, while outmoded in
London, will be new enough by the time they reach Calcutta."

A lady with such sound views on managing the domestic
budget as Miss Emma Roberts should not have remained long
in single blessedness.

II

Those were not the days of ocean greyhounds, covering the
distance between England and India in a couple of weeks. Nor
was there then any Suez Canal route to shorten the long miles
that had to be traversed. Thus, when Lola and her spouse
embarked from England in an East Indiaman, the voyage took
nearly five months to accomplish, with calls at Madeira, St.
Helena, and the Cape, before the welcome cry, " Land
Ahead ! " was heard and anchor was dropped at Calcutta.

Lola's first acquaintance with India's coral strand had been
made as a child of five. Now she was returning as a married
woman. Yet she was scarcely eighteen. She did not stop
in Calcutta long, for her husband's regiment was in the
Punjaub, and a peremptory message from the brigadier
required him to rejoin as soon as possible. It was at Kurnaul
(as it was then spelled) that Lola began her experience of
garrison life. Among the other officers she met there was a
young subaltern of the Bengal Artillery, who, in the years to
come, was to make a name for himself as " Lawrence of
Lucknow."

The year 1838 was, for both the Company's troops and the
Queen's Army, an eventful one where India was concerned.

During the spring Lord Auckland, the newly-appointed Governor-General, hatched the foolish and ill-conceived policy which led to the first Afghan war. His idea (so far as he had one) was, with the help of Brown Bess and British bayonets, to replace Dost Muhammed, who had sat on the throne there for twenty years without giving any real trouble, by an incompetent upstart of his own nomination, Shah Shuja.

Lieutenant James's regiment, the 21st Bengal Native Infantry, was among those selected to join the expeditionary force appointed to "uphold the prestige of the British Raj"; and, as was the custom at that time, Lola, mounted on an elephant (which she shared with the colonel's better half), and followed by a train of baggage camels and a pack of fox-hounds complete, accompanied her husband to the frontier. The other ladies included Mrs. McNaghten and Mrs. Robert Sale and the Governor-General's two daughters. It is just possible that Macaulay had a glimpse of Lola, for a con-temporary letter says that " he turned out to wish the party farewell."

The " Army of the Indus " was given a good send off by a loyal native prince, Ranjeet Singh (the " Lion of the Pun-jaub "), who, on their march up country, entertained the column in a rest-camp at Lahore with " showy pageants and gay doings," among which were nautch dances, cock-fights, and theatricals. He meant well, no doubt, but he contrived to upset a chaplain, who declared himself shocked that a " bevy of dancing prostitutes should appear in the presence of the ladies of the family of a British Governor-General." Judging from a luscious account that Lola gives of a big durbar, to which all the officers and their wives were bidden, these strictures were not unjustifiable. Thus, after Lord Auckland (" in sky blue inexpressibles ") and his host had delivered patriotic speeches (with florid allusions to the " British Raj," the " Sahib Log," and the " Great White Queen," and all the rest of it) gifts were distributed among the assembled company. Some of these were of an embarrassing description, since they took the form of " beautiful Circassian slave maidens, covered with very little beyond precious gems." To the obvious annoyance, however, of a number of prospective recipients, " the Rajah was officially informed that English custom and military regulations alike did not permit Her Majesty's warriors to accept such tokens of goodwill."

But, if they could not receive them, the guests had to make presents in turn, and Ranjeet Singh for his part had no qualms about accepting them. With true Oriental politeness, and " without moving a muscle," he registered rapture at a " miscellaneous collection of imitation gold and silver trinkets and rusty old pistols offered him on behalf of the Honourable East India Company."

A correspondent of the *Calcutta Englishman* was much impressed. " The particular gift," he says, " before which the Maharajah bent with the devotion of a *preux chevalier* was a full-length portrait of our gracious little Queen, from the brush of the Hon. Miss Eden herself."

In a letter from Lord Auckland's military secretary, the Hon. William Osborne, there is an account of these doings at Lahore :

> Ranjeet has entertained us all most handsomely. No one in the camp is allowed to purchase a single thing ; and a list is sent round twice a week in which you put down just what you require, and it is furnished at his expense. It costs him 25,000 rupees a day. Nothing could exceed his liberality and friendship during the whole of the Governor-General's visit.

A second durbar, held at Simla, was accompanied by much florid imagery, all of which had to be interpreted for the benefit of Lord Auckland. " It took a quarter of an hour," says his sister, " to satisfy him about the Maharajah's health, and to ascertain that the roses had bloomed in the garden of friendship, and the nightingales had sung in the bowers of affection sweeter than ever since the two Powers had approached each other."

The Afghan campaign, as ill conceived as it was ill carried out, followed its appointed course. That is to say, it was punctuated by "regrettable incidents" and quarrels among the generals (two of whom, Sir Henry Fane and Sir John Keane, were not on speaking terms) ; and, with the Afghans living to fight another day, a "success for British arms" was announced. Thereupon, the column returned to India, bands playing, elephants trumpeting a salute, and guns thundering a welcome. "The war," declared His Excellency (who had received an earldom) in an official despatch, "is all over." Unfortunately, however, it was all over Afghanistan, with the result that there had to be another campaign in the following year. This time, not even Lord Auckland's imagination could call it "successful."

"There will be a great deal of prize money," was the complacent fashion in which Miss Eden summed up the situation. "Another man has been put on the Khelat throne, so that business is finished." But it was not finished. It was only just beginning. "Within six months," says Edward Thompson, "Khelat was recaptured by a son of the slain Khan, Lord Auckland's puppet ejected, and the English commander of the garrison murdered."

Although the expedition that followed was the subject of a highly eulogistic despatch from the Commander-in-Chief and the big-wigs at headquarters, a number of "regrettable incidents" were officially admitted. As a result, a regiment of Light Cavalry was disbanded, "as a punishment for poltroonery in the hour of trial and the dastards struck off the Army List."

Later on, when Lord Ellenborough was Governor-General, a bombastic memorandum, addressed "To all the Princes and Chiefs and People of India," was issued by him :

"Our victorious army bears the gates of the Temple of Somnauth in triumph from Afghanistan, and the despoiled

tomb of Sultan Mahmood looks down upon the ruins of
Ghuznee. The insult of 800 years is at last avenged !

" To you I shall commit this glorious trophy of successful
war. You will yourselves with all honour transmit the gates
of sandalwood to the restored Temple of Somnauth.

" May that good Providence, which has hitherto so mani-
festly protected me, still extend to me its favour, that I may
so use the power entrusted to my hands to advance your
prosperity and happiness by placing the union of our two
countries upon foundations that may render it eternal."

There was a good deal more in a similar style, for his lord-
ship loved composing florid despatches. But this one had a
bad reception when it was sent home to England. " At this
puerile piece of business," says the plain spoken Stocqueler,
" the commonsense of the British community at large revolted.
The ministers of religion protested against it as a most un-
pardonable homage to an idolatrous temple. Ridiculed by
the Press of India and England, and laughed at by the members of his own party in Parliament, Lord Ellenborough
halted the gates at Agra, and postponed the completion of the
monstrous folly he had more than begun to perpetrate."

Severe as was this criticism, it was not unmerited. Ellenborough's theatrical bombast, like that of Napoleon at the
Pyramids, recoiled upon him, bringing a hornets' nest about
his own ears and leading to his recall. As a matter of fact, too,
the gates which he held in such reverence were found to be
replicas of the pair that the Sultan Mahmood had pilfered
from Somnauth ; and were not of sandalwood at all, but of
common deal.

III

While following the drum from camp to camp and from
station to station, Lola spent several months in Bareilly, a
town that was afterwards to play an important part in the
Mutiny. Colonel Durand, an officer who was present when
the city was captured in 1858, says that the bungalow she
occupied there was destroyed. Yet, the mutineers, he

noticed, had spared the bath house that had been built for her in the compound.

During the hot weather of 1839, young Mrs. James, accompanied by her husband, went off to Simla for a month on a visit to her mother, who, yielding to pressure, had at last held out the olive-branch. The welcome, however—except from Captain Craigie, who still had a warm corner in his heart for her—was somewhat frigid.

There is a reference to this visit in *Up the Country*, a once popular book by Lord Auckland's sister, the Hon. Emily Eden. Following the coy fashion of the period, however, she always refrained from giving a name in full, but would merely allude to people as " Colonel A," " Mr. B," " Mrs. C," and " Miss D," etc. Still, the identities of " Mrs. J " and " Mrs. C " in this extract are clear enough :

September 8, 1839.

Simla is much moved just now by the arrival of a Mrs. J, who has been talked of as a great beauty all the year, and that drives every other woman quite distracted. . . . Mrs. J is the daughter of a Mrs. C, who is still very handsome herself, and whose husband is deputy-adjutant-general, or some military authority of that kind. She sent this only child to be educated at home, and went home herself two years ago to see her. In the same ship was Mr. J, a poor ensign, going home on sick leave. He told her he was engaged to be married, consulted her about his prospects, and in the meantime privately married this child at school. It was enough to provoke any mother ; but, as it now cannot be helped, we have all been trying to persuade her for the last year to make it up. She has withstood it till now, but at last has consented to ask them for a month, and they arrived three days ago.

The rush on the road was remarkable. But nothing could be more satisfactory than the result, for Mrs. J

looked lovely, and Mrs. C has set up for her a very grand
jonpaun, with bearers in fine orange and brown liveries ;
and J is a sort of smart-looking man with bright waistcoats and bright teeth, with a showy horse, and he rode
along in an attitude of respectful attention to *ma belle
mère*. Altogether, it was an imposing sight, and I cannot
see any way out of it but magnanimous admiration.

During this visit to Simla the couple were duly bidden to
dine at Auckland House, on Elysium Hill, where they met
His Excellency.

" We had a dinner yesterday," wrote their hostess. " Mrs.
J is undoubtedly very pretty, and such a merry unaffected
girl. She is only seventeen now, and does not look so old ;
and when one thinks that she is married to a junior lieutenant
in the Indian Army, fifteen years older than herself, and that
they have 160 rupees a month, and are to pass their whole
lives in India, I do not wonder at Mrs. C's resentment at her
having run away from school."

Writing to Lady Teresa Lister in England, Miss Eden
gives an entertaining account of Simla at this date :

Everybody has been pleased and amused, except the two
clergymen who are here, and who have begun a course of
sermons against what they call a destructive torrent of worldly
gaiety. They had much better preach against the destructive
torrent of rain which has now set in for the next three months,
and not only washes away all gaiety, but all the paths, in the
literal sense, which lead to it. . . . I do not count Simla as
any grievance—nice climate, beautiful place, constant fresh
air, plenty of fleas, not much society, everything that is
desirable.

In another letter, this indefatigable correspondent
remarks :

Here, society is not much trouble, nor much anything
else. We give sundry dinners and occasional balls, and have
hit upon one popular device. Our band plays twice a week on

one of the hills here, and we send ices and refreshments to the listeners, and it makes a nice little reunion with very little trouble.

A further reference to the amenities of Government House at Simla during the Aucklands' regime is instructive, as showing that it was not a case of all work and no play :

There are about ninety-six ladies here whose husbands are gone to the wars, and about twenty-six gentlemen—at least, there will, with good luck, be about that number. We have a very dancing set of aides-de-camp just now, and they are utterly desperate at the notion of our having no balls. I suppose we must begin on one in a fortnight ; but it will be difficult, and there are several young ladies here with whom some of our gentlemen are much smitten. As they will have no rivals here, I am horribly afraid the flirtations may become serious, and then we shall lose some active aides-de-camp, and they will find themselves on ensign's pay with a wife to keep. However, they *will* have these balls, so it is not my fault.

After she had left Simla and its round of gaieties, Lola was to have another meeting with the hospitable Aucklands. This took place in camp at Kurnaul, " a great ugly canton- ment, all barracks and dust and guns and soldiers." Miss Eden, who was accompanying her brother on a tour through the district, wrote to her sister in England :

November 13, 1839.

We were at home in the evening, and it was an im- mense party ; but, except that pretty Mrs. J, who was at Simla, and who looked like a star among the others, the women were all plain.

A couple of days later, she added some further particulars :

We left Kurnaul yesterday morning. Little Mrs. J was so unhappy at our going that we asked her to come

Benjamin Lumley.   Lessee of Her Majesty's Theatre

Lola Montez, " Spanish Dancer."   Début at Her Majesty's Theatre

and pass the day here, and brought her with us. She
went from tent to tent and chattered all day and visited
her friend, Mrs. M, who is with the camp. I gave her
a pink silk gown, and it was altogether a very happy day
for her evidently. It ended in her going back to Kurnaul on my elephant, with E.N. by her side, and Mr. J
sitting behind. She had never been on an elephant
before, and thought it delightful.

She is very pretty, and a good little thing apparently.
But they are very poor, and she is very young and lively,
and if she falls into bad hands, she would laugh herself
into foolish scrapes. At present the husband and wife
are very fond of each other, but a girl who marries at
fifteen hardly knows what she likes.

When she wrote this passage, Miss Eden might have been
a Sibyl, for her words were to become abundantly true.

IV

Except when on active service, officers of the Company's
Army were not overworked. Everything was left to the
sergeants and corporals ; and, while Thomas Atkins and Jack
Sepoy trudged in the dust and sweated and drilled in their
absurd stocks and tight tunics, the commissioned ranks,
lolling in barracks, killed the long hours as they pleased.

Following form, Captain James (the Afghan business had
brought him a step in rank) did a certain amount of tiger-
shooting and pig-sticking, and a good deal of brandy-swilling,
combined with card-playing and gambling. As a husband, he
was not a conspicuous success. " He slept," complained
Lola, feeling herself neglected, " like a boa-constrictor,"
and, during the intervals of wakefulness, " drank too much
porter." The result was, there were quarrels, instead of
love-making, for they both had tempers.

" Runaway matches, like runaway horses," Lola had once
written, " are almost sure to end in a smash-up." In this

case there was a " smash-up," for Tom James was not always sleeping and drinking. He had other activities. If fond of a glass, he was also fond of a lass. The one among them for whom he evinced a special fondness was a Mrs. Lomer, the wife of a brother officer, the adjutant of his regiment. His partiality was reciprocated.

One morning when, without any suspicion of what was in store for them, Mrs. James and Adjutant Lomer sat down to their *chota-hazree*, two members of the accustomed breakfast party were missing. Enquiries having been set on foot, the fact was elicited that Captain James and Mrs. Lomer had gone out for an early ride. It must have been a long one, thought the camp, as they did not appear at dinner that evening. Messengers sent to look for them came back with a disturbing report. This was to the effect that the couple had slipped off to the Nilgiri Hills and had decided to stop there.

The next morning a panting native brought a letter from the errant lady addressed to her furious spouse. This missive is (without explaining how he got it) reproduced by an American journalist, T. Everett Harré, in a series of articles, *The Heavenly Sinner* : " I suggest," runs an extract, " you come to your senses and give me my freedom . . . I am going with a man of parts who knows how to give a woman the attentions she craves, and is himself glad to shake off a young chit of a wife who is too brainless to appreciate him."

A first-class sensation. The entire cantonment throbbed and buzzed with excitement. The colonel fumed ; the adjutant cursed ; and there was talk of bringing the Don Juan Captain James to a court-martial for " conduct unbecoming an officer and a gentleman." But Lola, as was her custom, took it philosophically, doubtless reflecting that she was well rid of a spouse for whom she no longer cared, and went back to her mother in Calcutta.

Mrs. Craigie's maternal heart-strings should have been wrung by the unhappy position of her daughter. They were not wrung. The clandestine marriage, with the upsetting of her own plans, still rankled and remained unforgiven and unforgotten. As a result, when she asked for shelter and sympathy, Lola received a very frigid welcome. Her step-father, however, took her part, and declared that his bungalow was open to her until other arrangements could be made for her future. Not being possessed of much imagination, his idea was that she should leave India temporarily and stop for a few months in Scotland with his brother, Mr. David Craigie, a man of substance and Provost of Perth. After an interval for reflection there, he felt that the differences of opinion that had arisen between her husband and herself would become adjusted, and the young couple resume marital relations. Accordingly, he wrote to his brother, asking him to meet her when she arrived in London and escort her to Perth.

Lola, however, while professing complete agreement, had other views as to her future. She wanted neither a reconcili-ation with her husband nor a second experience of life with the Craigie family in Scotland. One such had been more than sufficient, but she was careful not to breathe a word on the subject. She kept her own counsel, and matured her own plans.

CHAPTER III

THE CONSISTORY COURT

I

SAILING from Calcutta for London in an East India-man, at the end of 1840, Lola was consigned by her step-father to the " special care " of a Mrs. Sturgis who was among the passengers. He obviously felt the part-ing. " Big salt tears," says Lola, " coursed down his cheeks," when he wished her a last farewell. He also gave her his blessing; and, what was more negotiable, a cheque for £1000. The two never met again.

But although she had left India's coral strand, a memory of her lingered there for many years. In this connection, Sir Walter Lawrence says that he once found himself in a canton-ment that had been deserted so long that it was swallowed up by the ever advancing jungle. " A wizened villager," he says, " recalled a high-spirited and beautiful girl, the young wife of an officer, who would creep up and push him into the water. ' Ah,' he said, with a smile of affection, ' she was a *badmash*, but she was always very kind to me.' She was better known afterwards as Lola Montez."

At Madras a number of fresh comers joined the good ship *Larkins* in which Lola was proceeding to England. Among them was a certain Captain Lennox, aide-de-camp to Lord Elphinstone, the Governor. An agreeable young man, and very different from the missionaries and civil servants who formed the bulk of the other male passengers. Lola and himself were soon on good terms. " Too good," was the acid comment of the ladies in whose society Captain Lennox exhibited no interest. The couple were inseparable. They sat at the same table in the saloon ; they paced the deck together, arm in arm, on the long hot nights, preferring dark and unfrequented corners ; their chairs adjoined ; their cabins adjoined ; and, so the shocked whisper ran, they sometimes mistook the one for the other.

" Anybody can make a mistake in the dark," said Lola, when Mrs. Sturgis, remembering Captain Craigie's injunctions, and resolved at all costs to fulfil her trust, ventured on a remonstrance.

Ninety years ago, travellers had to " rough it ; " and the conditions governing a voyage from India to England were very different from those that now obtain. None of the modern amenities had any place in the accepted routine. Thus, no deck sports ; no jazz band ; no swimming-pool ; no cocktail bar ; not even a sweepstake on the day's run.

But time had to be killed ; and, as a young grass widow, Mrs. James felt that flirting was the best way of getting through it. Captain Lennox was the only man on board ship with whom she had anything in common. He was sympathetic, good-looking, and attentive. Also, he swore that he was " madly in love with her." The old, old story ; but it did its work. Before the vessel berthed in London docks, Lola had come to a decision. A momentous decision. She would give David Craigie the slip, and, listening to his blandishments, cast in her lot with George Lennox.

" I'll look after you," he said reassuringly. " Trust me for that, my dear."

Lola did trust him. In fact, she trusted him to such an extent that, on reaching London, she stopped with him at the Imperial Hotel in Covent Garden ; and then, when the manageress of that establishment took upon herself to make pointed criticisms, at his rooms in Pall Mall.

Naturally enough, this sort of thing could not be hushed up for long. Meaning nods and winks greeted the dashing Lennox when he appeared at his club. Tongues wagged briskly. Some of them even wagged in distant Calcutta, where they were heard by Lola's husband. Ignoring his own amorous dalliance with a brother officer's spouse, he elected to feel injured. Resolved to assert himself, he got into touch with his London solicitors and instructed them to take the preliminary steps to dissolve his marriage. The first of these was to bring an action for what was then politely dubbed "crim. con." against the man he alleged to have " wronged " him.

The lawyers would not be hurried ; and things moved in leisurely fashion. Still, they moved to their appointed end ; and, the necessary red tape being unwound, interrogatories administered, and the evidence of prying chambermaids and hotel servants collected and examined, in May, 1841, the case of James *v.* Lennox got into the list and was heard by Lord Denman and a special jury in the Court of Queen's Bench. Sir William Follett, the Solicitor-General, was briefed on behalf of the plaintiff, and Frederick Thesiger appeared for Captain Lennox.

In his opening address, Sir William Follett (who had not been too well instructed) told the jury that the petitioner and his wife " had lived very happily together in India, and that the return of Mrs. James to England was due to a fall from her horse at Calcutta." While on the passage home, he continued, pulling out his *vox humana* stop, the ship touched at Madras, where the defendant came on board ; and, " during the long voyage, an intimacy sprang up between Mrs. James and himself which developed in a fashion that left the outraged husband no choice but to institute the present proceedings to recover damages for having been wantonly robbed of the affection and society of his consort."

At this point, counsel for Captain Lennox (who, in pusillanimous fashion, had loved and sailed away, rather than stop and help the woman he had compromised) cut short his learned friend's tearful eloquence by admitting that he was prepared to accept a verdict, with £1000 damages. As the judge agreed, the case was abruptly terminated.

This, however, was only the first round. In December of the following year, the next step was adopted, and a suit for divorce was commenced in the Consistory Court. As neither Mrs. James nor the Lothario-like Captain Lennox put in an appearance, Dr. Lushington, declaring himself satisfied that misconduct had been committed, pronounced a decree *a mensa et thoro*. All that this amounted to was merely a judicial separation.

The report in *The Times* only ran to a dozen lines. Considering that the paper cost fivepence a copy, this was not a very liberal allowance. Still, readers had better value in respect of another action in " high life " that was heard the same day, that of Lord and Lady Graves, which had a full column allotted it.

II

This was all that the public knew of the case. It did not seem much on which to blast a young wife's reputation. Dr. Lushington, the judge of the Consistory Court, however, knew a good deal more about the business than did the general public. This was because, during the preliminary hearing, held some months earlier and attended only by counsel and solicitors, a number of damaging facts had transpired.

Mrs. James, said learned counsel for the petitioner, had " been guilty of behaviour at which a crocodile would tremble and blush." A serious charge to bring against a young woman. Still, in answer to the judge, he professed himself equipped with ample evidence to support it. His first witness was a retired civil servant, a Mr. Browne Roberts, who had known the respondent's husband, first, as a bachelor in India, and afterwards as a married man in Dublin. At the beginning of 1841, he had received a call, he said, from a Major McMullen to whom Captain Craigie had written, asking him to take charge of his step-daughter on her arrival in London and see her off to his relatives in Scotland. When, however, the major offered this hospitality, it was refused. Thereupon, Mr.

Roberts had himself called at the Imperial Hotel, Covent Garden, and suggested that she should come and stop with his wife ; and this invitation was also refused.

Not much in this perhaps, but a good deal in what followed. Mrs. Elizabeth Walters, the manageress of the Imperial Hotel, said that on February 21, 1841, " a lady and gentleman arrived in a hackney cab, with luggage marked G. Lennox and Mrs. James, and booked a double room." Mrs. Walters had not, she admitted, " actually discovered them undressed, or sharing the bed," but " she would not have been surprised to have done so." Accordingly, when her travelling companion left the next morning, she taxed Mrs. James with misconduct. After telling her to " mind her own business," Mrs. James had declared that she and Captain Lennox were on the point of being married, and had then packed up and left the establishment.

" What exactly did she say ? " enquired the judge.

" She said, ' what I choose to do is my own affair and nobody else's.' "

On leaving the somewhat arid hospitality of the Covent Garden Hotel, Mrs. James had removed to a lodging-house just off Pall Mall, where she stopped for a month. Mrs. Martin, the proprietress, told the court that, during this period, Captain Lennox settled the bill, and " called there every day, often stopping till all hours of the night."

The testimony of Mrs. Sarah Watson, the sister of Captain James, was that her brother had written to her in the autumn of 1840, saying that his wife had been thrown from her horse and was coming to England for medical treatment ; and that he had written to his aunt, Mrs. Rae, of Edinburgh, suggesting that his wife should stop with her. Mrs. Watson, having " been told things," then called on Mrs. James in Covent Garden. " I spoke to her," she said, " of the shocking rumour that Captain Lennox had passed a night with her there, and pointed out the unutterable ruin that would result from a continuance of such deplorable conduct. I begged her to entrust herself to the care of Mrs. Rae. My entreaties were ineffectual. She positively declared, affirming with an oath, that she would do nothing of the kind."

Among the passengers on board the East Indiaman by which Mrs. James had voyaged to England was Mrs. Ingram, the captain's wife. " The conduct of Mrs. James," she said, " was unguarded in the extreme, and her general behaviour was what is sometimes called flirting." Captain Ingram, who followed, had a still more disturbing story to recount. " On several occasions," he said, " I heard Mrs. James address the gentleman who joined us at Madras as ' Dear Lennox,' and she would even admit him to the privacy of her cabin while the other passengers were attending divine service on deck. When I spoke to her about it, she answered me in a very cool fashion."

All this was distinctly damaging. The real sensation, however, was provided by Caroline Marden, a stewardess.

" During the voyage from Madras," she told the astonished judge, " I more than once saw Captain Lennox lacing up Mrs. James's stays."

" Did you see anything else ? " faltered counsel.

" Yes, I also saw her actually putting on her stockings while Captain Lennox was in her cabin ! "

There were limits to intimacies between the sexes. This was clearly among them. For a man to assist in adjusting a woman's stays, and watch her changing her stockings, could, in the opinion of the learned and experienced Dr. Lushington, only lead to one result. The worst result. Hence, he had no difficulty in pronouncing the decree for which the husband was applying.

III

All James had got for his activities in bringing his action was a divorce *a mensa et thoro*, that is, " from bed and board." But, while it was all he got, this measure of relief was probably all he wanted, as he was not contemplating a second experiment in matrimony, either with Mrs. Lomer or anybody else. Where his discarded wife was concerned, she would have to shift for herself. She no longer had any legal claim upon him ; nor could she marry again during his lifetime. Her position was a somewhat pathetic one. Thus, she was alone and friendless ; besmirched in reputation ; abandoned by her husband ; and deserted by her lover. But she still had her youth and her courage.

The London of the 1840's, where Lola found herself cast adrift, was a curious microcosm and full of contrasts. A mixture of unabashed blackguardism and cloistered prudery ; of double-beds and primness ; of humbug and frankness ; of liberty and restraint ; of lust and license ; of brutal horseplay passing for " wit," and of candour marching with cant. The working classes scarcely called their souls their own ; women and children mercilessly exploited by smug profiteers ; the " Song of the Shirt " ; Gradgrind and Boanerges holding high festival ; Tom and Jerry (on their last legs) and Corinthians wrenching off door knockers and upsetting policemen ; and Exeter Hall and the Cider Cellars both in full swing. Altogether, an ill place of sojourn for an unprotected young woman.

Exactly how this one supported herself during the next few months is not very clear, for, if she kept a diary, she never published it. According, however, to a Sunday organ, " she entangled the virtuous Earl of Malmesbury in a delicate kind of newspaper correspondence, an assertion having been made in public that she visited that pious nobleman at his own house." An odd story (of American origin, and quite unfounded) has it that, about this period, she established contact with a certain Jean François Montez, " an individual of immense wealth who lavished a fortune on her " ; and Edward Blanchard, a hack dramatist of Drury Lane, contributes the somewhat unhelpful remark, " She became a Bohemian." Perhaps she did. But she had to discover a second career that would bring a little more grist to the mill. Such a course was imperative, since the balance of the £1000 her stepfather had given her would not last indefinitely. Looking round, she felt that, all things considered, the stage offered the best prospects of earning a livelihood. Not a very novel decision. Nowadays, as an attractive young woman, with a little capital in her possession, she would have had more choice. Thus, she might have opened a hat shop, or run tea-rooms, or bred pet dogs, become a mannequin, or a dance club hostess, or even " gone on the films." But none of these avenues to feminine employment existed in the eighteen-forties. Hence, it was the footlights or nothing.

She had the sense to put herself in the hands of an in-structress. The one she selected was Fanny Kelly (" the only woman to whom Charles Lamb had screwed up sufficient courage to propose marriage "), who conducted a school of acting. Being honest, as well as capable, Miss Kelly took the measure of the would-be Ophelia very promptly.

" You'll never make an actress," was her decision. " You've no talent for it."

But, if the applicant had no talent, the other saw that she had something else. This was a pair of shapely legs, which, as a ballet-dancer, could yet twinkle in front of the footlights.

This opinion being shared by its recipient, she lost no time in adopting it. As a preliminary, she went to Madrid. There, under expert tuition, she learned to rattle the castanets, and practised the bolero and the cachucha, as well as the classic arabesques and entrechats and the technique accompanying them. But she did not advance much beyond the simplest steps, for the time at her disposal was short, and the art of the ballerina is not to be acquired without years of unceasing study.

According to a French journalist, an " English Milord " made Lola's acquaintance in Madrid. This was Lord Malmesbury, " who was so dazzled by the purity of her Spanish accent that he adopted her as a *compagnon de voyage*, and shared with her the horrors of bad cooking and the joys of nights in Granada." This fact, however, if it be a fact, is not to be found in the volume of "memoirs" that he afterwards published.

Still, it seems that Lord Malmesbury did meet Lola. His own account of the incident is that, on returning to England from abroad, in the spring of the year 1843, he was asked by the Spanish Consul at Southampton to escort to London a young woman who had just landed there. He found her, he says, "a remarkably handsome person, who was in deep mourning and who appeared to be in great distress." While they were alone in the railway carriage, he improved the occasion and extracted from his travelling companion the story of her life.

"She informed me," he says, "in bad English that she was the widow of Don Diego Leon, who had lately been shot by the Carlists after he was taken prisoner, and that she was going to London to sell some Spanish property that she possessed, and give lessons in singing, as she was very poor."

Notwithstanding his diplomatic training, Lord Malmesbury swallowed this story, as well as much else with which it was embroidered. One thing led to another; and the acquaintance thus fortuitously begun in a railway carriage was continued in London. There he got up a concert for her benefit at his town house, where, in addition to singing Castilian ballads, his protégée sold veils and fans among the audience ; and he also gave her an introduction to a theatrical manager, with results that neither of them had foreseen.

CHAPTER IV

FLARE OF THE FOOTLIGHTS

I

TIMES change. When Lola returned to London a passage through the divorce court was not regarded as a necessary qualification for stage aspirants. Also, being well aware that, to ensure a good reception, a foreign-sounding name was desirable, this one decided to adopt that of Lola Montez. This, she felt, would, among other advantages, effectively mask her identity with that of Mrs. Thomas James, an identity she was anxious to shed.

Her plans were soon made. On the morning after her arrival, she presented her letter of introduction to the impressario of Her Majesty's Theatre, in the Haymarket. This position was held by an affable Hebrew, one Benjamin Lumley, an ex-solicitor, who had abandoned his parchments and bills of costs and acquired a lease of Her Majesty's. The house had long been looked upon as something of a white elephant in the theatrical jungle ; but Lumley, being pushful and knowledgeable, soon built up a valuable following and set the establishment on its legs.

As luck would have it, Lola's interview with him came at just the right moment, for he was alternating ballet with opera and was in want of a fresh attraction. Convinced that he recognised it in his caller (or, perhaps, anxious to please Lord Malmesbury), he offered her an engagement there and then to dance a *pas seul* between the acts of *Il Barbiere di Seviglia*.

" If you make a hit," he said, " you shall have a contract for the rest of the season. It all depends on yourself."

Lola, wanting nothing better, left the managerial office, treading on air.

As was his custom, Lumley cultivated the critics, and would receive them in his sanctum whenever he had a novel attraction to submit.

" I have a surprise for you in my next programme," he said, when the champagne and cigars had been discussed. " This is that I have secured Donna Lola, a Spanish dancer, direct from Seville. She is, I assure you, deliciously beautiful and remarkably accomplished. I pledge you my word, gentlemen, she will create a positive *furore* here."

In 1843 dramatic critics had the privilege of attending rehearsals and penetrating behind the scenes. One of their number, adopting the pseudonym " Q," has left an account of the manner in which he first met Lola Montez. He had called on Lumley for a gossip, and was invited by that authority to descend to the stage and watch his new acquisition practising a dance there.

" At that period," he says, " her figure was even more attractive than her face, lovely as the latter was. Lithe and graceful as a young fawn, every movement she made was instinct with melody. Her dark eyes were blazing and flashing with excitement, for she felt that I was willing to admire her. . . . As she swept round the stage, her slender waist swayed to the music, and her graceful head and neck bent with it like a flower that bends with the impulse given to its stem by the fitful temper of the wind."

Lumley was tactful enough to leave the pressman alone with the star. As the latter promised to " give her a good puff in his paper," Lola, who never missed an opportunity, made herself specially agreeable to him. Her bright eyes did their work. " When we separated," says " Q " in his reminiscences, " I found myself tumbled heels over head into the profound depths of that which the French call a *grande passion*."

Lumley's next step was to draw up an announcement of the promised novelty for inclusion in the programme :

HER MAJESTY'S THEATRE

June 3, 1843

SPECIAL ATTRACTION !

Mr. Benjamin Lumley begs to announce that, between the acts of the Opera, DONNA LOLA MONTEZ, of the Teatro Real, Seville, will have the honour to make her first appearance in England in the Original Spanish dance El Oleano.

After the cast list had been set out the rest of the reading matter on the programme was given up to advertisements. Some of them would appear to have been selected rather at haphazard. At any rate, their special appeal to music lovers was a little difficult to follow. Thus, one was of " Jackson's patent enema machines, as patronised by the nobility (either sex) when travelling "; another of " Mrs. Rodd's anatomical ladies' stays (which ensure the wearer a figure of astonishing symmetry "; and another of a " Brilliant burlesque ballad, ' Get along, Rosey,' sung with the most positive triumph every evening by Madame Vestris."

With much satisfaction, Manager Lumley, taking a preliminary peep at the crowded house, saw that a particularly " smart " audience was assembled on the night of June 3. The list of " fashionables " he handed to the reporters resembled an extract from the pages of Messrs. Burke and Debrett. Thus, the Royal Box was graced by the Queen Dowager, with the King of Hanover and Prince Edward of Saxe-Weimar for her guests ; and, dotted about the pit tier (then the fashionable part of the house) were the Duke and Duchess of Wellington, the Marquess and Marchioness of Granby, Lord and Lady Brougham, and the Baroness de Rothschild, with the Belgian Minister, Count Esterhazy, and Baron Talleyrand. Even the occupants of the pit had to accept an official intimation that " only black trousers will be allowed." Her Majesty's had a standard, and Lumley insisted on its observance.

That long familiar feature, "Fops' Alley," having disappeared from the auditorium, the modish thing for unattached men was to make up a party and hire an omnibus-box ; and from that position to pronounce judgment upon the legs of the dancers pirouetting in wispy gauze on the stage. Then, when the curtain fell, they would be privileged to go behind the scenes and chat with the coryphées.

On the evening of Lola's début one of the omnibus-boxes was occupied by Lord Ranelagh, a raffish mid-Victorian roué, who had brought with him a select party of " Corinthians " in frilled shirts and flowered waistcoats. It was observed that he paid but languid attention to the opera. As soon, however, as the promised novelty, *El Oleano*, was reached, he exhibited a sudden interest and pushed his chair forward.

" We shall see some fun in a moment," he whispered. " Mind you fellows keep quiet until I give the word."

II

A little ominous, perhaps, that the Haymarket entrepreneur should bear the same name as the Calcutta judge who had unsuccessfully sought her hand. But Lola experienced no qualms. As she stood at the wings, in a black satin bodice and much flounced pink silk skirt, waiting for her cue, Lumley passed her with a nod of encouragement.

" Capital," he said, rubbing his whiskers. " Most attractive. You'll be a big success, my dear."

As he moved off, a bell tinkled in the prompt corner. In response, the conductor lifted his baton ; the heavy curtains were drawn aside ; and, under a cross-fire of opera glasses, Lola bounded on to the stage and executed her initial piroutte. There was a sudden hush, as, at the finish of the number, she stepped up to the footlights and awaited the verdict. Had she made good, or not ? In a moment, however, she knew that all was well, for a storm of applause and clapping of hands filled the air. Lumley, from his place in the wings, beamed approval. His enterprise was to be rewarded. The débutante was a success. No doubt about it. She should have a contract from him before any other manager should step in and snap her up.

We do not believe (scribbled a critic, hurriedly jotting down his impressions, to be expanded when he got back to his office) that Donna Lola smiled once throughout her performance. As she withdrew, numbers of bouquets fell on to the stage. But the proud one of Seville did not deign to return to pick them up, and one of the gentlemen in livery was deputed for that purpose. When, however, her measure was encored, she stepped down from her pinnacle and actually condescended to accept an additional bouquet that had been tossed by a fair one from a box.

Her Majesty's Theatre (added a colleague) may now be said to be in its full zenith of grandeur and perfection of beauty and splendour, and variety and fame of the ballet. A new Spanish Donna has been introduced. Although the visitation was unheralded by the customary flourish of trumpeting *on dits*, it was extremely successful. The young lady came and saw and conquered. Many floral offerings were shot at her as a compliment, and the useful M. Coulos—ever at hand in such an emergency— assisted very industriously in picking them up. As for *El Oleano*, this is a sort of cachucha ; and it certainly gives Donna Lola Montez an opportunity of introducing herself to the public under a very captivating aspect. . . . A lovely picture she is to contemplate. There is before you the very perfection of Spanish beauty—the tall handsome figure, the full lustrous eye, the joyous animated countenance, and the dark raven tresses. You gaze upon the Donna with delight and admiration.

It was just after the third item on her programme and while she stood before the curtain, bowing and smiling her acknowledgments, that there was an unexpected interruption. An ominous hiss suddenly split the air. The sound came from the occupants of the stage box in which Lord Ranelagh and his party had ensconced themselves. As at a prearranged signal, the occupants of the opposite box took it up and repeated it. The audience gasped in astonishment, and looked to Lord Ranelagh for a solution. He supplied one promptly. " Egad ! " he exclaimed in a loud voice, " that's not Lola Montez at all. It's Betsy James, an Irish girl. Ladies and gentlemen, we're being properly swindled ! "

" Swindled " was an ugly word. The pit and gallery, feeling that they were in some mysterious fashion being defrauded, followed the cue thus given them, and a volume of hisses and cat-calls sprang from the throats that, a moment earlier, had bellowed vociferous cheers. The great Michael Costa, who was conducting, dropped his baton in astonishment, and, refusing to pick it up again, left his desk. There is a theory that it was this untoward incident that led him to transfer himself from the Haymarket to Covent Garden. Quite possible. Musicians are temperamental folk.

It was left for Lumley to deal with the situation. He did so by ringing down the curtain, while Lola, in tears and fury, rushed off to her dressing-room.

III

Perhaps they left early, but none of the critics saw anything of this *dénouement*. What, however, they did see they described in rapturous, not to say, florid terms :

> We saw, as in a dream (declared one of them), an Elssler or a Taglioni descend from the clouds, under the traits of a new dancer, whose fervent admirers lavished on her all the enthusiasm and applause with which the rare perfection of her predecessors has been rewarded.

On Saturday last, between the acts of the opera, Donna Lola Montez was announced to appear on the programme at Her Majesty's. A thousand ardent spectators were in feverish anxiety to see her. Donna Lola enchanted everyone. There was throughout a graceful flowing of the arms—not an angle discernible—an indescribable softness in her attitude and suppleness in her limbs which, developed in a thousand positions (without infringing on the Opera laws), were the most intoxicating and womanly that can be imagined. We never remember seeing the *habitués*—both young and old—taken by more agreeable surprise than the bewitching lady excited. She was rapturously encored, and the stage strewn with bouquets.

Lord Ranelagh and his friends must have grinned when they read this gush.

" I saw Lumley immediately after the fall of the curtain," says a reporter who was admitted behind the scenes. " He was surrounded by the professors of morality from the omnibus-box, who said that Donna Lola was positively not to reappear. They pointed out to him that it was absolutely essential to have none but exemplary characters in the ballet ; but they did not tell him where he would procure females who would have no objection to exhibiting their legs in pink silk fleshings. As Lumley could not afford to offend his patrons, he was compelled to accept the *fiat* of these virtuous scions of a moral and ultra-scrupulous aristocracy. Carlotta Grisi might have had a score of lovers ; but, then, she had never turned up her charming little nose at my Lord Ranelagh."

It was an age when the theatre had to kow-tow to the patron. Unless My Lord approved, Mr. Crummles had no choice but to ring down the curtain. As the Ranelagh faction very emphatically disapproved, Lumley was compelled to give the recruit her marching-orders.

Lola's *première* had thus become her *dernière*.

By the way, a Sunday paper, writing some time afterwards, was guilty of a serious slip in its account of the episode, and mistook Lord Ranelagh for the Duke of Cambridge. " The newcomer," says this critic, " was recognised as Mrs. James by a Prince of the Blood and his companions in the omnibus-box. Her beauty could not save her from insult ; and, to avenge themselves on Mr. Lumley, for some pique, these chivalrous English gentlemen of the upper classes hooted a woman from the stage."

What was behind Lord Ranelagh's cowardly attack on the débutante ? There was a simple explanation, and not one that redounded to his credit in any way. It was that, during her " Bohemian " period, he had endeavoured to fill the empty niche left in her affections by the departure of that light-o'-love, Captain Lennox, and had been repulsed for his pains. A bad loser, my Lord nursed resentment. He would teach a mere ballet-dancer to snap her fingers at him. His opportunity came sooner than he imagined. He made the most of it.

Fond as he was of biting, Lord Ranelagh was, some years afterwards, himself bitten. He took a prominent part in an unsavoury scandal that fluttered mid-Victorian dovecotes, when a Bond Street " beauty specialist," known as Madame Rachel, was clapped into prison for swindling a wealthy and amorous widow. This was a Mrs. Borrodaile, whom " Madame " had gulled by declaring that Lord Ranelagh's one desire was to share his coronet with her. Although the raffish peer denied all complicity, he did not come out of the business too well.

" The peculiar prominence he has attained," remarked an obituarist, " has not always been of an enviable description. There are probably few men who have had so many charges of the most varied and disagreeable nature made against them. The resultant obloquy to which he had thus been exposed is great, nor has it vanished, as it properly should have done, with the charges themselves."

This, however, was looking ahead. The comments of 1843 came first. " In the clubs that night," we read, " the bucks and bloods laughed heartily when they discussed the mishap of the proud beauty who had scorned the advances of my Lord." Lola Montez, however, did not regard it as anything at which to laugh. She may, as she boasted, have had a dash of Spanish blood in her veins, but she certainly had none of George Washington's, for she immediately sat down and wrote a circular letter to all the London papers. In this she sought to correct what she described as a " false impression." Swallowing it as gospel, a number of them printed it in full :

To the Editor.

SIR :

Since I had the honour of dancing at Her Majesty's Theatre, on Saturday, the 3rd inst. (when I was received by the English public in so kind and flattering a manner) I have been cruelly annoyed by reports that I am not really the person I pretend to be, but that I have long been known in London as a woman of disreputable character. I entreat you, Sir, to allow me, through the medium of your respected journal, to assure you and the public, in the most positive and unqualified manner, that there is not a word of truth in such a statement.

I am a native of Seville ; and in the year 1833, when ten years old, was sent to a Catholic lady at Bath, where I remained seven months, and was then taken back to my parents in Spain. From that period, until the 14th of April, when I landed in England, *I have never set foot in this country, and I never saw London before in my life.*

In apologising for the favour I ask you, I feel sure that you will kindly consider the anxiety of myself and my friends to remove from the public any impression to my disadvantage. My lawyer has received instructions to proceed against all the parties who have calumniated me.

Believe me to be your obedient and humble servant,

LOLA MONTEZ.

June 13, 1843.

Ballet-dancers cannot, when making their débuts, be expected to remember everything ; and this one had obviously forgotten her sojourn in India, just as she had forgotten her marriage to Thomas James (and the subsequent Consistory Court action), as well as her amorous dalliance with Captain Lennox during the previous year.

" In spite of the encouraging reception accorded Donna Lola Montez, she has not danced again," remarked a critic in the *Examiner*. " What is the reason ? "

Lumley could have supplied the information. He did so, some years afterwards, in his book, *Reminiscences of the Opera* :

> It is not my intention to rake up the world-wide stories of this strange and fascinating woman. Perhaps it will be sufficient to say frankly that I was, in this instance, fairly " taken in." A Noble Lord (afterwards closely connected with the Foreign Office) had introduced the lady to my notice as the daughter of a celebrated *Spanish* Patriot and martyr, representing her merits as a dancer in so strong a light that her " appearance " was granted.
>
> . . . But this spurious Spanish lady had no real knowledge of that which she professed. The whole affair was an imposture ; and on the very night of her first appearance the truth exploded. On the discovery of the truth, I declined to allow the English adventuress, for such she was, another appearance on my boards. In spite of the expostulations of the " friends " of the lady —in spite of the deprecatory letters in which she earnestly

Viscount Ranelagh, who organised a cabal against Lola Montez

Abbé Liszt : Musician and Lover

denied her English origin—in spite even of the desire expressed in high places to witness her strange performance—I remained inflexible.

The " Noble Lord " thus referred to in this pompous disclaimer was Lord Malmesbury.

IV

If she had a quick temper, Lola Montez had a good heart, and was always ready to lend a helping hand to others. In this connection Edward Fitzball, a hack dramatist with whom things were not going well, has a story of how she volunteered to assist in a benefit performance that was being got up to set him on his legs. It was difficult to secure attractions ; and the beneficiare, realising that, as was the custom in such cases, he would have to make good any deficit himself, was feeling depressed.

" This benefit," he says, " which I fully expected would prove to be a decided loss, annoyed me sadly. I was sauntering along Regent Street when I met Stretton, the popular singer, whose own benefit was just coming off. He said that he had secured every attraction worthy of the public, and that there was no hope for me, ' unless,' he added, ' you could secure Lola Montez.'

" ' Pray, who is that ? ' I said in my ignorance.

" ' Lola Montez is a lady who appeared the other night at Her Majesty's Theatre as a dancer, but, due to some aristocratic disturbance, has left in disgust. The papers were full of it. I offered her £50 to dance for me, and met with a decided refusal. Hence, I see no hope for you.' "

Fitzball, however, thinking it worth while taking a chance, hurried to Lola's lodgings and begged her to contribute to the programme he was offering. He had not expected to be successful, since he knew that she was smarting under a sense of injury. To his surprise and delight, however, she promised her services, and refused to accept any payment.

Overjoyed at the success of his embassy, Fitzball rushed off to the printers and had the hoardings plastered with bills, directing special attention to the novelty :

THEATRE ROYAL, COVENT GARDEN
Monday, July 10, 1843.
COLOSSAL ATTRACTION !
(For the Benefit of Mr. Fitzball)
EXTRAORDINARY COMBINATION OF TALENT !

During the evening the celebrated DONNA LOLA MONTEZ (whose recent performance created so pronounced a sensation at Her Majesty's Theatre) will execute, by special request, her remarkable dance, " El Oleano."

N.B.—This will positively be the Donna's only appearance in London, as she departs on Thursday next for St. Petersburg.

" The theatre," says Fitzball, in his account of the evening, " was crammed. Lola Montez arrived in a splendid carriage, accompanied by her maid. When she was dressed, she enquired if I thought her costume would be approved. I have seen sylphs and female forms of the most dazzling beauty in ballets and fairy dramas, but the most dazzling and perfect form I ever did gaze upon was that of Lola Montez in her white and gold attire studded with diamonds. Her bounding before the public was the signal for general applause and admiration. On the conclusion of her performance, there was a rapturous and universal call for her reappearance."

CHAPTER V

A PASSIONATE PILGRIMAGE

I

THE " departure for St. Petersburg " was a stretch of Fitzball's imagination. Where Lola did go when she left England was not to Russia, but to Belgium. The visit was not a success, as none of the theatres in Brussels at which she applied for an engagement exhibited any interest in ballet-dancers, whether they came from Seville, or elsewhere. A spell of ill luck followed ; and, if her own account of this period is to be trusted, she was reduced to such a pass that in the Belgian capital she became familiar with the inside of pawnshops and had to sing in the streets, to secure a lodging. But this " singing in the streets " business was, if a picturesque one, not an original touch. It is still in active use, as a stock portion of the autobiographical equipment of every stage and film heroine who wants " publicity." Further, if Lola Montez ever did anything of the kind, it was not for long. A " rich man "—she had a knack of establishing contact with them—promptly came to the rescue ; and, assisted by, it is said, the mysterious Jean François Montez, who had followed her from London, she shook the inhospitable dust of the Brussels boulevards off her feet.

It was in Berlin that, in the autumn of 1843, long delayed Fortune smiled on her. A novelty being wanted, she secured an engagement to dance at a fête organised by Frederick William IV in honour of his son-in-law, the Czar Nicholas, and a posse of Grand Dukes then visiting Potsdam. The autocrat of all the Russias expressed himself as highly pleased with the

newcomer's efforts. The Berliners followed suit. Lola was
" made " ; and every night for a month on end she was booked
up to dance somewhere.

While in the German capital, she is said to have had an
encounter with the arm of the law. The story is that, mounted
on a blood horse, she attended a review held in honour of the
King and the Czar ; and her steed, being somewhat mettlesome, carried her at full tilt across the parade ground and into
the midst of the royal party assembled at the saluting-point.

When an indignant policeman, bellowing *Verboten !* at the
top of his voice, rushed up and clung to the bridle, he received
for his pains a vigorous cut from her whip. The next morning
a summons was delivered to the daring Amazon, ordering her
to appear before a magistrate and answer a charge of " insulting
the uniform." Thereupon, Lola, feeling that the general
atmosphere was unfavourable, packed her trunks. She managed to get away just in time, as a warrant for her arrest was
actually being made out. But if she did not leave Berlin with
all the honours of war, it is at any rate recorded that " she left
this city of pigs with a high head and a snapping of her fan."

The Odyssey continued. The next place where she halted
was Dresden. There the pilgrim swam into the orbit of
Franz Liszt, who happened to be giving a series of recitals.
Born in 1811—the " year of the Comet "—he was at the
height of his powers when Lola Montez flashed across his
path. During an early visit to England, as a " boy prodigy,"
he had gathered considerable laurels. Windsor Castle had
smiled upon him, and he had played to George IV and to
Queen Victoria. The chance encounter with Lola was a
fateful one for both of them. But, as it happened, the virtuoso
rather welcomed the prospect of a fresh intrigue just then.
Wearied of the romanticism of the phalanx of feminine
admirers, who clustered about him like bees, he found this
one, with her beauty and vivacious charm, to have a special
appeal for him. He responded to it avidly. The two became
inseparable.

One evening, while *Rienzi* was being performed, his latest charmer accompanied Liszt to the Opera House, and, during an interval, joined him in the dressing-room of Josef Tichatschek, the tenor. Hearing that he was there, Wagner was coming to speak to him, " when he saw that his companion was a painted and bejewelled woman with insolent eyes." Thereupon, if his biographer is to be trusted, " the composer turned and fled." Lola had routed " Rienzi."

Musicians will be musicians ; and Liszt was no exception. With his love affairs and his long catalogue of " conquests " in half the capitals of Europe, he was generally regarded as a Don Juan of the keyboard. It is said by James Huneker that, on leaving Dresden, Lola joined him in Constantinople. In her memoirs she says nothing about wandering along the shores of the Bosphorus in his company. Still, she says a good deal about Sir Stratford Canning, the British Ambassador, by whom, she declares, she was given a letter to the Chief Eunuch, admitting her to the Sultan's harem. But this, like many of her other statements, must be taken with a generous pinch of salt.

During that memorable summer Liszt was specially invited to Bonn, to unveil the Beethoven monument that had been erected there. The ceremony attracted a distinguished gathering, and was witnessed by the King and Queen of Russia, together with Queen Victoria and Prince Albert. It was also witnessed by Lola Montez, who accompanied Liszt. She was promptly recognised by Ignatz Moscheles ; and, when they discovered her presence, the reception committee were so upset that they had her barred from the hotel in which rooms had been engaged for the guest of honour. But it took more than this to keep her in the background. While the speeches were in full swing, she forced her way into the banquet-hall, and won over the prudish burghers by jumping on the table and dancing to them.

The Prince Consort was shocked at the " liberty." Frederick

William, however, being more broad-minded, cracked a Teutonic jest.

" Lola is a Lorelei ! " he declared, with an appreciative grin, when the episode was reported to him. " What will she be up to next ? "

An inevitable result of Liszt's dalliance with his new Calypso in the various capitals that they visited together during the months that followed was to shatter the relations that had existed for years between himself and Madame d'Agoult. The virtuoso emerged from the business badly, for the woman he had discarded in summary fashion for a younger and more attractive one had sacrificed her name and her reputation for his sake, and had also presented him with three pledges of mutual affection. Infuriated at his callousness, she afterwards, as " Daniel Stern," relieved her outraged feelings in a novel (" written to calm her agitated soul "), *Nélida*, where Liszt, under a transparent disguise, figured as " Guermann Regnier."

But the pace was too hot to last. Still, it was Liszt, and not Lola, who cooled first. " With Lola, as with others, known and unknown, it was," observes William Wallace, " *Da capo al Segno*." The story of the final rupture between them, as given by Guy de Pourtalès, has in it something of the element of farce:

> Liszt allowed her to make love to him, and amused himself with this dangerous sweetheart. But without any conviction, without any real curiosity. She annoyed, she irritated him during his hours of work. Before long he planned to escape, and, having arranged everything with the hotel porter, he departed without leaving any address, but not without having first locked this most wearisome of inamoratas up in her room. For twelve hours Lola raised a fearful uproar, breaking whatever she could lay her hands on.

Liszt, however, scenting this possibility, had settled the bill in advance.

But the incident does not redound to his credit, for the spectacle of a distinguished artist bribing a lackey to smuggle him out of an hotel and imprison in her bedroom the woman with whom he had been living, is a sorry one.

II

Having had enough of Germany for the time being, Lola decided to see what France had to offer. " The only place for a woman of spirit," she once said, " is Paris." Accordingly she betook herself there. As soon as she arrived, she secured lodgings in a modest hotel near the Palais Royal ; and, well aware of her limitations, took some dancing lessons from a ballet-master in the rue Lepelletier. When she had taken what she considered enough, she called on Léon Pillet, the director of the *Académie*.

" You have, of course, already heard of my immense success in London," she announced with an assured air.

M. Pillet had not heard of it. But this did not matter. As had been the case with Lumley before him, Lola's ravishing smile inflamed his susceptible heart ; and he promptly engaged her to dance in the ballet that was to follow Halévy's *Il Lazzarone*, then in active rehearsal.

Lola's début as a *première danseuse* was made on March 30, 1844. It was not a successful one. Far from it. The fact was, the Parisians, accustomed to the dreamy and sylph-like pirouettings of Cerito and Elssler and Taglioni, and their own Adèle Dumilâtre, could not appreciate the vigorous *cachuchas* and *boleros* now offered them. When they voiced their disapproval, Lola lost the one thing she could never keep—her temper. She made a *moue* at the audience ; and, if de Mirecourt is to be trusted, pulled off her garters (a second authority says a more intimate item of attire) and flung them with a gesture of contempt among the jeering crowd in the first row of stalls.

As may be imagined, the Press was unsympathetic towards this " demonstration."

" We will avoid damaging with our strictures," remarked *Le Constitutionnel* in its next issue, " a pretty young woman who, before making her début, has obviously not had time to study our preferences."

A much more devastating criticism was published in *Le Journal des Débats* by Jules Janin. He went out of his way, indeed, to be positively offensive. Nor did Théophile Gautier, who in his famous waistcoat of crimson velvet was present on this eventful evening, think very much of the would-be ballerina's efforts to win Paris.

> Beyond, he wrote, a pair of magnificent dark eyes, Mademoiselle Lola Montez has nothing suggestively Andalusian in her appearance. She talks poor Spanish, scarcely any French, and only tolerable English. The question is, to what country does she really belong ? We can affirm that she has small feet and shapely legs. The extent, however, to which these gifts serve her is quite another story.
>
> It must be admitted that the public's curiosity aroused by her altercations with the police of the North and her whip-cracking exploits among the Prussian gendarmes has not been satisfied. We imagine that Mademoiselle Lola would do better on horseback than on the stage.

An odd account, headed : " Singular Début of Lola Montez in Paris," was sent to New York by an American journalist :

" When, a few days ago, it was announced that two foreign dancers, Mlle Cerito and Mlle Lola Montez, had just entered the walls of Paris, the triumphs achieved by the Italian ballerina could not eclipse the horse-whipping exploits of Mlle Lola. ' Let us have Lola Montez ! ' exclaimed the stalls and pit. ' We want to see if her foot is as light as her hand ! ' Never did they witness a more astounding *entrée*. After her first leap, she stopped short on the tips of her toes, and, by a movement of prodigious rapidity, detached one of her garters from a lissome limb adjacent to her quivering thigh (innocent of *lingerie*) and flung it to the occupants of the front row of the orchestra. . . . Notwithstanding the effect produced by this piquant eccentricity, Mlle Lola has not met with the reception she anticipated ; and it has been deemed proper by the management to dispense with her reappearance."

But to give Lola her *congé* by word of mouth was a task which M. Pillet did not care to undertake. " So much was the haughty Amazon's riding-whip dreaded that a letter of dismissal was prudently delivered. As a result, bloodshed was avoided ; and Mlle Lola has solaced herself with the reflection that she has been the victim of the Machiavellian cabal of Russia, still angry at her routing of Muscovite gendarmes in Warsaw."

With reference to the Warsaw episode, the slipshod de Mirecourt says that she was dancing there in 1839. At that date, however, she was no nearer Warsaw than Calcutta. None the less, she did go there, but it was not until she had left Paris after her failure at the Académie Royale. According to herself, the Czar Nicholas, who remembered her in Berlin, invited her to visit St. Petersburg, and, having a month to spare, she accepted a preliminary engagement in the Polish capital.

This began well enough, for, if her terpsichorean abilities still left something to be desired, the Warsaw critics, ever susceptible to feminine charms, went into positive raptures about her personal attractions. One of them, indeed, became almost lyrical on the subject :

" Her soft silken hair," was this authority's opinion, " falls in luxuriant wealth down her back, its glistening hue rivalling that of the raven's wing ; on a slender and delicate neck— the whiteness of which eclipses swansdown—is poised a lovely face. . . . Where the proportions are concerned, Lola's little feet are somewhere between those of a Chinese maiden and those of the daintiest Parisienne imaginable. As for her bewitching calves, they suggest the steps of a Jacob's ladder transporting one up to heaven; and her ravishing figure resembles the Venus of Cnidus, that immortal masterpiece sculptured by the chisel of Praxiteles in the 104th Olympiad. As for her eyes, her very soul is enshrined in their blue depths."

There was a lot more—several columns more—in a similar strain.

As was to be expected, such a tribute attracted the attention of Prince Ivan Paskievich, the Viceroy of Poland. He had a weakness for pretty women; and, after the long succession of lumpy and heavy-footed ballerinas occupying the Warsaw stage, this new arrival sounded promising. When a trusted emissary reported that the critics " had not said half what they might," he resolved to make her acquaintance. His first step was to send her, through Madam Steinkeller, the wife of a banker, an invitation to have supper with him at his private house.

Lola, flattered by the invitation, and less clear-headed than usual, was sufficiently trusting to accept. She soon, however, discovered that his Excellency's intentions were strictly dishonourable, for he made her, she afterwards said, " a most indelicate proposition." Her response was to laugh in his face, and to tell him that " she had no wish to become his toy." Thereupon, Paskievich, furious at such a repulse (and unaccustomed to being thwarted by anyone, must less by a ballet-dancer), dismissed her with threats of reprisals. The first of these took the form of a visit from Colonel Abrahamowicz, the official charged with " preserving morality in the Warsaw theatres." He apparently interpreted his responsible functions in a fashion that left something to be desired, for Lola complained that " his conduct was so free that I took serious exception to it."

Paskievich then dealt his next card. This was to instruct his understrapper to fill the theatre with a rabble and have her hissed off the stage. Lola, however, was equal to the occasion. Advancing to the footlights, before the terror-stricken manager could stop her, she pointed to Colonel

Abrahamowicz, sitting in a box, and exclaimed : " Ladies and gentlemen, there is the dastard who attempts to revenge himself on a pure woman who has scorned his infamous suggestions ! I ask your protection ! "

Accompanied by M. Lesniowski, the editor of the *Warsaw Gazette*, she returned to her lodgings, wondering what would happen next. She was soon to discover, for the angry Colonel and a squad of police arrived with a warrant for her arrest as an " undesirable." When, however, they announced their purpose, she flourished a pistol in their faces and declared that she would put a bullet through the first of them who came near her. Realising that she meant what she said, and not anxious to qualify for cheap martyrdom, Colonel Abrahamowicz was tactician enough to withdraw. In the meantime, the public, learning what had happened, sided with Lola and raised lusty shouts of " Down with the Viceroy ! Long live the Montez ! "

Paskievich, who had crushed with an iron hand the rebellion of 1831, had a short and sharp way with incipient revolutionaries ; and, calling out the troops, cleared the streets at the point of the bayonet. While they were thus occupied, Lola slipped off to the French consul and suggested that he should grant her his protection as a national. With characteristic gallantry, he met her wishes. None the less, she had to leave Warsaw the next morning, under escort to the frontier.

There were reprisals for a number of those who had taken her part. Thus the manager of the theatre and the editor of the *Warsaw Gazette* were dismissed ; M. Steinkeller was imprisoned ; and a dozen students were publicly flogged.

" Tranquillity has been restored," was the official view of the situation.

According to Lola herself (not, by the way, a very sound authority) she went straight from Warsaw and the clutches of the lustful Paskievich to St. Petersburg. Considering, however, that Poland was at that period under the domination of the Czar, it is highly improbable that, after her expulsion,

she could have set foot in Russia without a passport. Had
she been sufficiently daring to make the experiment, she
would assuredly have been clapped into fetters and packed
off to Siberia.

Lola's motto was "courage, and shuffle the cards."
Undeterred by her previous failure there, she went back to
Paris, to try her luck a second time.

Luck came to her very soon, for she had scarcely arrived in
the capital when she encountered a young Englishman,
Mr. Francis Leigh, an ex-officer of the 10th Hussars. Within
a week the two were on such intimate terms that they set up
housekeeping together. But the harmony was shattered
abruptly by Lola, who, in a jealous fit, one day fired a pistol
at her "protector." As this was more than he could be
expected to stand, Mr. Leigh, deciding that they could not
continue living under the same roof, severed the relationship.

III

In 1845 the Paris of Louis-Philippe was, when Lola resumed
her acquaintance with it, a pleasant city in which to live. The
star of Baron Haussmann had not yet arisen ; and the capital's
vulgarisation under the Second Empire had not then begun
John Bull still gave it a wide berth ; nor, except for a few stray
specimens, were there any hordes of tourists to gape at the
" Froggies." Everything was cheap ; and most things were
nice. Paris really was *La ville lumière*. Dull care had been
given its marching orders. All that was required of a man
was that he should be witty, and of a woman that she should
be entertaining. The world of the boulevards—with its cafés
and restaurants and theatres—was the accepted rallying point
of the authors and poets, the painters and musicians, and
the lights twinkling in the theatrical and journalistic firma-
ments, the men in velveteen jackets and peg-top trousers, the
women in flounced skirts and shawls and elastic-sided boots.
The mode of the moment.

Lola settled down among them, and was given a warm

welcome. Among others with whom she was soon on friendly terms was the famous (or, perhaps, it would be better to say, notorious) Alphonsine Plessis. The Lady of the Camelias had a large heart and a wide circle ; and Liszt, who was also back in Paris, was to be found among the guests attending her " receptions " at her house on the Boulevard de la Madeleine. Lola, who never cherished rancour, was prepared to let bygones be bygones, and resumed relations with him. But this time they were short lived, for the maestro was already dangling after another charmer, and, as was his habit, left for Weimar without saying farewell. Lola took his defection philosophically. As a matter of fact, she rather welcomed it, for it solved a situation that was fast threatening to become awkward. This was that she herself had now formed an intimacy with somebody else.

Her new acquaintance was Charles Dujarier, a young man of five and twenty, and a journalist of some distinction, being part proprietor and feuilleton editor of *La Presse*. Lola met him in the friendly atmosphere of a Bohemian café, where formal introductions were not insisted upon. As was the custom in such an atmosphere, the friendship ripened rapidly. Within a week of their first meeting the two set up house-keeping together in the rue Lafitte. Before long there was talk of marriage. But it did not get beyond talk, for Lola had put her head in the matrimonial noose once—in her opinion, once too often—and she had no desire to do so a second time. Apart from this consideration, she was probably well aware that her divorce from the philandering Thomas James had never been completed.

As Dujarier's acknowledged mistress, Lola was accepted without demur as one of themselves by the literary and artistic " set " thronging the cafés and salons they frequented. Gautier and Sue, with Claudin and Méry and Dumas, were those habitués of whom she saw most ; and Ferdinand Bac (but nobody else) says that she was on intimate terms with the austere M. Guizot.

Gustave Claudin declared that he met Lola Montez in Paris in the spring of 1841. That she made an impression on him is evident from a passage in his *Souvenirs* :

> Lola Montez was a charmer. There was something—I do not quite know what—about her appearance that was provocative and voluptuous, and which attracted one. She had a white skin, hair suggestive of the tendrils of honeysuckle, and a mouth that could be compared with a pomegranate. Added to this was a ravishing figure, charming feet, and perfect grace. Unfortunately, as a dancer, she had very little talent.
>
> Towards the year 1845 the author of these notes saw much of her. She wanted him to write her memoirs, and gave him some material for them. . . . She was born in Seville in 1823, with a French officer for a god-father and (as is the custom in Spain) the city of Seville for a godmother. The adventures of her life were written out by her in an exercise-book. She told me that, at a ball in Calcutta, she had once refused to waltz with a wealthy gentleman who was so encrusted with diamonds that he resembled a snuff-box. When he asked her the reason for refusing to dance, she replied : " Sir, I cannot dance with you because you have hurt my foot." The would-be waltzer was a chiropodist !

Writing, as he did, nearly fifty years after the episode to which he thus refers, Claudin's memory was a little shaky. Thus Lola Montez was born in Limerick in 1818, not, as he says, at Seville in 1823 ; nor could Claudin have met her in Paris in the spring of 1841, as she had not then left India.

Dujarier, according to Lola, was much impressed by her political acumen, and employed her on " secret service " for the Government, entrusting her as a preliminary with a " mission to St. Petersburg." The story is an obvious concoction, if merely because Dujarier, being little beyond a penny-a-liner hack, had no power to employ anybody on such a task. Still, Lola always stuck to it. Still, it is just possible that she may have gone to Russia at this period, for Nicholas was interested in the art of the ballet, and welcomed foreign exponents of Terpsichore from wherever they came. He was a familiar figure in the green-rooms of his capital. He patronised Taglioni and Elssler, and was always ready to make up any deficit in the box-office receipts. It only meant grinding more out of his army of serfs.

If she did go from Paris to Russia, Lola did not waste her time there, for, she says, she " nearly married Prince Schulkoski," whom she had already met in Berlin. This, she adds, was " one of the romances of her life." But something went wrong with it, for the princely wooer, " while furiously telegraphing kisses three times a day," was discovered to be enjoying the companionship of another charmer. Lola could put up with a great deal. There were, however, limits to her toleration, and this was one of them. First, Tom James ; then, George Lennox ; and now Prince Schulkoski. Masculine promises were no more substantial than pie-crust. Poor Lola was having a sad awakening. It is not remarkable that she formed the conclusion that men were " deceivers ever." After such an experience, nothing else was possible.

Among other items in her repertoire of alleged happenings in Russia at this period was one that certainly takes a good deal of swallowing. This was that, while having a " private audience " with the Czar himself and Count Benkendorf (the Chief of the Secret Police), an important visitor was announced. Thereupon, and to avoid her presence being known to the newcomer, she was locked up in a cupboard and left there for several hours. When the Czar came back, he was " full of apologies and insisted that she should accept from him a gift of a thousand roubles."

Other details follow :

" A great magnate conquers her at St. Petersburg ; Grand Dukes perform their tricks ; and Circassian Princes die for her. But soon she has enough of caviare and vodka. What, she wonders, is the good of becoming fuddled with drunkards and wasting valuable time on half-civilized Asiatics ? "

No good at all, was Lola's decision. Accordingly, she bade farewell to Russian hospitality, and, relinquishing all prospects of wearing the Muscovite diadem, returned to Paris and Dujarier. Her lover's influence secured her an engagement in *La Biche au Bois* at the Porte St. Martin Theatre ; but, as had happened at the Académie Royale, she was a " flop." The critics said so with no uncertain voice ; and the manager announced that he agreed with them. Clearly, then, the ballet was not her *métier*.

" Well, dancing isn't everything," said Lola, who always took a reverse in philosophical fashion.

CHAPTER VI

AN "AFFAIR OF HONOUR"

I

THE evening of March 7, 1845, was one pregnant with fate where Dujarier was concerned. He had received, and accepted, an invitation to a supper-party at the Frères-Provençaux restaurant, given by Mlle Anais Liévenne, a young actress from the Vaudeville company. Among the other *convives* gathered round the festive board were a quartet of attractive damsels, Atala Beauchene, Victorine Capon, Cecile John, and Alice Ozy, with, to keep them company, a trio of typical *flâneurs* in Rosemond de Beauvallon (a swarthy Creole from Guadaloupe, with ambitions to be considered a novelist), Roger de Beauvoir (a friend of Alphonse Karr, and whose other claim to distinction was that he had once challenged Balzac), and Saint-Agnan (an individual dubbed by journalists a " man-about-town "). Altogether, a gathering thoroughly representative of the theatre, the press, the world, and the half-world.

Lola was invited to join the party ; but, at Dujarier's special request, she excused herself. If, however, she had gone with him, the tragedy for which the evening was to be responsible might have been averted. Still, nobody can look ahead.

For some time, all went merrily as the proverbial marriage bell. The ladies were not too strait-laced ; dull care was banished. Food and drink without stint ; music and lights and laughter ; bright eyes and pretty faces. Champagne corks popped ; toasts were offered ; jests were cracked ; and tongues wagged.

But it did not last. The clouds were gathering; and presently the harmony was interrupted. Dujarier was to blame. Unable to carry his liquor well, or else, under the spell of her bright eyes, he went so far as to remark to his hostess : " My dear Anais, figure to yourself, in six months from now you and I will be sleeping together." The damsel's acknowledged cavalier, de Beauvallon, a stickler for propriety, took this amiss and declared the assertion to be unwarranted. Words followed. Warm words. Mlle Liévenne, however, being good-tempered, merely laughed, and peace was restored.

But the patched-up truce was only a temporary one. Feeling still ran high. A few minutes later, de Beauvallon picked another quarrel with Dujarier, this time complaining that he had neglected to publish a feuilleton of his, *Mémoires de M. Montholon*, that had been accepted by him. As was to be expected, the result of pestering the sub-editor at such a moment was to receive the sharp response that he " must wait his turn, and that, in the meantime, there were more important authors than himself to be considered."

With the idea of calming frayed nerves, somebody suggested that they should all adjourn for a flutter at lansquenet, then ousting écarté. The proposal was accepted ; and, the revellers having settled down, Saint-Agnan, having the best-lined wallet, took the bank.

Fortune did not smile on Dujarier. The luck seemed against him ; and, when the party broke up in the small hours, he was a couple of thousand francs to the bad. Worse than this, he was unable to settle his losses until he had borrowed the necessary billets from the head waiter. As a result, his temper was soured, his nerves on edge. Accordingly, when de Beauvallon was tactless enough to upset him again, he " answered somewhat abruptly."

This, however, was not all. The " wine being in, the wit was out." A woman's name cropped up, that of a certain Madame Albert, a young actress in whose affections Dujarier had, before Lola Montez appeared on the scene, been ousted by de Beauvallon. The recollection rankled, and he made some sneering reference to the subject. With an obvious effort, the other kept his temper and curtly remarking, " You will hear from me to-morrow, Monsieur," left the restaurant.

II

" It might have been thought," is the comment of Larousse, " that, with the fever of the wine abated, these happenings and the recollection of the indecorous words accompanying them would, by the next morning, have been forgotten."

But they were not forgotten. They were remembered. On the following afternoon, while Dujarier was in his office, lamenting the fact that he had made such a fool of himself, and wondering how he was to explain matters to Lola, two visitors were announced. One of them was the Comte de Flers and the other was the Vicomte d'Ecquevillez. With ceremonious bows, they stated the purport of their call. This was that they represented de Beauvallon, who " demanded satisfaction for the insults he had received from M. Dujarier."

The quarrel, however, was really one between two rival papers, *La Presse* and *Le Globe*, which had long been at daggers drawn. Granier de Cassagnac, the editor of *Le Globe*, was the brother-in-law of de Beauvallon, and Emile de Girardin, the proprietor of *La Presse*, had systematically held him up to ridicule in his columns. Hence, when the news of the restaurant fracas leaked out among the café gossipers, the result was that everybody said : " il n'y eut qu'une voix pour dire ' c'est le *Globe* qui veut se battre avec la *Presse*.' "

Dujarier, who had no stomach for fighting—except with his pen—would have backed out if he could. But he could not. Things had already gone too far. Accordingly, he referred the visitors to his friends, Arthur Bertrand (a godson of the Emperor) and Charles de Boignes, and then hurried off to consult them himself.

" Pistols for two and coffee for one," was their decision

when they heard what he had to tell them. There was, they were emphatic, no other way by which he could satisfy his " honour." The code demanded it.

Clutching at a straw, Dujarier next sought counsel of Alexandre Dumas.

" I don't know why I am fighting," he said.

If it came to that, Dumas shared his ignorance. Still, he insisted that a " meeting " was inevitable.

This was the case. For a Frenchman to refuse to " go out " —no matter what his reason—would be to incur social ignominy. He would be looked upon as a pariah ; not a hand would be offered him ; and he would have bundles of white feathers showered upon him by his former acquaintances.

It was all very ridiculous. Still, it must be remembered that " the period was one when journalists aped fine gentlemen, and killed themselves for nothing." Ferdinand Bac declares that this practice was " largely the fault of Dumas, who, in his romances, would describe lovely women throwing themselves between the combatants to effect their reconciliation."

Since a meeting could be a serious affair, the seconds were naturally anxious to protect themselves. Accordingly, the four of them, putting their heads together, drew up a document which, in the event of untoward consequences occurring, would, they felt, absolve them of responsibility :

" We, the undersigned, state that, as the result of a disagreement, M. de Beauvallon has provoked M. Dujarier in a fashion that makes it impossible for him to refuse an encounter. We ourselves have done all we can to reconcile these gentlemen ; and it is only at M. de Beauvallon's urgent demand that we are proceeding in the matter."

As the challenged party, Dujarier had the choice of weapons. The privilege, however, was not worth much to him. He had never handled cold steel, while his adversary was an expert fencer, and he was also such a poor marksman that he could not have made sure of hitting a haystack at twenty yards. Still, he reflected that, although de Beauvallon was unlikely to miss him with a rapier, he might possibly do so with a bullet. Accordingly, he elected for pistols.

When Dujarier came back to her that evening, Lola, with womanly intuition, saw that some trouble had befallen him. Under pressure, he admitted that he was about to fight a duel for which he had no stomach. At the same time, however, he led her to believe that his adversary was de Beauvoir, and not de Beauvallon.

Having thus calmed her fears, for she knew that de Beauvoir was no more a fire-eater than was he himself, he went off to have another consultation with his seconds.

" I shall not be back until late," he said, " as I am supping with Dumas. You must not stop up for me."

Instead, however, of returning that night, Dujarier, feeling that he could not face Lola and tell her the truth, stopped with one of his seconds. There he wrote and sealed a couple of letters, charging de Boignes to " deliver them if required by circumstances." The first was to his mother :

> If this letter reaches you, it will be because I shall be dead or else dangerously wounded. To-morrow morning I am going out to fight with pistols. My position requires it ; and, as a man of honour, I accept the challenge. If you, my good mother, should have cause to weep, it is better that you should shed tears for a son worthy of yourself than to shed them for a coward. I go to the combat in the spirit of a man who is calm and sure of himself. Justice is on my side.

A more difficult, although less flamboyant, letter to write was the second one, for its recipient would be the woman who had given him her heart : and was even then anxiously awaiting his return :

> MY EVER DEAREST LOLA :
>
> I want to explain why it was I slept by myself and did not come to you this morning. It is because I have

to fight a duel. All my calmness is required, and seeing you would have upset me. By two o'clock this afternoon everything will be over.

A thousand fond farewells to the dear little girl I love so much, and the thoughts of whom will be with me for ever.

Having written his letters, he proceeded to draw up his will. This document left, among specific bequests to his mother and sister, certain shares that he held in the Palais Royal to Lola Montez.

III

The date of the meeting was March 11, and the rendezvous was a retired spot in the Bois de Boulogne. A bitterly cold morning, with snow on the ground and heavy clouds in a leaden sky. As the clock struck the appointed hour, Dujarier, accompanied by his seconds, and M. de Guise, a medical man, drove up in a cab. They were the first to arrive.

After waiting for more than an hour, Dujarier was in such a nervous condition that his seconds declared he would be justified in leaving the field, since his adversary had not kept the appointment. Instead, however, of jumping at the chance, he took a swig at a flask of cognac. The potent spirit gave him some measure of Dutch courage, and his teeth stopped chattering.

" I will fight," he announced grandiloquently. " I am a Frenchman, and my honour is very dear to me."

It was to be put to the test, for a few minutes later de Beauvallon and his seconds arrived, with a tardy apology.

On behalf of their principal, Dujarier's seconds then made a last appeal for an amicable settlement. It was coldly received ; and they were told that " the insult offered was too serious to be wiped out by words." There being nothing else for it, the preliminaries were discussed, the conditions of the combat being that the adversaries should stand thirty paces apart, advance six paces, and then fire.

The pistols were furnished by d'Ecquevillez, and it had been expressly stipulated that his principal should not have handled them until that moment. When, however, Bertrand examined the pair, he remarked that, since the barrels were blackened and still warm to the touch, it was obvious that somebody had already practised with them. As, however, d'Ecquevillez swore that they had not been tried by de Beauvallon, the protest was withdrawn.

The distance being measured and the adversaries placed in position, the seconds stepped aside. Then, at a signal, the word was given. The first to fire was Dujarier. He was, however, so agitated that he sent a bullet wide of the mark. De Beauvallon, on the other hand, was perfectly cool and collected. He lifted his weapon and aimed with such deliberate care that de Boignes, unable to restrain himself, called out excitedly : " *Mais, tirez donc, Monsieur !* " With a nod, de Beauvallon pressed the trigger. There was an answering flash and a report ; and, as the smoke drifted away, Dujarier reeled and fell, blood gushing from his mouth and nostrils.

When Dr. de Guise examined him, he looked grave. He saw at once that the injury was serious. As a matter of fact, Dujarier was dead before they returned to Paris.

As the cab reached the house in the rue Lafitte, Lola, waiting there in an agony of suspense, heard the rumble of wheels. Rushing downstairs, she stepped back with a cry of terror, for three men were carrying a heavy burden into the hall. Instinctively, she realised that the worst had happened, that her suspense was at an end.

" Mademoiselle, we have ill tidings for you," said de Boignes.

" I know it," said Lola. " Dujarier is killed. I felt sure this would happen. You should not have let him fight."

The funeral of Dujarier, which took place a couple of days later in the cemetery at Montmartre, was attended by characteristic pomp. The velvet pall above his coffin was held by Balzac, Dumas, and Joseph Méry, and a flowery " oration " delivered at the graveside by Emile de Girardin :

" Whether it endure but a single day, or be deep and prolonged, Man's sorrow is always barren and profitless. It cannot restore to a disconsolate mother, bemoaning her untimely loss, the son for whom she weeps, or give him back to his friends. . . . Let the words written by Dujarier : ' I am about to fight a duel for the most absurd and futile of causes,' never be effaced from our memory. Farewell, Dujarier ! Rest in peace ! Let us carry away from the graveside the hope that the recollection of so lamentable an end will last long enough to shield others from a similar one. Let all mothers —still astounded and trembling—derive some measure of confidence from this hope, and pray to God for poor Dujarier with all the fervour of their souls ! "

As may be imagined, talk followed. A vast amount of talk, in the newspapers and elsewhere. " The topic was discussed," one reads, " at the royal table itself by the family of Louis-Philippe ; and Queen Amelie and Aunt Adelaide stigmatised the conduct of this wicked hussy, Lola Montez, in severe terms."

IV

After such an experience, Lola felt that she had had enough of France for a time. Accordingly, she went back to Germany. There she resumed relations with Liszt, who took her to a second Beethoven Festival at Bonn. While allowance could be made for the artistic temperament, this was considered to be straining it, and caustic remarks on the subject appeared in the press.

During the absence of Lola from Paris, the relatives of Dujarier had not been idle. Unpleasant whispers were heard that the dead man had not fallen in a fair fight ; and that the fatal bullet had come from a weapon with which his adversary had already practised. As this was contrary to the conditions of the encounter, the arm of the law reached out, and de Beauvallon and his seconds were called upon for an explanation. The one they furnished to them was deemed adequate by the authorities. Still, if " honour was satisfied,"

Fanny Elssler.   Predecessor of Lola Montez in Paris

Porte St. Martin Theatre, Paris, where Lola was a " flop "

the friends of de Beauvallon's victim were not. Accordingly, they set to work, and, pulling fresh strings, managed to get the official decision upset.

An article on the subject that appeared in *Le Droit* took a severe tone :

" The grounds alleged to be responsible for this deplorable business," declared an editorial, " were utterly frivolous. As a result, the public prosecutor has instructed an examining-magistrate to enquire into all the circumstances, and an autopsy will be held. It is possible that other measures will be adopted."

Other measures *were* adopted.

" All duels," was the austere comment of the examining-magistrate who conducted the enquiry, " are marked by folly, and some by deliberate baseness." Where this one was concerned, he hinted at something sinister, and asked pointed questions about the pistols that d'Ecquevillez had been obliging enough to furnish. The answer was that they belonged to M. de Cassignac, who, for his part, declared that, until the actual day of the meeting, they had been in the custody of the gunsmith from whom he had bought them. The gunsmith, however, M. Devismes, said that this was not the case ; and another witness declared that he had seen de Beauvallon having a little surreptitious practice with them in the garden.

The next thing that happened was that, before the magisterial enquiry was finished, de Beauvallon and d'Ecquevillez made a hurried departure from Paris. During their absence, it was decided to abandon further proceedings for want of evidence. Thinking himself safe, de Beauvallon then returned. But he was not safe. The Supreme Court cancelled the decision of the inferior one, and announced that he was to stand his trial for murder.

As public feeling ran high, and it was felt that an impartial jury could not have been secured in Paris, the trial was held at Rouen. The date was March 26, 1846. Attracted by the special circumstances of the case, the court was crowded.

" Nearly all those who were present," says Claudin, " belonged to the world of the boulevards." Albert Vandam was among the spectators ; and with him for a companion was a much more distinguished person, Gustave Flaubert.

V

All being in readiness, and the stage set for the drama that was about to be unfolded, the judges, in the traditional red robes, took their seats, with M. Letendre de Tourville as president of the Court. M. Salveton, the public prosecutor, and M. Rieff, the advocate-general, represented the Government ; and Mâitre Berryer and M. Léon Duval appeared respectively on behalf of the accused and the dead man's mother and sister.

As it had been suggested that de Beauvallon had purposely arrived late on the ground, in order to have some preliminary practice, he was told to give an account of his movements of the morning of the duel.

" I got up at seven o'clock," he said, " and went downstairs with the pistols which had been waiting for me at the concierge's when I returned home on the previous evening."

" The concierge remembers nothing of that," interrupted M. Duval. " This is a fresh fact. We must certainly consider it. What happened next ? "

" I went off in a cab to M. d'Ecquevillez, and handed the pistols to him. At half-past ten I returned home, to wait for my seconds. We arrived on the ground at half-past eleven. M. de Boignes received us coldly, with his hands in his pockets, and said : ' You do well to keep us waiting like this for you. Name of God ! this isn't a summer morning. We think there is not sufficient motive to fight a duel.' I answered frigidly, but politely, that I did not agree with him, and that I was in the hands of my seconds."

" But one of them, M. de Flers," remarked the President,

" thought the quarrel trifling and said so. Another thing.
Why did M. d'Ecquevillez tell us that the pistols belonged to
him ? Remember, he has given us details as to where he got
them."

" I ignore details," was the lofty response.

" If you do, we don't," returned the judge.

A vigorous denial was made by de Beauvallon to the suggestion that he was familiar with the pistols used in the duel.
To convince the jury that he was not to be believed, the
opposing counsel then told them that he had once pawned a
watch belonging to somebody else. When the judge expressed
himself shocked at such depravity, de Beauvallon, says a
report, " hung his head and wept."

Nor did d'Ecquevillez, the other defendant, cut a very
happy figure. His real name was said to be Vincent, and
aspersions were cast on his right to dub himself a " Count."
He swore he had never admitted that the pistols belonged to
him, and that de Beauvallon had borrowed them from the
gunsmith, Desvismes. The latter, however, calling on heaven
for support, declared the statement to be a " wicked in-
vention."

Believing in the efficacy of numbers in getting up their
case, forty-six witnesses were assembled by the prosecution.
Mlle Lièvenne, the first of them to be examined, brought with
her an atmosphere of the theatre, " adopting a flashy costume,
in deplorably bad taste." " This," says a chronicler, " took
the form of a blue velvet dress, a scarlet shawl, and a pearl-
grey mantle." Altogether, a striking colour-scheme. But
it did not help her. To the indignation of the examining-
counsel, she affected to remember nothing, declaring that
she had been " too busy at the supper-table, looking after
the company."

The other young women, described as " more or less
actresses," who had also been present, appeared to be suffering from a similar loss of memory. Their minds, they protested, were absolutely blank as to what had happened at the

restaurant and very little could be extracted from them. When they had given their evidence, they looked for seats in the body of the court. The Rouen ladies, however, having somewhat rigid standards, would not permit them to sit between the wind and their propriety.

" Things are coming to a pretty pass," they declared, " when play-actresses imagine they can sit beside respectable women like ourselves."

Thereupon, the discomfited damsels withdrew to the hard benches of the public gallery.

Dumas, subpœnaed as a witness, drove all the way from Paris in a four-horsed carriage, with Méry as a travelling companion. When he took his place on the stand, M. de Tourville, affecting judicial ignorance, enquired his profession.

" If," returned the other, striking an attitude, " I did not here happen to find myself in the country of the illustrious Corneille, I should call myself a dramatist."

" Just so," was the caustic response, " but there are degrees among dramatists."

Taking this for encouragement, Dumas launched out into a disquisition on the history of the duello through the ages that was nearly as long as one of his own serials. In the middle of it, a member of the jury, anxious to be in the limelight, asked him a question.

" How does it happen," he enquired, " that Dujarier, who considered that a man of fashion must fight at least one duel, had never prepared himself by learning to shoot and fence ? "

" I cannot tell you," was the reply. " My son, however, told me that he once accompanied him to a shooting-gallery. Out of twenty shots, he only hit the target twice."

Dumas made an exit as dramatic as his entry.

" I beg," he said, " that the honourable Court will permit me to return to Paris, where I have a new tragedy in five acts being performed this evening."

Lola Montez, garbed in heavy mourning, was the next summoned to give evidence.

" When," says one who was there, " she lifted her veil and removed her glove, to take the prescribed oath, a murmur of admiration ran through the gathering." To this an impressed reporter adds : " Her lovely eyes appeared to the judges of a deeper black than her lace ruffles."

The presiding judge had no qualms about enquiring her age ; and she had none about lopping five years off it and declaring that she was just twenty-one. Nor did she advance any objection to being described, with Gallic candour, as the " mistress of Dujarier."

During her evidence, Lola Montez, probably coached by Dumas, did just what was expected of her. Thus, she shed abundant tears, struck pathetic attitudes, and several times looked on the point of collapsing. But what she had to say amounted to very little. In fact, it was nothing more than an assertion that ill-feeling existed between Dujarier and de Cassagnac, the brother-in-law of de Beauvallon, and that the quarrel was connected with an alleged debt.

Dujarier, she said, had forbidden her to make de Beauvallon's acquaintance, or to attend the supper at the restaurant. He had returned from it in an excited condition at 6 o'clock the next morning and told her that he would have to accept a challenge.

" I was troubled about it," she said, " all day long. But for M. Bertrand's assurance that the encounter was to be with M. de Beauvoir, I would have gone to the police. You see, de Beauvoir was a high-minded gentleman, and would not have condescended to profit from the poor Dujarier's lack of skill."

" Did you not," enquired counsel, " say ' I am a woman of courage, and, if the meeting is in order, I will not stop it ' ? "

" Yes, but that was because I understood it was to be with de Beauvoir, and he would not willingly have harmed

Dujarier. When I heard it was to be with de Beauvallon I exclaimed, ' My God ! Dujarier is as good as dead ! ' "

" I myself," she added, " could handle a pistol more accurately than the poor Dujarier ; and, if he had wanted satisfaction, I should have been quite willing to have gone out with M. de Beauvallon myself."

A murmur of applause met this assurance. Lola's attitude appealed to the spectators. She was clearly a woman of spirit.

During the proceedings that followed some sharp things were said about M. Granier de Cassagnac, the accused's brother-in-law. Some of them were so bitter that at last he protested.

" Monsieur le President," he exclaimed hotly. " I cannot bear these abominable attacks on myself any longer."

" If you can't bear them, you can always leave the court," was the response.

" This gentleman's indignation does not disturb me in the least," said the public prosecutor. " I have already had experience of it, and I consider it to be artificial."

VI

After all the witnesses had been examined and cross-examined, and bullied and threatened in the approved fashion, Maître Duval addressed the jury on behalf of the dead man's relatives. In the course of this he delivered a powerful speech, full of passion and invective, drawing a parallel between this *affaire d'honneur* and the historic one between Alceste and Oronte in Molière's drama. According to him, Dujarier was a shining exemplar, while de Beauvallon was an unmitigated scoundrel, with a " past " of the worst description imaginable. Having once, years earlier, pledged a watch that did not belong to him, he had " no right to challenge anybody, much less a distinguished man of letters, such as the noble Dujarier." The various causes of the quarrel were discussed next. Counsel thought very little of them.

De Beauvallon had complained that Dujarier had " cut " him. " Is it an offence," enquired M. Duval, " for one man to avoid another ? Upon my word, M. de Beauvallon will have to kill a number of people if he wants to kill all those who decline the honour of his companionship." As for the gambling quarrel, this was not serious. What, however, was serious was that, on the morning of the encounter, de Beauvallon had gone to a shooting gallery and had some private practice with the very pistols that were afterwards used. This gave him an unfair advantage. " If," was the advocate's final effort to win a verdict, " M. de Beauvallon is acquitted, the result will be not only a victory for an improperly con- ducted duel, but the very custom of the duel itself will be dishonoured by such a decision."

Léon Duval having sat down, the President turned to the defendant's counsel.

" The word is with you, M. Berryer," he said.

Mâitre Berryer, a master of forensic oratory, began his address by contending that duelling was not prohibited by the law of France. In support he quoted Guizot's dictum : " Where the barbarian murders, the Frenchman seeks honourable combat ; legislation on the subject is profitless ; and this must be the case, since the duel is the complement of modern civilization."

The judges were unprepared to accept this view off-hand ; and, after consulting with the assessors, the President insisted that, whatever M. Berryer might say, duelling was illegal in France. Although he did not tell him so, it was also quite as illegal in England, where Lord Cardigan had, a little earlier, only just wriggled out of a conviction for taking part in one by a combination of false swearing and the subservience of his brother peers.

Not in the least upset, M. Berryer advanced another point. As might have been expected of so accomplished an advocate, he had little difficulty in demolishing the elaborate, but specious and unsupported, hypothesis built up by the other side. Hard facts did more with the stolid and unimaginative Rouen jury than did picturesque embroideries.

" Is the accusation true ? " demanded the President.

" On my honour and on my conscience, before God and before man," announced the foreman, " the declaration of the jury is that it is not true."

As a result of this finding, de Beauvallon was acquitted of the charge of murder. But he did not escape without penalty, for he was ordered to pay 20,000 francs " compensation " to the mother and Dujarier's relatives.

" He was the only son of his mother, and she was a widow." Convinced that there had been a miscarriage of justice and a vast amount of false swearing, the dead man's friends set to work to collect other evidence. By a stroke of luck, they got into touch with a gardener, who said that he had seen de Beauvallon, in company with d'Ecquevillez, having some surreptitious pistol practice on the morning of the duel. Thereupon, the pair of them were rearrested and tried for perjury. Being convicted, d'Ecquevillez was sentenced to ten years' imprisonment and de Beauvallon to eight years. But neither couple stopped in durance very long. The revolution of 1848 opened the doors of the Conciergerie and they made good their escape, the one of them to Spain, and the other to his Creole relatives in Guadeloupe.

CHAPTER VII

"HOOKING A PRINCE"

I

IMMEDIATELY after the Rouen trial, Lola left France, returning once more to Germany. Perhaps the Irish strain in her blood made her a little superstitious. At any rate, just before starting, she consulted a clairvoyante. She felt that she had her money's worth, for the Sibyl declared that she would " exercise much influence on a monarch and the destiny of a kingdom." A long shot, and, as it happened, quite a sound one.

Her intention being, as she had candidly informed Dumas, to " hook a prince," she studied the *Almanach de Gotha*, and familiarised herself with the positions and revenues of the various " notables " accorded niches therein.

Germany was obviously the best field to exploit, for that country just then was full of princes. As a matter of fact there were no less than thirty-six of them waiting to be " hooked." The first place to which she went on this errand was Baden, where, according to Ferdinand Bac, she " bewitched the future Emperor William I. The Prince, however, being warned of her syren spell, presently smiled and passed on."

Better luck befell the wanderer at her next attempt to establish intimate contact with a member of the *hoch geboren*, Henry LXXII. His principality, Reuss-Lobenstein-Ebersdorf (afterwards amalgamated with Thuringia), had the longest name, but the smallest area, of any in the kingdom, for it was only about the size of a pocket-handkerchief. But to Lola this was of no great consequence. What, however, was of consequence was that he was a millionaire (in thalers) and possessed an inflammable heart.

A great stickler for etiquette, he once published the following notice in his *Court Gazette* :

" For twenty years it has been my express injunction that every official shall always be alluded to by his correct title. This injunction, however, has not always been obeyed. In future, therefore, I shall impose a fine of one thaler on any member of my staff who neglects to refer to another by his proper title or description."

But that the Prince could unbend on occasion is revealed by another notification to his subjects :

" His Most Serene Highness and All-Highest Self has graciously condescended to approve the conduct of those six members of the Reuss militia who recently assisted to put out a fire. With his own All-Highest hand he is (on production of a satisfactory birth certificate) even prepared to shake that of the oldest among them."

Risking a prosecution for *lèse-majesté*, a local laureate described the incident in stirring verse. An extract from this effort, translated by Professor J. G. Legge, in his *Rhyme and Revolution in Germany*, is as follows :

HONOUR TO WHOM HONOUR IS DUE

Quite recently in Reuss
  Militia at a fire
(I'm sure it will rejoice you)
  Great credit did acquire.

When this, through a memorial,
  Their gracious Prince by Right
Had learned ; those territorials
  He to him did invite.

And when the good men shyly
  Stood up before him, each
His Gracious Highness highly
  Praised in a Gracious speech.

A solemn affidavit
(With parents' names and date)
Each then produced and gave it
—His birth certificate.

His Highness then demanded
The eldest of the band,
And clasped that horny-handed
With his All-Highest hand.

Now, this great deed recorded,
Who would not dwell for choice
Where heroes are rewarded
As in the land of Reuss ?

Where Lola was concerned, she very soon put a match to the inflammable, if arrogant, heart of Prince Henry, and, as a result, was " commanded " to accompany him to his miniature court at Ebersdorf. She did not, however, stop there very long, for, by her imperious attitude and contempt of etiquette, she disturbed the petty officials and bourgeois citizens surrounding it to such a degree that they made formal complaints to his High-and-Mightiness. At first he would not hear a word on the subject. Such was his favourite's position that criticism of her actions was perilously near *lèse-majesté* and incurred reprisals. As soon, however, as the amorous princeling discovered that his bank balance was being depleted considerably beyond the amount for which he had budgeted, he suffered a sudden spasm of virtue and issued marching-orders to the " Fair Impure," as his shocked and strait-laced Ebersdorfians dubbed the intruder among them. There was also some suggestion, advanced by a gardener, that she had a habit of taking a short cut across the princely flower-beds when she was in a hurry. This was the last straw.

" Leave my kingdom at once," exclaimed the furious Henry. " You are nothing but a feminine devil ! "

Not in the least discomfited by this change of opinion, Lola riposted by presenting a lengthy and detailed account for " services rendered " ; and, when it had been met (and not before), shook the dust of Reuss-Lobenstein-Ebersdorf from her pretty feet.

"You can keep your Thuringia," was her parting-shot. "I wouldn't have it as a gift."

The next places at which she halted were Homburg and Carlsbad, two resorts then beginning to become popular and attracting a wealthy crowd seeking a promised "cure" for their various ills. But, finding the barons apt to be close-fisted, and the smart young lieutenants without one *pfennig* in their pockets to rub against another, Lola was soon continuing her travels.

In September, 1846, she found herself in Wurtemburg, where, much to her annoyance, she discovered that a certain Amalia Stubenrauch, a prepossessing damsel, who would now be called a gold-digger, had conquered the spare affections of King William, on whom Lola herself had designs. But that large-hearted monarch had, as it happened, few affections to spare for anybody just then, for, when she encountered him at Stuttgart, he was on the point of being married to Princess Olga of Russia. A correspondent of the *Athenæum*, who was there to chronicle the wedding festivities for his paper, registered disapproval at her presence in the district. "From the capital of Wurtemburg," he announced sourly, "Lola Montez departed in the *schnellpost* for Munich, unimpeded by any luggage." Somebody else, however (perhaps a more careful observer), is emphatic that she "went off with three carts full of trunks." As she always had a considerable wardrobe, this is quite possible.

II

When, at the suggestion of Baron Maltitz (a Homburg acquaintance who had suggested that she should "try her luck in Munich"), Lola set off for Bavaria, that country was ruled by Ludwig I. A god-child of Marie-Antoinette, and the son of Prince Max Joseph of Zweibrucken and Princess Augusta of Hesse-Darmstadt, he was born at Salzburg in 1786 and had succeeded his father in 1825. As a young man,

he had served with the Bavarian troops under Napoleon, and
detesting the experience, had conceived a hatred of everything military. This hatred was so strongly developed that
he would not permit his sons to wear uniform. Under his
regime the military estimates were cut down to the bone.
The army, he said, was a " waste of money," and he grudged
every *pfennig* it cost the annual budget. He did his best to
abolish conscription, but had to abandon the effort. For all,
too, that he was a god-son of Marie-Antoinette, he had no
love for France.

Ludwig's sister, Louisa, exchanging her religion for a consort's crown, was the wife of the Czar Alexander I ; and he
himself was married to the Princess Theresa of Saxe-
Hildburghausen, a lady described as " plain, but exemplary."
Still, so far as personal appearance goes, Ludwig himself was
no Adonis. Nestitz, indeed, has pictured him as " having a
toothless jaw and an expressionless countenance." But his
consort did her duty ; and, at approved intervals, presented
him with a quiverful of four sons and three daughters. Of his
sons, one of them, Otto, was, as a lad of sixteen, selected by
the Congress of London to be King of Greece, much to the
fury of the Czar Nicholas, who held that this was a cunning,
if diplomatic, attempt to set up a Byzantine empire among the
Hellenes. " Were I," he said in a despatch on the subject,
" to give my countenance to such a step, I should nullify
myself in the eyes of my Church." Nesselrode, however, was
of another opinion. " It is unbecoming," he was daring
enough to inform his master, " for the Emperor of Russia to
question a step upon which the Greeks themselves are not in
entire accord." A remarkable utterance. Politicians had
gone to Siberia for less. Palmerston, too, had his way, and
Otto, escorted by a warship, left his fatherland. On arriving
in Athens, the joy-bells rang out and the columns of the
Parthenon were flood-lit. But the choice was not to the
popular taste ; and it was not long before Otto was extin-
guished, as well as the lights. By the irony of fate, he returned

to Munich on the very day that Ludwig had erected a Doric arch to commemorate the activities of the House of Wittelsbach in securing the Liberation of Greece.

Despite this untoward happening, Ludwig remained an ardent Phil-Hellene ; and, as such, conceived the idea of converting his capital into a mixture of Athens and Florence and a metropolis of all the arts. Under his fostering care, Munich was brought to bed of a succession of temples and columns, and sprouted pillars and porticoes in every direction. The slums and alleys and huddle of houses in the old enceinte were swept away, and replaced by broad boulevards, fringed with museums and churches and picture galleries. For many of the principal public buildings he went to good models. Thus, one of them, the Königsbau, was copied from the Pitti Palace ; a second from the Loggia de' Lanzi ; and a third from St. Paul's at Rome. He also built a Walhalla, at Ratisbon, in which to preserve the effigies of his more distinguished countrymen. Yet, although it ran to size, there was no niche in it for Luther.

In his patronage of the fine arts, Ludwig followed in the footsteps of the Medici. During his regime, he did much to raise the standard of taste among his subjects. Martin Wagner and von Hallerstein were commissioned by him to travel in Greece and Italy and secure choice sculpture and pictures for his galleries and museums. The best of them found a home in the Glyptothek and the Pinakothek, two enormous buildings in the Doric style, the cost of which he met from his privy purse. Another of his hobbies was to play the Maecenas ; and any budding author or artist who came to him with a manuscript in his pocket or a canvas under his arm was certain of a welcome.

We all have our little weaknesses. That of Ludwig of Bavaria was that he was a poet. He was so sure of this that he not only produced yards of turgid verse, defying every law of construction and metre, but he even had some of it printed. A volume of selections from his Muse, entitled *Walhalla's*

Genossen, was published for him by Baron Cotta, and, like
the Indian shawls of Queen Victoria, did regular duty as a
wedding-gift. One effort was dedicated " To Myself as
King," and another " To my Sister, the Empress of Austria " ;
and a number of choice extracts were translated and appeared
in an English guide-book.

Ignoring the divinity that should have hedged their
author, Heine was very caustic about this royal assault upon
Parnassus. Ludwig riposted by banishing him from the capital.
Still, if he disapproved of this one, he added to his library the
output of other bards, not necessarily German. But, while
Browning was there, Tennyson had no place on his shelves.
One, however, was found for Martin Tupper.

Ludwig cultivated friendly relations with England, and did
all he could (within limits) to promote an *entente*. Thus, on
the occasion of a chance visit to Munich by Lord Combermere, he " sent the distinguished traveller a message to the
effect that a horse and saddlery, with aide-de-camp complete,
were at his service." His companion, however, a member of
the Foreign Office Staff, who had forgotten to pack his uniform—or in John Bull fashion had declined to do so—did
not fare so well, since his name was struck off the list of
" eligibles " to attend the palace functions. Thereupon, says
Lord Combermere, he " wrote an angry letter to the chamberlain, commenting on the absurdity of the restriction."

But Ludwig's opinion of diplomatists was also somewhat
unflattering, for, of a certain embassy visited by him on his
travels, he wrote :

" A Theatre once—and now an Ambassador's dwelling.
   Still, thou are what thou wast—the abode of deception."

A strange mixture of Henry IV and Haroun-al-Raschid,
Ludwig of Bavaria was a man of contradictions. At one
moment he was lavishly generous ; at another, incredibly
mean. He could be an autocrat to his finger tips, and insist
on the observance of the most minute points of etiquette ;

and he could also be as democratic as anybody who ever waved a red flag. Thus, he would often walk through the streets as a private citizen, and without an escort. Yet, when he did so, he insisted on being recognised and having compliments paid him. The traffic had to be held up and hats doffed at his approach.

Nowadays, he would probably have been clapped into a museum as a curiosity.

Such, then, was the monarch whose path was to be crossed, with historic and unexpected consequences to each of them, by Lola Montez.

III

On arriving in Munich, Lola called on the manager of the Hof Theatre. As this individual already knew of her Paris fiasco, instead of an engagement from him, she met with a rebuff. Quite undisturbed, however, by such an experience, she hurried off to the palace, and commanded the astonished door-keeper to take her straight to the King.

The flunkey referred her to Count Rechberg, the aide-de-camp on duty. With him Lola had more success. Boldness conquered where bashfulness would have failed. After a single swift glance, Count Rechberg decided that the applicant was eligible for admission to the " Presence," and reported the fact to his master.

But Ludwig already knew something of the candidate for terpsichorean honours. As it happened, that very morning he had received from Herr Frays, the director of the Hof Theatre, a letter, telling him that, on the advice of his *première-danseuse*, Fräulein Frenzal, he had refused to give her an engagement. Count Rechberg's florid description of her charms, however, decided His Majesty to use his own judgment. But he did not give in easily.

" Is it suggested," he demanded acidly, " that I should receive all these would-be ballerinas and put them through their paces ? They come here by the dozen. Why am I troubled with such nonsense ? "

" Sire," returned Rechberg, greatly daring, but with Lola's magnetism still upon him, " you will not regret it. I assure you this one is an exception. She is delightful. That is the only word for it. Never have I seen anybody to equal her. Such grace, such charm, such——"

" Pooh ! " interrupted Ludwig, cutting short the threatened rhapsodies, " your swan is probably a goose. Most of them are. Still, now that she's here, let her come in. If she isn't any good, I'll soon send her about her business."

Brave words, but they availed him nothing. Ludwig shot one glance at the woman who stood before him, and capitulated utterly.

A sudden thrill passed through him. His sixty years fell away in a flash. A river of blood surged through his sexagenarian arteries. His boast recoiled upon himself. Rechberg had not deceived him.

" What has happened to me ? " he muttered feebly. " I am bewitched." Then, as the newcomer stood smiling at him in all her warm loveliness, he found his tongue.

" Mademoiselle, you say you can dance. Well, let me see what you can do. Count Rechberg, you may leave us."

" Do I dance here, in this room, Your Majesty ? "

" Certainly."

Lola wanted nothing better. The opportunity for which she had been planning and scheming ever since she left Paris had come at last. Well, she would make the most of it. Not in the least perturbed that there was no accompaniment, and no audience but His Majesty, she executed a *pas seul* there and then. It was a " royal performance," and eminently successful. Her feet tripped lightly across the polished floor, and danced their way straight into Ludwig's heart.

" You shall dance before the public," he announced. " I will myself give orders to the director of the Hof Theatre."

Luise von Kobell, when a schoolgirl, encountered her by chance just after her arrival, and thus records the impression she received :

As I was walking in the Briennerstrasse, not far from the Bayersdorf Palace, I saw a veiled lady, wearing a black gown and carrying a fan, coming towards me. Something flashed across my vision, and I suddenly stood still, completely dazzled by the eyes into which I stared, and which shone from a pale countenance that lit up with a laughing expression at my bewilderment. Then she swept past me ; and I, forgetting what my governess had said about looking round, stared after her until she disappeared. . . . " That," said my father, when I reached home and recounted my adventure, " must have been Lola Montez, the Spanish dancer."

The next evening little Fräulein von Kobell saw her again at the Hof Theatre, where her first appearance before the Munich public was made on October 10, 1846.

Lola Montez assumed the centre of the stage. She was not dressed in the customary tights and short skirts of a ballerina, but in a Spanish costume of silk and lace, in which shone at intervals a diamond. It seemed as if fire darted from her wonderful blue eyes, and she bowed like one of the Graces at the King in the royal box. She danced after the manner of her country, bending on her hips and alternating one posture with another, each rivalling the former one in beauty.

While she was dancing she held the attention of all ; everybody's eyes followed her sinuous movements, now indicative of glowing passion, now of frolicsomeness. Not until she ceased her rhythmic swayings was the spell interrupted. The audience went mad with rapture, and the entire dance had to be repeated over and over again.

Ludwig, ensconced in the royal box, could not take his eyes off her. During an *entr'acte* he scribbled a verse :

Happy movements, clear and near,
Are in thy living grace.
Supple and tender, as a deer
Art thou, of Andalusian race !

" *Wunderschön !* " declared an admiring aide-de-camp to whom he showed it.

" *Kolossal !* " echoed a second, not to be outdone in recognising laureateship.

As, however, the cheers were mingled with a few hisses (" due to the report that the newcomer was an English Freemason, and wanted to destroy the Catholic religion "), the next evening the management took the precaution of filling the pit with a leather-lunged and horny-handed *claque*. This time the bill consisted of a comedy, *Der Weiberseind von Benedix*, followed by a cachucha and a fandango with Herr Opsermann for a dancing-partner.

Lola's success was assured ; and Herr Frays, who had started by refusing to let her appear, was now full of grovelling apologies. He offered her a contract. But Lola, having other ideas as to how her time should be employed in Munich, would not accept it.

" Thank you for nothing," she said. " When I asked you for an engagement, you told me I was not good enough to dance in your theatre. Well, I have now proved to both Fräulein Frenzal and yourself that I am. That is all I care about, and I shall not dance again, either for you or for **anybody else.**"

If she had known enough German, she would probably have added : " Put that in your pipe and smoke it ! "

Munich in those days must have proved attractive to people with small incomes. Thus, Edward Wilberforce, who spent some years there, says that meat was fivepence a pound, beer twopence-halfpenny a quart, and servants' wages eight shillings a month. But there were drawbacks.

" The city," says an English guide-book of this period, " has the reputation of being a very dissolute capital." Yet it swarmed with churches. The police, too, exercised a strict watch upon the hotel registers ; and, as a result of their activities, a " French visitor was separated from his feminine companion on grounds of public morality."

" None of your Parisian looseness for us ! " said the City Fathers.

But Lola appears to have avoided any such rigid censorship. At any rate, a certain Auguste Papon (a mixture of pimp and *souteneur*), whom she had met in Paris, happened to be in Munich at the same time as herself. The intimacy was revived ; and, as he did not possess the entrée to the Court, for some weeks they lived together at the Hotel Maulich. In the spring of 1847 a young Guardsman found himself in the town, on his way back to England from Kissengen. He records that, not knowing who she was, he sat next Lola Montez at dinner one evening, and gives an instance of her quick temper. " On the floor between us," he says, " was an ice-pail, with a bottle of champagne. A sudden quarrel occurred with her neighbour, a Bavarian lieutenant ; and, applying her foot to the bucket, she sent it flying the length of the room."

IV

Lola certainly made the running. Five days after she first met him, Ludwig summoned all the officials of the Court, and astonished (and shocked) them by introducing her with the remark : " Gentlemen, I have the honour to present to you my best friend. See to it that you accord her every possible respect." He also compelled his long suffering spouse to admit her to the Order of the Chanoines of St. Thérèse, a distinction for which—considering her some-what lurid " past "—this new recipient was scarcely eligible.

When he heard that instructions had been issued for paying special compliments to her, Mr. *Punch* registered severe disapproval.

" It is a good joke," he remarked, " to call upon others to

uphold the dignity of one who is always at some freak or other to lower herself."

When she first sailed in dramatic fashion into the orbit of Bavaria's sovereign, Lola Montez was just twenty-seven. In the full noontide of her beauty and allurement, she was well equipped with what the modern jargon calls sex-appeal. Big-bosomed and with generously swelling curves, " her form," says Eduard Fuchs, " was provocation incarnate." Fuchs, who was an expert on the subject of feminine attractions, knew what he was talking about. " Shameless and impudent," adds Heinrich von Treitschke, " and as insatiable in her voluptuous desires as Sempronia, she could converse with charm among friends ; manage mettlesome horses ; sing in thrilling fashion ; and recite amorous poems in Spanish. The King, an admirer of feminine beauty, yielded to her magic. It was as if she had given him a love philtre. For her he forgot himself ; he forgot the world ; and he even forgot his royal dignity."

The fact that Lola always wore a Byronic collar helped the theory, held by many, that she was a daughter of the poet. But her real reason for adopting the style was that she had a lovely neck, and this set it off to the best advantage. She studied the art of dress and gave it an immense amount of care. Where this matter was concerned, no trouble or care was too much. Her favourite material was velvet, which she considered—and quite justifiably—to exercise an erotic effect on men of a certain age. She was insistent, too, that the contours of her figure (" her quivering thighs and all the demesnes adjacent thereto ") should be clearly revealed, and in a distinctly provocative fashion. This, of course, was not far removed from exhibitionism. As a result, bourgeois opinion was outraged. The wives of the petty officials shopping in the Marienplatz shuddered, and clutched their ample skirts when they saw her ; anxious mothers instructed dumpy Fräuleins " not to look like the foreign woman." There is no authoritative record that any of them did so.

CHAPTER VIII

LUDWIG THE LOVER

I

LOLA MONTEZ had done better than "hook a prince." A lot better. She had now "hooked" a sovereign. Her ripe warm beauty sent the thin blood coursing afresh through Ludwig's sluggish veins. There it wrought a miracle. He was turned sixty, but he felt sixteen.

The conversation of Robert Burns is said to have "swept a duchess off her feet." Perhaps it did. But that of Lola Montez had a similar effect on a monarch. Under the magic of her spell, this one became rejuvenated. The years were stripped from him; he was once more a boy. With his charmer beside him, he would wander through the Nymphenburg Woods and under the elms in the Englischer Garten, telling her of his dreams and fancies. His passion for Greece was forgotten. Pericles was now Romeo.

> *In dem Suden ist die Liebe,*
> *Da ist Licht und da ist Glut !*

that is,

> In the south there is love,
> There is light and there is heat.

sang Ludwig.

Yet Lola Montez was not by any means the first who ever burst into the responsive heart of Ludwig I. She had many predecessors there. One of them was an Italian syren. But that Lola soon ousted her is clear from a poetical effort of which the royal troubadour was delivered. This begins :

Tropfen der Seligkeit und ein Meer von bitteren Leiden
Die Italienerin gab—Seligkeit, Seligkeit nur
Lässest Du mich entzündend, begeistert, befändig empfinden,
In der Spanierin fand Liebe und Leben ich nur !

A free rendering of this passionate heart throb would read very much as follows :

Drops of bliss and a sea of bitter sorrow
    The Italian woman gave me. Bliss, only bliss,
Thou gav'st my enraptured heart and soul and spirit.
    In the Spanish woman alone have I found Love and Life !

Ludwig had a prettier name for his inamorata than the " feminine devil " of Henry LXXII of Reuss. He called her the " Lovely Andalusian " and the " Woman of Spain." She also inspired him to fresh poetic flights. One of these ran :

Thine eyes are blue as heavenly vaults
    Touched by the balmy air ;
And like the raven's plumage is
    Thy dark and glistening hair !

There were several more verses.

A feature of the Residenz Palace was a collection of old masters. Wanting to add a young mistress, Ludwig allotted a place of honour among them to a portrait of Lola Montez, from the brush of Josef Stieler. The work was well done, for the artist was inspired by his subject ; and he painted her wearing a costume of black velvet, with a touch of colour added by red carnations in her head-dress.

Ludwig's heart being large, *Die Schönheitengalerie* (as the " Gallery of Beauties " was called) filled two separate rooms. The one qualification for securing a niche on the walls being a pretty face, the collection included the Princess Alexandra of Bavaria (daughter of the King of Greece), the Archduchess Sophie of Austria, and the Baroness de Krüdener (catalogued as the " spiritual sister " of the Czar Alexander I), a popular actress, Charlotte Hagen, a ballet-dancer, Antoinette Wallinger, and the daughters of the Court butcher and the municipal town-crier. To these were added a quartet of

Englishwomen, in Lady Milbanke (the wife of the British Minister), Lady Ellenborough, Lady Jane Erskine, and Lady Teresa Spence. It was to this gallery that Ludwig was accustomed to retire for a couple of hours every evening, to " meditate " on the charms of its occupants. Being, however, possessed of generous instincts, and always ready (within limits) to share his good things, the public were admitted on Sunday afternoons.

But Ludwig could scratch, as well as purr. On one occasion he chanced to meet a lady who had figured among the occupants of the *Schönheiten.* She was considerably past the first flush of youth, and Ludwig, exercising his prerogative, affected not to remember her.

" But, Sire," she protested, " I used to be in your gallery."

" That, madame," was the response, " must have been a very long time ago. You would certainly not be there now."

II

From her modest hotel, where, soon tiring of his society, she left Auguste Papon to stay by himself, Lola took up fresh quarters in a small villa which the King had placed at her disposal in the Theresienstrasse, a boulevard conveniently near the Hofgarten and the Palace. While comfortable enough, it was held to be merely a temporary arrangement. There was not enough room in it for Lola to expand her wings. She wanted to establish a *salon* and to give receptions. Accordingly, she demanded something more suitable. It meant spending money, and Ludwig had already, he reflected, spent a great deal on her whims and fancies. Still, under pressure, he came round, and, agreeing that there must be a fitting nest for his love-bird (with a perch in it for himself), he summoned his architect, Metzger, and instructed him to build one in the more fashionable Barerstrasse.

" No expense is to be spared," he said.

None was spared.

The new dwelling, which adjoined the Karolinen Platz, was really a bijou palace, modelled on the Italian style. Everything in it was of the best, for Ludwig had cash and Lola had taste. Thus, her toilet-set was of silver ware ; her china and glass came from Dresden : the rooms were filled with costly nicknacks ; mirrors and cabinets and vases and bronzes ; richly-bound books on the shelves ; and valuable tapestries and pictures on the walls. French elegance, added to Munich art, with a touch of solid English comfort in the shape of easy chairs and couches.

To check a playful habit that the Munich mob had of throwing bricks through them, when they had drunk more beer than they could carry, the windows were fitted with iron grilles. As a further precaution, a mounted officer always accompanied the Barerstrasse châtelaine when she was driving in public, and sentries stood at the door, to keep the curious at a respectful distance.

A description of the Barerstrasse nest was sent to London by a privileged journalist who had inspected it :

" The style of luxury in which Lola Montez lives here passes all bounds. Nothing to equal it has been met with in Munich. It might almost be an Aladdin's palace ! The walls of her bed-chamber are hung with guipure and costly satin. The furniture is of Louis XV era, and the mantelpiece is of valuable Sèvres porcelain. The garden is filled with rare flowers, and the carriages and horses in the stables are the wonder and envy of the honest burghers."

" The Queen herself could not be better housed," said Lola delightedly, when she saw all the luxuries of which she was now the mistress.

" You are my Queen," declared Ludwig fondly.

While Lola, to please her patron, grappled with the intricacies of the German tongue, Ludwig, to please his charmer, took lessons from her in Spanish. She still stuck to her Andalusian upbringing, and is said (but the report lacks confirmation) to have introduced him to à Kempis. This, however, is probably a misprint for Don Quixote. None the less, her inspiration was such that her pupil could write :

> Thou dost not wound thy lover with heartless tricks ;
> Nor dost thou play with him wantonly.
> Thou art not for self ; thy nature is generous and kind.
> My beloved ! Thou art munificent and unchanging.
>
> .   .   .   .   .   .
>
> " Give me happiness ! " I begged with fierce longing.
> And happiness I received from thee, thou Woman of Spain !

Notwithstanding the suggestion implied by this assurance, Lola always insisted that her relations with the King were purely platonic. While this view is a little difficult to accept, it is significant that Ludwig's lawful spouse never objected to their " friendship." Her Majesty, however, was of a placid temperament. Perhaps, too, she thought that the fancy would not endure. If so, she was wrong, for, with the passage of time, the newcomer was obviously consolidating her position. " Lola Montez, of horse-whipping notoriety," remarked a journalist, " appears to be increasing in favour at the Court of Bavaria. The Queen calls her ' My dear,' and the ladies consider it their duty to caress the one who has all the world of Munich at her feet."

During the summer, Ludwig, divesting himself of the cares of state, retired to his castle at Bruckenau, picturesquely situated in the Fulda Forest ; and Lola, attended by a squadron of Cuirassiers, accompanied him to this retreat. There, as in the Nymphenburg Park, Ludwig dreamed dreams, while Lola amused herself with the officers of the escort. Halcyon days—and nights. They inspired His Majesty with yet another " poem " :

SONG OF WALHALLA

> Through the holy dome, oh come,
> Brothers, let us roam along ;
> Let from thousand throats the hum
> Rise, like rivers, swift and strong !

When the notes have died away
Let us clasp each other's hand ;
And, to high Heaven, let us pray
For our dearest Fatherland !

While she accorded it full value, Lola Montez did not depend on mere beauty for her power. She had a markedly sadistic vein in her composition ; and, when annoyed, was not above laying about her right and left with a dog-whip that she always carried. An impudent lackey would be flogged into submission, or set upon by a fierce mastiff that she kept at her heels. High office, too, meant nothing to her. She boxed the ears of Baron Pechman ; and, because he chanced to upset her, she encouraged her four-coated companion to tear the best trousers of Professor Lasaulx, the nephew of Görrez, a Cabinet Minister.

Her English bulldog (with apparently a strain of Presbyterian blood in him) had an unerring scent for Jesuits. He seemed to disapprove of their principles as much as his mistress did, and would attack them at sight. This animal would also appear to have been something of a prohibitionist. At any rate, he once bit a brewer's carman, delivering goods to a *bierkeller*. When the victim expostulated, Lola struck him with her whip. This infuriated the crowd to such an extent that she had to take refuge in a shop. There she happened to jostle a lieutenant, who, not recognising her, ventured on a protest. The next morning he received a challenge from a fire-eating comrade, alleging that he had " insulted a lady." Because the challenge was refused, a " court of honour " had him deprived of his commission.

III

What a distressed commentator has dubbed the " equivocal position " of Lola Montez at Munich also stuck in the gullet of the Cabinet, and heads were shaken. Public affronts were offered her. When she visited the Odéon Theatre, the stalls adjoining the one she occupied were promptly emptied.

" Respectable women drew back, exhibiting on their countenances disgust and terror." But the masculine members of
the audience were less exclusive, or perhaps made of sterner
material, for they displayed eagerness to fill up the vacant
stalls. " A new chivalry was born," says a chronicler of town
gossip, " and paladins were anxious to act as a buckler."

With the passage of time the infatuation of the Wittelsbach
Lovelace became so marked that it could not be ignored in
places beyond Munich. The Countess Bernstorff grew
seriously perturbed. " There has long been talk," she con-
fided to a friend, " as to whether King Ludwig would so far
presume on the kindness and indulgence of the Queen of
Prussia as to bring Lola Montez to Court during Her Majesty's
forthcoming stay in Munich." The problem, however, was
solved by the tactful action of Lola herself, who gave the
palace a wide berth until the visit had come to an end.

In his *Memoirs of Madam Jenny Lind-Goldschmidt* shocked
horror is similarly expressed by Canon Scott Holland at the
possibility of the Swedish Nightingale, who was arranging to
give a concert there, encountering Lola in her audience :

> The time fixed for this visit to Munich was, in one
> respect, most unpropitious ; and, for a young artist,
> unsupported by powerful moral protection, the visit
> itself might well have proved extremely unpleasant. It
> was impossible to sing at Court, for the reigning spirit in
> the household of King Ludwig I was the notorious Lola
> Montez, who was then at the climax of her ill-gotten
> power. To have been brought into contact with such a
> person would have been intolerable. An invitation to
> Court would have rendered such contact inevitable.

But if Jenny Lind adopted a lofty attitude and refused to
fulfil an engagement in the Bavarian capital, lest she should
have chanced to rub shoulders with Ludwig's mistress, other
visitors did not share these qualms. They arrived in battalions,
and evinced no disinclination to make her acquaintance.

" To the shame of the aristocracy and the arts," says a rigid commentator, " every day there were to be found at the feet of this Cyprian intruder a throng of princes and philosophers, authors and painters, and sculptors and musicians."

Fresh tactics to get her out of Munich were then adopted. When, however, somebody remarked that Ludwig was old enough to be her grandfather, she sent him away with a flea in his ear.

" It is ridiculous to talk like that," she said. " My Ludwig's heart is young. If you knew the strength of his passion, you would not credit him with being more than twenty ! "

As for Ludwig himself he was bombarded with anonymous letters and warnings, calling Lola by every evil name that occurred to the writers. She was La Pompadour and the Sempronia of Sallust in one, a " voluptuous woman," and a " flame of desire." There were also tearful protests from the higher clergy, who, headed by Archbishop Diepenbrock, were positive that the " dancing woman " was an emissary of Satan (sometimes they said of Lord Palmerston) sent from England to destroy the Catholic religion in Bavaria.

Ludwig was curt with His Grace. " You stick to your *stola*," he said, " and let me stick to my Lola."

A soft answer, perhaps ; but not a very satisfactory one.

" It is all very well for kings to have mistresses," was the opinion of the more broad-minded, " but they should select them from their own countrywomen. This one is a foreigner. Why should our hard-earned money be lavished on her ? " The grievance was, as it happened, well founded, for Lola was drawing 20,000 marks a year, wrung from the pockets of the tax-payers.

Baron Pechman, the Chief of Police, had a bad reception when he suggested that the populace might get out of control.

" If you can't manage the mob," said Ludwig, turning on him furiously, " I'll get someone who can. A change of air may do you good."

The next morning the discomfited Baron Pechman found himself *dégommé* and a successor appointed to his office.

The intrigue was too openly conducted to be " hushed up." Word of what was happening in Munich soon filtered through to Vienna. Queen Caroline-Augusta, Ludwig's sister, shook her head. " Alas," she sighed, " my wretched brother is always bringing fresh shame on me." She wrote him letters of tearful protest. They were ignored. She protested by word of mouth. Ludwig, in unbrotherly fashion, told her to " mind her own business." Caroline's next move was to take clerical counsel. " These creatures are always venal," said the Jesuits. " They only care for cash." An emissary was accordingly despatched to the Barerstrasse mansion, to convey an offer. Unfortunately, however, he had not advanced beyond " *Gnädige Frau, erlauben,*" when he himself capitulated to Lola's charms, and returned to the Hofburg, his task unaccomplished. Still, he must have made out some sort of story to save his face, for the Princess Mélanie wrote : " Our good Senfft has come back. He was unable to speak to Lola Montez. The poor country of Bavaria is in a sad condition, which gets worse every day."

The least disturbed individual appeared to be Queen Thérèse. Her attitude was one of placidity itself. But perhaps she was, by this time, accustomed to the dalliance of her Ludwig along the primrose path. Also, she probably knew by experience that it was not the smallest use making a fuss. The milk was spilled. To cry over it now would be a wasted effort.

The King's favourite was good " copy " for the Bavarian press ; and the Munich journals were filled with accounts of her activities. Not in the least upset by their uncomplimentary references to himself, Ludwig instructed his librarian, Herr Lichenthaler, to collect all the pasquinades, lampoons, squibs, and caricatures (many of them far from flattering, and others verging on the indecent) that appeared and have them sumptuously bound. It was not long before enough had been

assembled to fill half a dozen volumes. His idea was " to
preserve for posterity all this mountain of mud, as a witness
of Bavaria's shame." That somebody else was responsible
for the " shame " did not occur to him.

A choice specimen among the collection was one entitled
Lola Montez, oder Des Mench gehört dem Könige (" Lola
Montez, or the Wench who belongs to the King "). There
was also a scurrilous, and distinctly blasphemous, broadsheet,
purporting to be Lola's private version of the Lord's Prayer :

" Our Father, in whom throughout my life, I have never
yet had much belief, all's well with me. Hallowed be thy
name—so far as I am concerned. Thy kingdom come, that is,
my bags of gold, my polished diamonds, and my unpolished
Alemannia. Thy will be done, if thou wilt destroy my
enemies. Give me this day champagne and truffles and
pheasant, and all else that is delectable, for I have a very good
appetite. . . . Lead me not into temptation to return to this
country, for, even if I were bullet-proof, I might be arrested,
clapped into a cage, and six francs charged for a peep at me.
Amen ! "

IV

Those were the days when gentlemen (at any rate, Bavarians)
did not necessarily prefer blondes. Lola's raven locks were
much more to their taste. If she were not a success in the
ballet, she was certainly one in the boudoir. Of a hospitable
and gregarious disposition, she kept what amounted to open
house in her Barerstrasse villa. Every morning she held an
informal levée there, at which any stranger who sent in his
card was welcome to call and pay his respects ; and in the
evenings, when she was not dancing attendance on Ludwig at
the Palace, the Barerstrasse reception would be followed by a
soirée. These gatherings attracted—in addition to a throng
of artists and authors and musicians—professors and scholars
from all over Europe ; and, as Gertrude Aretz remarks, in
her admirable study, *The Elegant Woman* (with considerable
reference to this one) : " the best intellects of her century

helped to draw her victorious chariot. ¹ The uncultured mob, however, dubbed her a " Fair Impire " and a " Light o' Love," and flung even stronger and still more uncomplimentary epithets. Their subject, however, received them with a laugh. The shopkeepers, with an eye to business, embellished their wares with her portrait ; and the University students, headed by Fritz Peissner, serenaded her in front of her windows.

Lolita schön, wie Salamoni's Weiber.
Welch 'suszer Reis flog über dich dahin !

they sang in rousing chorus.

Among the students engaged in amassing light and learning at the University of Munich, there were a number of foreigners. One of them was a young American, Charles Godfrey Leland ("Hans Breitmann "), who had gone there, he says, to " study æsthetics." But this did not take up all his time, for, during the intervals of attending classes, he managed to see something of Lola Montez. " I must," he says, " have had a great moral influence on her, for, so far as I am aware, I am the only friend she ever had at whom she never threw a plate or a book, or attacked with a dagger, poker, broom, or other deadly weapon. . . . I always had a strange and great respect for her singular talents. There were few, indeed, if any there were, who really knew the depths of that wild Irish soul."

In another passage Leland offers further details : " The great, the tremendous, celebrity at that time in Munich was also an opera dancer, though not on the stage. This was Lola Montez, the King's last favourite. . . . She wished to run the whole kingdom and government, kick out the Jesuits, and kick up the devil, generally speaking.

" One of her most intimate friends was wont to tell her that she and I had many very strange characteristics in common, which we shared with no one else, while we differed utterly in other respects. It was very like both of us, for Lola, when defending the existence of the soul against an atheist, to tumble over a great trunk of books of the most varied kind, till she came to an old vellum-bound copy of *Apuleius*, and proceed to establish her views according to his subtle neo-Platonism. But she romanced and embroidered so much in conversation that she did not get credit for what she really knew."

Well, if it comes to that, Leland for his part was not above " romancing " and " embroidering." His books are full of these qualities. " Marvels," says a biographer, " fill his descriptions of student life at Munich. Interesting people figure in his reminiscences. . . . Prominent among them was Lola Montez, the King's favourite of the day, cordially hated by all Munich for an interference in public affairs, hardly to be expected from the ' very small, pale, and thin or *frèle* little person with beautiful blue eyes and curly black hair ' who flits across the pages of the Memoirs."

If this were Leland's real opinion of Lola's appearance, he must have formed it after drinking too much of the Munich beer of which he was so fond. He seems to have drunk a good deal at times, as he admits in one passage : " after the dinner and wine, I drank twelve *schoppens*." A dozen imperial pints would take some swallowing, and not leave the memory unclouded as to subsequent events.

v

Despite the alleged Spanish blood in her veins, Lola (with, perhaps, some dim stirring of memory for the far-off Montrose chapter) declared herself a staunch Protestant, and, like her pet bull dog, disavowed the Jesuits and all their works. Hence, she supported the Liberal Government ; and, as an earnest of her intentions, started operations by attempting to establish contact with von Abel, the head of the Ultramontane Ministry. He, however, affecting to be hurt at the bare suggestion, would have nothing to do with the " Scarlet Woman," as he did not scruple to call her. Following his example, the clerical press redoubled their attacks. As a result, Lola decided to form an opposition and to have a party of her own.   For this purpose she turned to some of the younger students, among whom she had a particular admirer in one Fritz Peissner.   In response to her smiles, he, together with Count Hirschberg and a number of his friends, embodied themselves in a special corps, pledged to act as her body-guard.   Its members elected to be known as the Alemannia, and invited her to accept the position of *Ehren-Schwester* (" honorary sister ").   Lola was quite agreeable, and recipro-cated by setting apart a room in her villa where the swash-bucklers could meet.   Not to be outdone in paying compliments, the Alemannia planted a tree in her garden on Christmas Day.   Their distinguishing badge (which would now probably be a black shirt) was a red cap.   As was inevitable, they were very soon at daggers drawn with the representatives of the other University Corps, who, having long-established traditions, looked upon the newcomers as upstarts, and fights between them were constantly occurring when they met in public.   Altogether, Ludwig had reason to regret his action in transferring the University from its original setting at Landshut.   On the other hand, Councillor Berks, a thick and thin champion of Lola (and not above taking her lap-dogs for an airing in the Hofgarten), supported the Alemannia, declaring them to be " an example to corrupt youth." Prince Leiningen retaliated by referring to him as " that wretched substitute for a minister, commonly held by public opinion in the deepest contempt."

The origin of the Alemannia was a little curious.   Two members of the Palatia Corps happened one afternoon, while peering through the windows of the Barerstrasse mansion, to see Lola entertaining a couple of their fellow-members.   This they held to be " an affront to the honour of the Palatia," and the offenders, glorying in their conduct, were expelled by the committee.   Thereupon, they joined with Fritz Peissner when he was thinking of establishing a fresh corps.

In her new position, Lola did not forget her old friends. Feeling her situation with Ludwig secure, she wrote to Liszt,

offering him " the highest order that Bavaria could grant."
He declined the suggestion, and sent word of her doings to
Madame d'Agoult :

> Apropos of this too celebrated Anglo-Spanish woman,
> have you heard that King Louis of Bavaria has demanded
> the sacrifice of her theatrical career ? and that he is
> keeping her at Munich (where he has bought her a house)
> in the quality of a favourite Sultanah ?

Later on, he returned to the subject :

> I have been specially pleased with a couple of allusions
> to Lola and this poor Mariette ; but, to be perfectly
> candid—and being afraid that you would find the subject
> a little indecorous—I began to reproach myself for having
> mentioned it to you in my last letter from Czernowitz.
>
> In speaking of Lola, you tell me that you defend her
> (which I do also, but not for the same reasons) because
> she stands for progress. Then, a page further on, in
> resuming the subject at Vienna, you find me very young
> to still believe in justice, not realising that, in this little
> circle of ideas and things, I represent in Europe a
> progressive and intelligent movement. " Alas ! Who
> represents anything in Europe to-day ? " you enquire
> with Bossuet.
>
> Well, then, Lola stands for the nineteenth century, and
> Daniel Stern stands for the woman of the ninth century ;
> and, were it not for having contributed to the repre-
> sentation of others, I too shall finish by representing
> something else, by means of the 25,000 francs of income
> it will be necessary for me to end up by securing.

CHAPTER IX

" MAÎTRESSE DU ROI "

I

THE rôle for which Lola cast herself was that of La Pompadour to the Louis XV of Ludwig I. She had been a coryphée. Now she was a courtesan. History was repeating itself. Like an Agnes Sorel or a Jane Shore before her, she held in Munich the semi-official and quite openly acknowledged position of the King's mistress. It is said of her that she was so proud of the title and all it implied, that she would add " Maîtresse du Roi " to her signature when communicating with understrappers at the palace. Ludwig, however, thought this going too far, and peremptorily forbade the practice. Lola gave way. Perhaps the only time on record. In return, however, she advanced a somewhat embarrassing demand.

" My position as a king's favourite," she said, " entitles me to the services of a confessor and a private chapel."

Ludwig was quite agreeable, and instructed Count Reisach, the Ultramontane Archbishop of Munich, to select a priest for this responsible office. His Grace, however, reported that all the clergy in a body had protested to him that, " fearing for their virtue, they could not conscientiously accept the post."

Disappointed at the rebuff, Lola herself then applied to Dr. Windischmann, the Vicar-General, telling him that if he would undertake the office she would reciprocate by securing him a bishopric. This dignitary, however, was not to be tempted. " Madame," he said, " my confessional is in the

Church of Notre-Dame ; and you can always go there when you want to accuse yourself of any of the numerous sins you have committed."

Nor would His Eminence, the Primate of Poland, give any help. All he would do was to get into his carriage and set off to expostulate with the King. But it was a wasted effort, for Ludwig insisted that his relations with the conscience-stricken postulant were "nothing more than platonic." Thereupon, "the superior clergy announced that the designs of Providence were indeed inscrutable to mere mortals, but they trusted that His Majesty would at any rate change his mistress." Ludwig, however, brooking no interference with his amours, refused to do anything of the kind.

"What are you thinking about ? " he stormed. "How dare you hint that I am the man to roll myself in the mud of the gutter ? My feelings for this lady are of the most lofty and high-minded description. If you drive me to extremes, heaven alone knows what will happen ! "

His Eminence met the outburst by whispering in the ear of the Bishop of Augsburg that the King was "possessed." As for the Bishop of Augsburg, he "wept every day." A leaky prelate.

"It is a paradox," was the expert opinion of Archbishop Diepenbrock, "that the more shameful she is, the more beautiful is a courtesan." A "Day of Humiliation," with a special prayer composed by himself, was his suggestion for mending matters ; and Madame von Krudener, not to be outdone in coming to the rescue, preached the neces-sity of "public penance." Thus taken to task, Ludwig solemnly declared in writing that he had "never exacted the last favours " from Lola Montez, and furnished the entire episcopal bench with a copy of this declaration.

"That only makes his folly the greater," was the caustic comment of Canitz, who was not to be deluded by eye-wash of this description.

With the passage of time, Lola's influence at the Palace

grew stronger. Before long, it became abundantly clear to the Ministry that she was the real channel of approach to the King and, in fact, his political Egeria. " During that period," says T. Everett Harré, " when she was known throughout the world as the ' Uncrowned Queen of Bavaria,' Lola Montez wielded a power perhaps enjoyed by no woman since the Empress Theodora, the circus mime and courtesan, was raised to imperial estate by the Emperor Justinian." Well aware of this fact, and much as they objected to it, the Cabinet, headed by von Abel, began by attempting to win her to their side. When they failed, they put their thick heads together, and, announcing that she was an emissary of Palmerston— just as La Paiva was credited with being in Bismarck's employ —they hinted that her room was preferable to her company. The hints having no effect, other measures were adopted. Thus, Ludwig's sister offered her a handsome sum (for the second time) to leave the country, and Metternich improved on it ; the Bishop of Augsburg, drying his tears, composed another and longer special prayer ; the Cabinet threatened to resign ; and caricatures and scurrilous paragraphs once more appeared in Munich journals. But all to no purpose. Lola refused to budge. Nothing could shake her resolve. *J'y suis, j'y reste*, might well have been her motto.

" I will leave Bavaria," she said, " when it suits me, and not before."

II

For ten years Ludwig had been under the thumb of the Ultramontanes and the clerical ministry of Carl von Abel. He was getting more than a little tired of the combination. The advance of Lola Montez widened the breach. To get rid of him, accordingly, he offered von Abel the appointment of Bavarian Minister at Brussels. The offer, however, was not accepted. Asked for his reason, von Abel said that he " wanted to stop where he was and keep an eye on things."

At this date Bavaria was Catholic to a man—and a woman— and the Ultramontanes held the reins of government. While

Residenz Palace, Munich, in 1848.   Residence of Ludwig I

" Command " Portrait.   In the " Gallery of Beauties," Munich

one would have been enough, they professed to have two
grievances. One was the " political poison " of the Liberal
opposition ; and the other was the " moral perversion " of
the King. In March matters came to a crisis. A number of
University professors, headed by the rigid Lasaulx, held an
indignation meeting in support of the Ultramontane Cabinet
and " their efforts to espouse the cause of good morals." This
activity on the part of a secular body was resented by the
clergy, who considered that they, and not the University, were
the official custodians of the public's "morals." But if it upset
the clergy, it upset Ludwig still more ; and, to mark his
displeasure, he summarily dismissed four of the lecturers he
himself had appointed. As the general body of students sided
with them, they " demonstrated " in front of the house of
Lola Montez, whom they held responsible.

What began as a very ordinary disturbance soon developed
into something serious. Tempers ran high ; brickbats were
thrown, and windows smashed ; there were collisions with
the police, who endeavoured to arrest the ringleaders ; and
finally the Karolinen Platz had to be cleared by a squadron of
Cuirassiers. The Alemannia, joining arms, forced a passage
through which Lola managed to slip to safety and reach the
gates of the Residenz. But it was, as she said, " a near
thing."

The crowd relieved their feelings by breaking a few more
windows ; and a couple of Alemannia, detached from their
comrades, were ducked in the Isar.

" *Vivat, Lola !* " bellowed one contingent.

" *Pereat, Lola !* " bellowed the opposition.

Accounts of the disturbance filtered through to England.
There they attracted much attention and acid criticism.

" A lady," remarked the *Examiner*, " has overthrown the
Holy Alliance of Southern Germany. Lola Montez, whose
affecting testimony during the trial of those who killed
Dujarier in a duel cannot but be remembered, was driven by
that catastrophe to seek her fortunes in other realms. Chance

brought her to Munich, the Sovereign of which capital has divided his time between poetry and the arts, gallantry and devotion."

" What Paphian cestus," was another sour comment, " does Lola wind round the blade of her poniard ? We all remember how much the respectable Juno was indebted to the bewitching girdle of a less regular fair one, but the properties of that talisman are still undescribed."

The *Thunderer*, in its capacity as a European watch-dog, had its eye on Ludwig and his dalliance along the primrose path. Disapproval was registered. " The King of Bavaria," solemnly announced a leading article, " has entirely forgotten the duties and dignities of his position."

Freiherr zu Canitz, however, who had succeeded von Bülow as Minister for Foreign Affairs, looked upon Ludwig's lapse with more indulgence. " It is not," he wrote from the Wilhelmstrasse, " the first time by any means that kings have chosen to live with dancers. While such conduct is not, perhaps, strictly laudable, we can disregard it if it be accompanied by a certain measure of decorum. Still, a combination of ruler-ship and dalliance with a vagrant charmer is a phenomenon that is as much out of place as is an attempt to govern a country by writing sonnets."

Availing herself of what was then, as now, looked upon as a natural safety-valve, Lola herself wrote to the *Times*, giving her own version of these happenings :

> I left Paris in June last on a professional trip ; and, among other arrangements, decided upon visiting Munich where, for the first time, I had the honour of appearing before His Majesty and receiving from him marks of appreciation, which is not a very unusual thing for a pro-fessional person to receive at a foreign Court.
>
> I had not been here a week before I discovered that there was a plot existing in the town to get me out of it, and that the party was the Jesuit Party. . . . When they saw

that I was not likely to leave them, they tried what
bribery would do ; and actually offered me 50,000 fcs. a
year if I would quit Bavaria and promise never to return.
This, as you may imagine, opened my eyes ; and, as I
indignantly refused their offer, they have since not left
a stone unturned to get rid of me. . . . Within this last
week a Jesuit professor of philosophy at the university
here, named Lasaulx, was removed. Thereupon, the
party paid and hired a mob to insult me and break the
windows of my house.

. . . Knowing that your columns are always open to
protect anyone unjustly accused, and more especially
when that one is an unprotected female, makes me rely
upon you for the insertion of this ; and I have the
honour to subscribe myself, your obliged servant,

LOLA MONTEZ.

A couple of weeks later Printing House Square was favoured
with a second epistle :

To the Editor of " The Times."

MUNICH,
March 31.

SIR :—In consequence of the numerous reports circulated in various papers regarding myself and family,
I beg of you, through the medium of your widely circulated journal, to insert the following :

I was born at Seville in the year 1833 ; my father was a
Spanish officer in the service of Don Carlos ; my mother,
a lady of Irish extraction, born at the Havannah, and
married to an Irish gentleman, which, I suppose, is the
cause of my being called sometimes Irish and sometimes
English, and " Betsy Watson," and " Mrs. James," etc.

I beg leave to say that my name is Maria Dolores
Porres Montez, and I have never changed that name.

As for my theatrical qualifications, I never had the
presumption to think I had any. Circumstances obliged

me to adopt the stage as a profession, which profession I have now renounced for ever, having become a natural-ised Bavarian, and intending in future making Munich my residence.

Trusting that you will give this insertion, I have the honour to remain, Sir,

Your obedient servant,

LOLA MONTEZ.

The assumption that she had ever been known as " Betsy Watson " was due to the fact that she was said at one period to have lived under this name in Dublin, " protected there by an Irishman of rank and fortune." With regard to the rest of the letter, this was much the same as the one she had circulated after her London fiasco. It was very far from being well founded. Still, she had repeated this story so often that she had probably come to believe in it herself.

As *The Times* at that period was not read in Munich to any great extent, Lola, wanting a larger public, sent a letter to the *Allegemeine Zeitung*. This, she thought, would secure her a measure of sympathy not accorded her elsewhere :

" I object to being made a target for countless malicious attacks—public and private, written and printed—some whis-pered in secret, and others uttered to the world. I therefore now stigmatise as a wicked liar and perverter of the truth any individual who shall, without proving it, disseminate any report to my detriment."

The letter was duly published. The attacks, however, did not end. On the contrary, they redoubled in virulence. All sorts of fresh charges were brought against her. Many of them were quite unfounded, and deliberately ignored much that might have been put to her credit. Lola had not done nearly as much harm as some of Ludwig's lights o' love. Her predecessors, however, had made themselves subservient to the Jesuits and clericals. When her friends sent protests to the editor, refuge was taken in the stereotyped reply :

" pressure on our space does not permit us to continue this correspondence."

By those who wished her ill, any stick was good enough with which to beat Lola Montez. Thus, when a dignitary died— no matter what the medical diagnosis—it was announced in the gutter press that he died of " grief, caused by the national shame." The alleged last words of a certain politician were declared to be : " I die because I cannot continue living under the orders of a strumpet who rules our dear Bavaria as if she were a princess." Ludwig took it calmly. " The real trouble with this poor fellow," he said, " is that he never experienced the revivifying effects of the love of a beautiful woman." A popular prescription. The local doctors, however, were coy about recommending it to their patients.

That the Munich disturbances had an aftermath is clear from a news item that appeared in the *Cologne Gazette* ot July, 3, 1847. Lola, wanting a change of air and scene, had gone on a tour, travelling *incognita* and without any escort. Still, as she was to discover, it was impossible for her to move without being recognised :

> According to letters from Bavaria, it is obvious that the animosities excited against Lola Montez earlier in the year are far from having subsided. On passing through Nuremberg, she was received with coldness, but decency. At Bamberg, however, it was very different. At the railway station she was hissed and hooted, and, stones being thrown at her carriage, she presented her pistols and threatened to punish her assailants. The upper classes were thoroughly ashamed of such excesses ; and the chief magistrate has been instructed to appoint a deputation of the leading citizens to apologise to Mademoiselle.

In a letter to his brother, dated July 7, 1847, a University student says : " Lola Montez was near being assassinated three days ago," but he gives no particulars. Hence, it was probably gossip picked up in a beer hall.

III

A grievance felt by Lola was that she was not accorded recognition among the aristocracy. But there was an obvious remedy. This was to grant her a coronet. After all, historic examples were to hand by the dozen. In modern times the mistress of Frederick William III had been made a duchess. Hence, Lola felt that she should be at least a countess.

" What special services have you rendered Bavaria ? " bluntly demanded the minister to whom she first advanced the suggestion.

" If nothing else, I have given the King many happy days," was Lola's response.

Curiosity was then exhibited as to whether she was sufficiently *hoch-geboren*, or not. The applicant herself had no doubts on the subject. Her father, Ensign Gilbert, she said, had the blood of Cœur-de-Lion in his veins, and her mother's ancestors were among the Council of the Inquisition.

When the matter was referred to him, Ludwig was sympathetic and readily promised his help. But as she was a foreigner, she would, he pointed out, have to start by becoming naturalised as a Bavarian subject ; and, under the constitution, the necessary indigenate certificate must bear the signature of a Cabinet Minister. For this purpose, and never thinking that the slightest difficulty would be advanced, he had one drawn up and sent to Count Otto von Steinberg. Much to his annoyance and surprise, however, that individual, " suddenly developing conscientious objections," excused himself. Thereupon, von Abel, as head of the Government, was instructed to secure another signature.

" Do not worry. It will be settled to-morrow," announced Ludwig, when Lola enquired the reason of the hitch.

He was, however, speaking without his book. The Ministry, Ultramontane to a man, could swallow a good deal, in order to retain their portfolios (and salaries), but this, they felt, was asking too much of them. In unctuous terms, and taking refuge in offended virtue, they declared they would resign, rather than countenance the grant of Bavarian nationality for " the foreign woman." Neither pressure nor threats would shake them. Ludwig could do what he pleased ; and they would do what they pleased.

The manifesto in which the Cabinet's decision was delivered is little short of an historic document :

MUNICH.

February 11, 1847.

Sir : Public life has its moments when those entrusted by their Sovereign with the proper conduct of public affairs have to make their choice between renouncing the duties to which they are pledged by loyalty and devotion, and, by discharging those duties in conscientious fashion, incurring the displeasure of their beloved Sovereign. We, the faithful servants of Your Majesty, have now found ourselves in this situation owing to the decision to grant Bavarian nationality to Senora Lola Montez. As we cannot forget the duties that our oath compels us to observe, we cannot flinch in our resolve. . . .

It is abundantly clear that reverence for the Throne is becoming weakened in the minds of your subjects ; and little is now heard in all directions but blame and disapproval. National sentiment is wounded, because the country considers itself to be under the dominion of a foreign woman of evil reputation. The obvious facts are such that it is impossible to adopt any other view. . . . The public journals print the most shocking anecdotes, together with the most degrading attacks on your Royal Majesty. As a sample of this, we append a copy of No. 5 of the *Ulner Chronic.* The vigilance of the police is powerless to check the circulation of these journals, and they are read everywhere. . . . Not only is the Government being jeopardised, but also the very existence of the Crown. Hence, the delight of such as wish ill to the Throne, and the anguish of such as are loyal to Your Majesty. The fidelity of the army, too, is threatened. Ere long, the forces of the Crown will become a prey to profound disaffection ; and where could we look for help, should this occur and this last bulwark totter ?

The hearts of the undersigned loyal and obedient servants are torn with grief. This statement they submit to you is not one of visionaries. It is the melancholy result of observations made by them during the exercise of their functions for several months past. Each of the undersigned is ready and willing to surrender everything to his Sovereign. They have given you repeated proofs of their fidelity ; and it is now nothing less than their sacred duty to direct the attention of your Majesty to the dangers confronting him. Our humble prayer, to which we beg you to listen, is not governed by any desire to run counter to your Royal will. It is put forward solely with a view to ending a condition of affairs which is inimical to the well-being and happiness of a beloved monarch. Should, however, your Majesty not think fit to grant their petition, we, your Ministers, will then have no alternative but to tender the resignation of the portfolios with which you have entrusted them.

The signatories to this precious " manifesto " were von Abel, von Gumpenberg (Minister of War), von Schrenk, and von Seinsheim (Councillors of State). Much to their hurt astonishment, their resignations were accepted. Nor was there any lack of candidates for the vacant portfolios. Ludwig, prompted by Lola, filled up the gaps at once. Georg von Maurer (who reciprocated by signing her certificate of naturalisation) was appointed Minister of Justice and Foreign Affairs, and Freiherr Friederich zu Rhein was the new Minister of Public Worship and Finance.

The students, not prepared to let slip a chance of asserting
themselves, paraded the streets with a fresh song :

> *Da kam Senorra Lolala,*
> *Sturzt Abel und Consorten ;*
> *Ach war sie doch jetz wieder da,*
> *Und jagte fort den——*

Despite the fact that he was indebted for his appointment
to her, Maurer attempted to snub Lola and refused to speak
to her the next time they met. For his pains, he found himself, in December, 1847, dismissed from office. There was,
however, joy in the ranks of the clerical party, for, to their
horror, he happened to be a Protestant.

" I have now a new ministry, and there are no more Jesuits
in Bavaria," announced Ludwig with much complacence.
As was his custom when a national crisis occurred, he was also
delivered of a sonnet, commencing :

> You who have wished to hold me in thrall, tremble !
> Greatly do I esteem the important affair
> Which has ever on divested you of your power !

But the fallen ministers had the sympathy of Vienna.
Count Senfft, the Austrian envoy at Munich, gave a banquet
in their honour. Lola reported this to Ludwig, and Ludwig
gave Senfft his *congé*.

What had annoyed the Wittelsbach Lovelace more than
anything else about the business was that the memorandum in
which von Abel and his colleagues had expressed their candid
opinion of Lola Montez found its way into the *Augsburger
Zeitung* and a number of Paris journals. This was regarded
by him as a breach of confidence. Enquiries revealed the fact
that von Abel's sister had been surreptitiously shown a
copy of the document, and, not prepared to keep such a tit-
bit of gossip to herself, had disclosed its contents to a reporter.
After this, the fat, so to speak, was in the fire ; and nothing
that Ludwig could do could prevent the affair becoming
public property. As a result, it formed the basis of

innumerable articles in the press of Europe, and the worst possible construction was put on it.

The erudite Dr. Döllinger, between whom and Lola Montez no love was lost, was much upset by the situation and wrote a long letter on the subject :

> The existing ministry were fully awake to the encroachments of the notorious Lola Montez ; and in view of the destruction which menaced both the throne and the country, they secretly resolved to address a petition to Ludwig I, humbly praying him to dismiss his favourite, and setting forth the grounds on which they based their request.
>
> Rumours of this business soon got afloat. People began to whisper ; and one fine day a sister of one of the ministers, goaded by curiosity, discovered the petition. She imparted the news in the strictest confidence to her most intimate friends ; and they, in their turn, secretly read the memorial, with the result that, some time after the important document had been safely restored to its hiding-place, its contents appeared, nobody knew how, in the newspapers.
>
> The panic of the ministers was great ; the King's displeasure was still greater. He suspected treachery, and considered the publication of such a petition treasonable. Remonstrances were of no avail ; the ministers were dismissed, and their adherents fled in every direction. I, who had been nominated a member of the Chamber by the University, but against my will, had to resign office at the bidding of the King. His Majesty was greatly incensed, and meanwhile the excited populace were assembling in crowds before the house of Lola Montez.

Döllinger was a difficult man to cross. He had doubts— serious doubts—concerning a number of matters. Among them was one of the infallibility of the Pope. What was more, he was

daring enough to express these doubts. The wrath of the
Vatican could only be appeased by ex-communicating him
from the Church. He, however, added to his contumacy by
surviving until his ninety-second year.

IV

Appreciating on which side its bread was buttered, the new
ministry had no qualms as to the eligibility of Lola Montez
for the honour of a coronet in the Bavarian peerage. This
having been granted her, the next step was to select a suitable
territorial title.

Ludwig ran an exploring finger down the columns of a
gazetteer. There he saw two names, Landshut and Feldberg,
that struck him as suggestive. Combined, they made up
Landsfeld. Nothing could be better.

" I have it," he said. " Countess of Landsfeld, I salute
you ! "

Thereupon the Court archivist was instructed to prepare
the necessary document :

> " We, Ludwig, King of Bavaria, etc., hereby make public
> to all concerned that We have resolved to raise Maria von
> Porres and Montez, of noble Spanish descent, to the
> dignity of Countess of Landsfeld of this Our kingdom.
> Whilst we impart to her the dignity of a Countess, with
> all the rights, honours and prerogatives connected there-
> with, it is Our desire that she have and enjoy the follow-
> ing escutcheon on a German four-quartered shield :
> In the first field, red, an upright white sword with golden
> handle ; in the second, blue, a golden-crowned lion
> rampant ; the third, blue, a silver dolphin ; and in the
> fourth, white, a pale red rose. This shield shall be
> surmounted by the coronet of a Countess.
>
> " Be this notified to all the authorities and to Our
> subjects in general, with a view to not only recog-
> nising the said Maria as Countess of Landsfeld, but also

to supporting her in that dignity ; and it is Our will that whoever shall act contrary to these provisions shall be summoned by Our Attorney-General and there and then be condemned to make public and private atonement.

" For Our confirmation of the above we have affixed Our royal name to this document and placed on it the seal of Our kingdom.

" Given at Aschaffensberg, this 14th of August, in the 1847th year after the birth of Christ, our Lord, and in the 22nd year of Our Government."

This did not miss the eagle eye of *Punch*, in whose columns appeared a caustic reference :

"The armorial bearings of the new COUNTESS OF LANDSFELD, the ex-*coryphée* of Her Majesty's Theatre, have been designed, but we think they are hardly so appropriate as they might have been. We have therefore made some slight modifications of the original, which we hope will prove satisfactory."

The suggested " modifications " were to substitute a parasol for the sword, a bull-dog for the lion, and a pot of rouge for the rose. Were such an adjunct of the toilet table then in existence, a lipstick would probably have been added.

V

With her title and heraldic honours complete, plus a generous allowance on which to support them, and a palace in which to live, Lola Montez cut a very considerable dash in Munich. Two sentries marched up and down in front of her gate, and two mounted orderlies (instead of one, as had previously been the case) accompanied her whenever she left the house in the Barerstrasse.

While by far the most important of them, Ludwig was not by any means the only competitor for Lola's favours. Men of wealth and position—the bearers of high-sounding titles—with politicians and place-hunters, fluttered round her. It is to her credit that she sent them about their business.

" The peculiar relations existing between the King of Bavaria and the Countess of Landsfeld," remarked an apologist, " are not of a coarse or vulgar character. His Majesty has a highly developed poetic mind, and thus sees his favourite through his imagination, and regards her with affectionate respect."

This found a responsive echo in another quarter, and some sharp raps on the knuckles were administered to the Bavarian moralists by a Paris journal :

" Why do you interfere with the amours of your good Ludwig ? We don't say he should not have observed rather more discretion or have avoided compromising his dignity. Still, a monarch, like a simple citizen, is surely free to love where he pleases. In selecting Lola Montez, the amorous Ludwig proves that he loves equality and, as a true democrat, can identify himself with the public. Let him espouse his servant girl, if he wants to. Personally, we would rather see the Bavarians excite themselves about their constitution than about the banishment of a royal favourite. The King of Bavaria turns his mistress into a Countess ; his subjects refuse to recognise her ; and a section of the students clamour for her head. Happy days of Montespan, of Pompadour, of Dubarry, of Potemkin, of Orloff, where have you gone ? "

In the summer of 1847 the Paris Courts were occupied with a long outstanding claim against Lola Montez. This was to the effect that, when she was appearing at the Porte St. Martin, she had run up a bill for certain intimate undergarments and had neglected to settle the account. The result was, she received a solicitor's letter in Munich. She answered it in the following terms:

MUNICH,
September 25, 1847.

MONSIEUR BLOQUE,

As I have never given any orders to Messrs. Hamon and Company, tailors, rue de Helder, they have no claim on me ; and I am positively compelled to repudiate the bill for 1371 francs which you have the effrontery to demand in the name of this firm.

Last spring Monsieur Leigh made me a present of a riding-habit and certain other articles which he ordered for me, and I consider that it is to him you should now address yourself.

Accept, Monsieur, etc.,

COUNTESS DE LANDSFELD.

Not being prepared to accept this view, the Paris firm's next step was to bring an action for the recovery of the alleged debt. Once more, Lola repudiated liability, this time on the grounds that the creditors had kept back some dress material belonging to herself. The defence to this charge was that, " on being informed by their representative that real ladies could not wear such common stuff, she had said she did not want it back." The court, however, held that the debt had been incurred ; and, " as she considered it beneath her dignity to appear, either in person or by counsel," judgment for 2,500 francs was given against her.

Count Bernstorff, a not particularly brilliant diplomatist, had an idea (shared, by the way, with a good many others) that Frederick William IV, King of Prussia, was at one time under Lola's spell. He was allowed to think so by reason of a letter that the King had sent him from Sans Souci in the autumn of 1847 :

" I am charging you, my dear Count, with a commission, the performance of which demands a certain degree of that measure of delicacy which I recognise you to possess. The commission is somewhat beyond the accepted limits of what is purely diplomatic in character. . . . It is a matter of handing a certain trinket to a certain lady. The trinket is of little value, but, from causes you will be able to appreciate, the lady's favour is of very high value to myself. All depends on the manner in which the gift is presented. This should be sufficiently flattering to increase the value of the offering and to cause its unworthiness to be overlooked. My acquaintance with the lady, and my respect for her, should be adroitly described and made the most of, as must also be my desire to be remembered at her hands.

" You will, of course, immediately perceive that I am alluding to Donna Maria de Dolores de los Montez, Countess of Landsfeld."

It was not until he turned over the page that the horror-struck Bernstorff saw that the King was playing a character-istic jest on him ; and he realised that the intended recipient of the gift was his wife, the Countess von Bernstorff, " as a souvenir of my gratitude for the many agreeable hours passed under your hospitable roof last month."

CHAPTER X

BURSTING OF THE STORM

I

THE beauty of Lola Montez was a lever. As such, it disturbed the equilibrium of the Cabinet; for the time being, it even checked the dominion of Rome. But the odds were against her. The Jesuits were still a power, and would not brook any interference.

Metternich's wife, the Princess Mélanie, who had the family *flair* for politics, marked the course of events.

"Lola Montes," she wrote, "has actually been created Countess of Landsfeld. She is really a member of the Radical Party. . . . Rechberg, who has just arrived from Brazil, was alarmed on his journey at Munich by the events of which this town is the theatre. The shocking conduct of Lola Montes will finish by plunging the country into revolution."

This was looking ahead. Still, not very far ahead. The correspondent of a London paper in the Bavarian capital did not mince his words. " The indignation," he wrote, " against the King on account of his scandalous conduct, has been roused to the highest pitch. . . . King Ludwig, who possesses many good qualities, is, unfortunately, a very licentious old man. . . . Neither the tears of the Queen, nor the entreaties of his sons, nor the public's indignation, could influence the old monarch, who has become the slave of his silly passion and of the caprices of a Spanish dancer and Parisian lorette."

Once more, Ludwig " dropped into verse," and relieved his feelings about his enemies. This time, however, the verse was blank :

You have driven me from my Paradise,
You have closed it for ever with iron grilles.
You have turned my days into bitterness.
You would even like to make me hate you
Because I have loved too much to please your withered spirits.

The perfume of my spring-time is dissipated,
But my courage still remains.
Youth, always bounding in my dreams, rests there,
Embracing my heart with fresh force !

You who would like to see me covered with shame,
Tremble !
You have committed sins against me and vomited injuries.
Your wicked acts have judged you.
There has never been anything to equal them !

Already the clouds disappear ;
The storm passes ;
The sky lights up ;
I bless the dawn.
Ungrateful worms, creep back to your darkness !

There were repercussions across the Atlantic, where the rôle played by Lola Montez in Bavarian circles was arousing considerable interest. American women saw in it a message of encouragement for the aspirations they themselves were cherishing. " The moral indignation which her political opponents exhibited," said a leading jurist, " was unfortunately a mere sham. They had not only tolerated, but had actually patronised, a female who formerly held the equivocal position which the Countess of Landsfeld recently held, because the former made herself subservient to the then dominant party."

But, just as Lola had staunch friends in Munich, so had she pronounced enemies. Conspicuous among them was Johann Görres, a leading Ultramontane who held the position of professor of history at the University. He could not say anything strong enough against the King's mistress, and did all he could to upset her influence with him. As he had a " following," some measure of success attended his efforts. It was on his death, in January 1848, that matters came to a head. The rival factions dividing the various students' corps made his funeral the occasion of a free fight among themselves. The mob joined in, and clamoured for the dismissal of the " Andalusian Woman." A hothead suggested that she should be driven from the town. The cry was taken up, and a rush set in towards her house in the Barerstrasse. As there was an agreeable prospect of loot, half the scum of the city swelled the mob. Bricks were hurled through the windows ; and, until the police arrived, things began to look ugly.

Lola, as cool as a cucumber, appeared on the balcony, a glass of champagne in one hand, and a box of chocolates in the other.

" I drink to your good healths," she said contemptuously, as she drained her glass and tossed bon-bons among the crowd.

Not appreciating this gesture, or regarding it as an impertinence, the temper of the rabble grew threatening. They shouted vulgar insults ; and there was talk of battering in the doors and setting the house on fire. This might have happened, had not Ludwig himself, who never lacked personal courage, plunged into the throng and, offering Lola his arm, escorted her to the Residenz.

The disturbances continued, for tempers had reached fever pitch. Troops hastily summoned from the nearest barracks patrolled the streets. A furious crowd assembled in front of the Rathaus ; the burgomaster, fearing for his position, talked of reading the Riot Act ; a number of arrests were made ; and it was not until the next afternoon that the coast was sufficiently clear for Lola to return to the Barerstrasse, triumphantly escorted by some members of the Alemannia. When, however, they left her there, they were set upon by detachments of the Palatia Corps, who still cherished a grudge against them.

Lola's own account of these happenings, and written as if by a detached onlooker, is picturesque, if somewhat imaginative :

" They came with cannons and guns and swords, with the voices of ten thousand devils, and surrounded her little castle.

Against the entreaties of her friends, she presented herself before the infuriated mob which demanded her life. . . . A thousand guns were pointed at her, and a hundred fat and apoplectic voices fiercely demanded that she should cause the repeal of what she had done. In language of great mildness— for it was no time to scold—she answered that it was impossible for her to accede to such a request ; and that what had been done by her had been done for the good of the people and the honour of Bavaria."

After this " demonstration," there was a calm. But not for long. On the evening of February 10, a rabble assembled in front of the Palace, raising cries of : " Down with Lola Montez ! " " Down with the King's strumpet ! " As the protestors consisted largely of students (whom Thiersch, the rector, being no disciplinarian, could not keep in check), Ludwig's response was drastic. He ordered the University to be shut, and all its members who did not live in Munich to leave the town within twenty-four hours. This was a tactical blunder, and was in great measure responsible for the more serious repercussions of the following month. Apart, too, from other considerations, the edict hit the pockets of the local tradesmen, since the absence of a couple of thousand hungry and thirsty customers had an adverse effect on the consumption of sauerkraut and beer.

As she was still " news " in Paris, a gossiping columnist suggested her return there :

> Lola Montez laments the Notre-Dame de Lorette district, the joyous little supper-parties at the Café Anglais, and the theatrical first nights viewed from stage boxes. " Ah," she must reflect, as she looks upon her coronet trodden underfoot and hears the sinister murmurs of the Munich mob, " how delightful Paris would be this evening ! What a grand success I would be in the new ballet at the Opera or at a ball at the Winter Garden ! " Alas, my poor Lola, your whip is broken ; your prestige

is gone ; you have lost your talisman. Do not battle
against the jealous Bavarians. Come back to Paris,
instead. If the Porte St. Martin won't have you, you
can always rejoin the corps de ballet at the Opera.

Lola, however, did not accept the invitation. She was vir-
tually a prisoner in her own house, where, the next afternoon,
a furious gathering assembled, threatening to wreak vengeance
on her. Never lacking a high measure of courage, she appeared
on the balcony and told them to do their worst. They did it
and attempted to effect an entrance by breaking down the door.
But for the action of the Alemannia, rallying to her help, she
might have been severely handled.

One of her bodyguard managed to make his way to the
nearest barracks and summon assistance. Thereupon, the
bugles rang out the alarm ; the drums beat a warning call.
In response, a squadron of Cuirassiers clattered up the Barerstrasse ; sabres rattled ; and the rioters fled precipitously.

Prince Wallerstein, who combined the office of Minister of
Public Worship with that of Treasurer of the Royal Household, leaping into the breach, harangued the mob ; and Prince
Vrede, a strong adherent to the " whiff of grapeshot " remedy
for a disturbance, suggested firing on the ringleaders. Although
the suggestion was not accepted, hundreds of arrests were made
before some semblance of order was restored. But the rioting
was only checked temporarily. A couple of days later it started
afresh. The temper of the troops being upset, Captain Bauer
(a young officer whom Lola had patronised) took it upon
himself to give them the word to charge. Sabres flashed, and
there were many broken heads and a good deal of bloodshed.

The Alemannia, thinking discretion the better part of
valour, barricaded themselves in the restaurant of one Herr
Rothmanner, where they fortified themselves with vast
quantities of beer. Becoming quarrelsome, their leader,
Count Hirschberg, drew his sword and was threatened with
arrest by a schutzmannschaft. Thereupon, his comrades sent
word to Lola. She answered the call, and rushed to the house.

It was a characteristic, but mad, gesture, for she was promptly recognised and pursued by a furious mob. Nobody would give her sanctuary ; and the Swiss Guards on duty there shut the doors of the Austrian Legation in her face. Thereupon, she fled to the Theatiner Church, where she took refuge. But she did not stop there long ; and, for her own safety, a military escort arrived to conduct her to the main guard-room. As soon as the coast was comparatively clear, she was smuggled out by a back entrance and making her way on foot to the Barerstrasse, hid in the garden.

In the meantime fresh attempts were being made to storm her house. Suddenly, a figure, dishevelled and bare-headed, appeared on the threshold and confronted the rioters.

" You are behaving like a pack of vulgar blackguards," he exclaimed, " and not like true Bavarians at all. I give you my word, the house is empty. Leave it in peace."

A gallant gesture, and a last act of homage to the building that had sheltered the woman he loved. The mob, recognising the speaker, uncovered instinctively. *Heil, unserm König, Heil!* they shouted. A chorus swelled ; the troops presented arms.

" It is an orgy of ingratitude," said Ludwig, as he watched the rabble dancing with glee before the house. " The Jesuits are responsible. If my Lola had been called Loyala, she could still have stopped here."

To Dr. Stahl, Bishop of Wurzburg, who had criticised his conduct, he addressed himself more strongly. " Should a single hair of one I hold dear to me be injured," he informed that prelate, " I shall exhibit no mercy."

Palmerston, who stood no nonsense from anybody, wrote a very snappy letter to Sir John Milbanke, British Minister at Munich :

" Pray tell Prince Wallerstein that, if he wishes the British and Bavarian Governments to be on good terms, he will abstain from any attempt to interfere with our diplomatic arrangements, as such attempts on his part are as offensive as they will be fruitless."

II

As Ludwig had said, the Barerstrasse nest was empty, for its occupant had managed to slip out of it and reach Lindeau. From there, on February 23, she wrote a long letter to a friend in England, giving a somewhat highly coloured (and not altogether accurate) version of these happenings :

In the morning, the nobles, with Count A.—V—[Arco Valley] and a number of officers, were mixed up with the commonest people. The Countess P [Preysing] I saw myself, with other women—I cannot call them *ladies*— actually at their head. Hearing that the entire city—with nobles, officers, and countesses—were making for my residence, I looked upon myself as already out of the land of the living. I had all my windows shuttered, and hid all my jewels ; and then, having a clear conscience and a firm trust in God, calmly awaited my fate. The ruffians, egged on by a countess and a baroness, had stones, sticks, axes, and firearms, all to frighten and kill one poor inoffensive woman ! They positively clamoured for my blood.

I must tell you that all my faithful and devoted servants, with some others of my real friends, were in the house with me. I begged them to leave by the garden, but they said, poor fellows, they would die for me. . . . Seeing the eminent danger of my friends, and not thinking of myself, I ordered my carriage while the blackguards were endeavouring to break down the gates. My good George, the coachman, helped me to rush through the door and we set off at a furious gallop. Many pistol shots were fired at me, but I was in God's care and avoided the bullets.

My escape was most miraculous. At a distance of two hours from Munich I left my carriage and in Bluthenberg sought the protection of a brave honest man, by whom I was given shelter. Presently, some officers galloped up and demanded me. My benefactor declared I was not there, and his daughters said my carriage had passed. When they were gone, his good wife helped me to dress as a peasant girl, and I rushed out of the house, across fields, ditches, and forests. Being so well disguised, I resolved to return to Munich. It was a dreadful spectacle. The Palace blockaded ; buildings plundered ; and anarchy in all directions. Seeing nothing but death if I stopped there, I left for Lindeau, from whence I am writing to you.

. . . Count Arco Valley has been distributing money like dirt to all classes, and the priests have stirred up the mob. Nobody is safe in Munich. The good, noble King has told everyone he will never leave me. Of that he is quite determined. The game is not up. I shall, till death, stick to the King ; but God knows what will happen next.

I forgot to tell you that my enemies have announced in the German papers that the students are my *lovers* ! They could not credit them with the loyal devotion they have ever had for the King and myself.

Marie de Landsfeld.

Writing in his diary on March 14, 1848, Frederick Cavendish, a budding diplomatist, whom Palmerston had appointed as attaché at Vienna, remarks :

" There has been the devil of a disturbance in Munich ; and the King's mistress, Lola Montez, has been forced to fly for her life. She has been the curse of Bavaria, yet the King is still infatuated with her."

Scarcely diplomatic language. Still, not far from the truth.

A rigorous press censorship was exercised. The Munich papers had to print what they were told, and nothing else. As a result, an inspired article appeared in the *Allegemeine Zeitung*, of Augsburg, declaring that the Ultramontanes were responsible for the *émeute*. " Herr von Abel," in the opinion of a colleague, Heinrich von Treitsche, " took advantage of the opportunity to espouse a sudden championship of morals, and made *les convenances* an excuse for resigning what had long been to him a dangerous office."

Döllinger himself always declared that he became an Ultramontane against his will, and that he only joined the Ministry at the earnest request of von Abel. This was probably true enough, for he was much happier among his books than among the politicians. With his nose decidedly out of joint, he relieved his feelings in a lengthy epistle to his friend, Madame Rio. Years afterwards this letter came into the hands of Dom Gougaud, O.S.B., who published it in the *Irish Ecclesiastical Record.* Among the more important passages were the following :

Since you left M[unich] the impudence of L[ola] M[ontez] and the infatuation of her admirers have been constantly increasing. Our Members of Parliament, which have been convocated to an extraordinary session on account of a railway loan, did not dare, or did not deem it expedient, to interfere. The only thing that was done, but without producing any effect in high quarters, was that the Chamber of Deputies unanimously voted a protestation against the deposition of the professors. Then came the change of Ministers. Prince Wallerstein, who is a sort of Bavarian Thiers, selfish and unprincipled, only bent upon maintaining himself in the possession of the *portefeuille*, which is the glorious end that in his estimation sanctifies the means—this man of unscrupulous memory came in again, together with an obscure individual, a mere creature of L[ola] M[ontez], M. Berks. . . . Meanwhile the crisis was brought about by the students of the University. L[ola] M[ontez] had succeeded in seducing a few of these, who, finding themselves immediately shunned and rejected by their fellow-students, formed a separate society or club, calling itself *Alemannia*, which from its beginning was publicly

King of Bavaria. " *Ludwig the Lover* "

Lola Montez in caricature.   " Lola on the Allemannen Hound "

understood to be distinguished by the King's special favour and protection. In the course of two or three months they rose to the number of nineteen or twenty, easily recognised by the red caps and ribbons they wore. For L[ola] M[ontez] they formed a sort of male harem, and the particulars which have since transpired, and which, of course, I must not pollute your ears with, leave no doubt that she is a second Messalina.

The indignation of the students, who felt all this as a degradation of the University and an affront cast upon their character, was general. The *Alemanni* were treated as outcasts, whose very presence was pollution.

. . . L[ola] M[ontez] had already been heard threatening that if the students continued to show themselves hostile to her favourites she would have the University closed. At last, on the 10th February, a royal mandate came forth, declaring the University to be suspended for the entire year.

Next morning it was evident that a decisive crisis was coming on ; the students paraded in procession through the streets, when, suddenly, the *gendarmerie*, commanded by one of L. M.'s favourites, made an attack upon them and wounded two of them. This, of course, served only to kindle the flames of general indignation. The citizens threatened to appear in arms, and the people made preparations for storming the house of L[ola] M[ontez].

Towards 8 o'clock in the morning of the 11th, the appalling intelligence was communicated to the K[ing] that L. M.'s life was in imminent danger. Meanwhile several members of the royal family had tried to make an impression on the K.'s mind. When his own tools, who, up to that moment, had been pushing him on, told him that L.'s life was in jeopardy, and that the regiments refused to fight, he began to yield. But even then his behaviour left no doubt that the personal safety of L[ola] M[ontez] was his paramount motive. He himself ran

to her house, which the mob had begun to pluck down ;
regardless of all royal dignity, he exposed his person to
all the humiliation which the intercourse with an infuriated mob might subject him to. . . . Certainly, that day
was the most disgraceful royalty has yet had in Bavaria.

. . . You will find it natural that the first announcement of L.M.'s forced departure begot universal exulta-
tion. In the streets one met only smiling countenances ;
new hopes were kindled. People wished, and therefore
believed, that the K[ing] having at last become aware of
the true state of the nation's mind, had made a noble
sacrifice. A few days were sufficient to undeceive
them. The K.'s mind was in a sort of fearful excitement,
alternating between fits of depression and thoughts of
vengeance. . . . It is impossible to foresee what things
will lead to, and where the persecution is to stop. The
opinion gains credit that his intention is to bring L[ola]
M[ontez] back. Evidently he is acting, not only from a
thirst for vengeance, but also under the fatal influence
of an irresistible and sinister passion for that woman.

A few days later, Ludwig, to test public opinion, went to
the Opera.

" I have lost my taste for spectacles," he said to his companion, " but I wish to see if I am still King in the hearts of
the people I have served."

He was not long in doubt, for the moment he entered his
box the audience stood up and cheered him vigorously. This
was enough ; and, without waiting for the curtain to rise, he
returned to the Palace.

" After all, my subjects still trust me," he said. " I was
sure of them."

III

There was another display of loyalty elsewhere. The
Munich garrison, under Ludwig's second son, Prince Luitpold, took a fresh oath *en masse*, swearing fidelity to the new

constitution. It was, however, a little late in the day. Things had gone too far ; and Lola, who had merely gone a few leagues from the capital, had not gone far enough. That was the trouble. She was still able to pull strings, and to make her influence felt in various directions. Nor would she show the white feather or succumb to the threats of rowdies.

It was from Lindeau that, disguised as a boy (then a somewhat more difficult job than now), Lola, greatly daring, ventured back to the arms of Ludwig. But she only stopped with him a couple of hours, for she had been followed, and was still being hunted by the rabble of the town. Before, however, resuming her journey, she endeavoured to get into touch with her faithful *Alemannia*. " I beg you," she wrote to the proprietor of the café they frequented, " to tell me where Herr Peissner has gone." The landlord, fearing reprisals, withheld the knowledge. If he had given it, he would probably have had his premises wrecked. Safety first !

In this juncture, Ludwig, acting like a mental deficient, announced that there was only one adequate explanation for Lola's conduct. This was that she was " possessed of an evil spirit " which had to be exorcised before things should get worse. Lending a ready ear to every quack in Bavaria, he sent her under escort to Weinsberg, to the clinic of a Dr. Justinus Kerner, who had established himself there as a mesmerist.

" You are to drive the devil out of her," were the instructions given him.

Fearing that his spells and incantations might, after all, not prove effective, and thus convict him for a charlatan, the man of science felt uneasy. Still, an order was an order, especially when it came from a King, and he promised to do his best. On the day that his patient arrived, he wrote to his married daughter, Emma Niendorf. A free translation of this letter, which is given in full by Dr. von Tim Klein (in his *Der Vorkamfdeutscher Einheit und Freiheit*), would read :

Yesterday there arrived here Lola Montez ; and, until further instructions come from Munich, I am detaining her in my tower, where guard is being kept by three of the *Alemannia*. That the King should have selected me of all people to send her to is most annoying. But he was assured that she was possessed of a devil, and that the devil in her could be driven out by me at Weinsberg. Still, the case is one of interest.

As a preliminary to my magneto-magic treatment, I am beginning by subjecting her to a fasting-cure. This means that every day all she is to have is a quarter of a wafer and thirteen drops of raspberry juice.

" *Sage es aber niemanden ! Verbrenne diesen Brief !* (" But don't tell anybody about it ; burn this letter ") was the exorcist's final injunction.

To live up to his reputation for wonder-working, the mystic had an Æolian harp in each of the windows of his house, so arranged that Ariel-like voices would float through the summer breezes.

" It is magic," said the peasants, crossing themselves devoutly when they heard the sound.

But the harp-obligato proved no more effective than the reduced dieting and early attempt to popularise slimming. After a couple of days, accordingly, the regime was varied by the substitution of asses' milk for the raspberry juice. Much to his annoyance, however, the specialist had to report to another correspondent, Sophie Schwab, that his patient was not deriving any real benefit, and that the troublesome " devil " had not been dislodged.

As was to be expected, Lola, having a healthy appetite and objecting to short rations, gave the mesmerist the slip and hurried back to her Ludwig. After a few words with him, she left for Stahrenberg.

Ludwig sat down and wrote another " poem." Appropriately enough, this was entitled " Lamentation."

CHAPTER XI

A FALLEN STAR

I

EVEN with Lola Montez out of the way and the University doors re-opened, it was not a case of all quiet on the Munich front. Far from it. Berks, the new Minister of the Interior, who had always supported her, still remained in office ; and Lola herself continued from a distance to pull strings. Some of them were effective.

But Lola Montez, or no Lola Montez, there was in the eyes of his exasperated subjects more than enough to make them thoroughly dissatisfied with the Wittelsbach regime, as carried out by Ludwig. The Cabinet had become very nearly inarticulate ; public funds had been squandered on all sorts of grandiose and unnecessary schemes ; and the clerical element had long been allowed to ride roughshod over the constitution. Altogether, the " Ministry of Dawn," brought into existence with such a flourish of trumpets after the dismissal of von Abel and his colleagues, had not proved the anticipated success. Instead of getting better, things had got worse ; and, although it had not actually been suggested, the idea of substituting the monarchy by a republic was being discussed in many quarters.

The editor of the *Annual Register*, abandoning his customary attitude of an impartial historian, dealt out a sharp rap on the knuckles to the Royal Troubadour :

" The discreditable conduct of the doting old King of Bavaria, in his open *liaison* with a wandering actress who had assumed the name of Lola Montez (but who was in reality

the eloped wife of an Englishman, and whom he had created a
Bavarian Countess by the title of Gräfin de Landsfeld), had
thoroughly alienated the hearts of his subjects."

As the result of a solemn conclave at the Rathaus, an ulti-
matum was delivered by the Cabinet ; and Ludwig was
informed, without any beating about the bush, that unless he
wanted to plunge the country into revolution, Lola Montez
must leave the kingdom.   Ludwig yielded ; and forgetful of,
or else deliberately ignoring, the fact that he had once written
a passionate threnody, in which he declared :

> " And though thou be forsaken by all the world,
>   Yet, never wilt thou be abandoned by me ! "

he could find it in his heart to issue a decree expelling her
from his realms.

To this end, on March 17, he signed two separate Orders
in Council.

I

> " We, Ludwig, by the Grace of God, King of Bavaria,
> etc., think it necessary to give notice that the Countess of
> Landsfeld has ceased to possess the rights of naturali-
> sation."

2

> " Since the Countess of Landsfeld does not give up
> her design of disturbing the peace of the capital and
> country, all the judicial authorities of the kingdom are
> hereby ordered to arrest the said Countess wherever she
> may be discovered.   They are to carry her to the nearest
> fortress, where she is to be kept in custody."

Events moved rapidly.   A few days later Lola was arrested
by Prince Wallerstein (whom she herself had put into power
when his stock had fallen) and deported, as an " undesirable
alien," to Switzerland.

Woman-like, she had the last word.

" I am leaving Bavaria," she said, " but, before very long,
your King will also leave."

Everybody had something to say about the business. Most people had a lot to say. The wires hummed; and the foreign correspondents in Munich filled columns with long accounts of the recent disturbances in Munich and their origin. No two accounts were similar.

"The people insisted," says Edward Cayley, in his *European Revolutions of* 1848, " on the dismissal of the King's mistress. She was sent away, but, trusting to the King's dotage, she came back, police or no police. . . . This was a climax to which the people were unprepared to submit, not that they were any more virtuous than their Sovereign." Another publicist, Edward Maurice, puts it a little differently: " In Bavaria the power exercised by Lola Montez over Ludwig had long been distasteful to the sterner reformers." This was true enough; but the Müncheners disliked the Jesuits still more, asserting that it was with them that Lola shared the conscience of the King. The Liberals were ready for action, and welcomed the opportunity of asserting themselves.

As soon as Lola was really out of the country, her Barerstrasse mansion was searched from attic to cellar by the Munich police. Since, in order to justify the search, they had to discover something compromising, they announced that they had discovered " proofs " that Lord Palmerston and Mazzini were in active correspondence with the King's ex-mistress; and that the go-between for the British Foreign Office was a Jew called Loeb. This individual was an artist who had been employed to decorate the house. Seized with pangs of remorse, he is said to have gone to Ludwig and confessed having intercepted Lola's correspondence with Mazzini and engineered the rioting. He further declared that large sums of money had been sent her from abroad. Historians, however, have no knowledge of this; nor was the nature of the " proofs " ever revealed.

Lola's villa in the Barerstrasse afterwards became the new home of the British Legation. It was demolished in 1914;

and not even a wall plaque now marks her one-time occupancy. As for the Residenz Palace where she dallied with Ludwig, this building is now a museum, and as such echoes to the tramp of tourists and the snapping of cameras. *Sic transit*, etc.

II

When Lola, hunted from pillar to post, eventually left Munich for Switzerland, it was in the company of Auguste Papon, who, on the grounds of " moral turpitude," had already been given his marching-orders. He described himself as a " courier." His passport, however, bore the less exalted description of " cook." It was probably the more correct one. The faithful Fritz Peissner, anxious to be of service to the woman he loved, and for whom he had already risked his life, joined her at Constance, together with two other members of the *Alemannia*, Count Hirschberg and Lieutenant Nussbaum. But they only stopped a few days.

Anxious to get into touch with them, Lola wrote to the landlord at their last address :

SIR,　　　　　　　　　　　　　　　　*2 March*, 1848.

In case the students of the Alemannia Society have left your hotel, I beg you to inform my servant, the bearer of this letter, where Monsieur Peissner, for whom he has a parcel to deliver, has gone.

Receive in advance my distinguished sentiments.

COUNTESS OF LANDSFELD.

Lola's first halt in Switzerland (a country she described as " that little Republic which, like a majestic eagle, lies in the midst of the vultures and cormorants of Europe ") was at Geneva. An error of judgment, for the austere citizens of Calvin's town, setting a somewhat lofty standard among visitors, were impervious to her blandishments. " They were," she complained, " as chilly as their own icicles." At Berne, however, to which she went next, she had better luck. This was because she met there an impressionable young Chargé d'affaires attached to the

British Legation, whom she found " somewhat younger than Ludwig, but more than twice as silly." An *entente* was soon established. " Sometimes riding, and sometimes driving she would appear in public, accompanied by her youthful adorer."

The official was Robert Peel, a son of the distinguished statesman, and was afterwards to become third baronet. In a curious little work, typical of the period, *The Black Book of the British Aristocracy*, there is an acid allusion to the matter : " This bright youth has just taken under his protection the notorious Lola Montez, and was lately to be observed walking with her, in true diplomatic style, in the streets of a Swiss town."

It was about this period that it occurred to a theatrical manager in London, looking for a novelty, that there was material for a stirring drama written round the career of Lola Montez. No sooner said than done ; and a hack dramatist, who was kept on the premises, was commissioned to set to work. Locked up in his garret with a bottle of brandy, at the end of a week he delivered the script. This being approved by the management, it was put into rehearsal, and the hoardings plastered with bills :

THEATRE ROYAL, HAYMARKET
(Under the Patronage of Her Gracious Majesty The Queen, His Royal Highness Prince Albert, and the Élite of Rank and Fashion.)   On Wednesday, April 26, 1848, will be produced a New and Original and Apropos Sketch entitled :
" Lola Montez, or The Countess for an Hour."

" An hour." This was about as long as it lasted, for the reception by the critics was distinctly chilly. " We cannot," announced one of them, " applaud the motives that governed the production of a farce introducing a mock sovereign and his mistress. In our opinion the piece is extremely objectionable."

The Lord Chamberlain apparently shared this view, for he had the play withdrawn after the second performance.

"*Es gibt kein Zurück*" ("There is to be no coming back") had been Ludwig's last words to her. But Lola did not take the injunction seriously. According to a letter in the *Deutsche Zeitung*, she was back in Munich within a week, travelling under the "protection" of Baron Möller, a Russian diplomatist. Entering the Palace surreptitiously, she extracted a cheque for 50,000 florins from Ludwig. As it was drawn on Rothschild's bank at Frankfort, she hurried off there, and returned to Switzerland the same evening, "with a bagful of notes."

To convince his readers that he was well behind the scenes, Papon gives a letter which he asserts was written by Ludwig to a correspondent some months later :

> I wish to know from you if my dear Countess would like her annuity assured by having it paid into a private bank, or if she would rather I deposited a million francs with the Bank of England. . . . I am already being blamed for giving her too much. As the revolutionaries seize upon any pretext to assert themselves, it is important to avoid directing attention to her just now. Still, I want my dearly loved Countess to be satisfied. I repeat that the whole world cannot part me from her.

While he was with her in Switzerland, Papon strung together a pamphlet : *Lola Montez, Mémoires accompagnés de lettres intimes de S.M. le Roi de Bavière et de Lola Montez, ornés des portraits, sur originaux donnés par eux à l'auteur*, purporting to be written by their subject. "I owe my readers," he makes her say smugly, "the exact truth. They must judge between my enemies and myself." But, in his character of a Peeping Tom, very little truth was expended by Papon. Thus, he declares that, during her sojourn in the land of the mountains and William Tell, she had a series of *affaires* with a "baron," a "muscular artisan," and an "intrepid sailor." He also has a story to the effect that "two pure-blooded English ladies, the bearers of illustrious names," called on her uninvited ; and

that this circumstance annoyed her so much that she made her
pet monkey attack them.

But Auguste Papon cannot be considered a very reliable
authority. A decidedly odd fish, he claimed to be an ex-
officer and also dubbed himself a marquis. For all his
pretensions, however, he was merely a *chevalier d'industrie*,
living on his wits ; and, masquerading as a priest, he was
afterwards convicted of swindling and sent to prison.

III

A doughty, but anonymous, champion jumped into the
breach and issued a counterblast to Papon's effort in the shape
of a second pamphlet, headed " A Reply." But this was not
any more remarkable for its accuracy than the original. Thus,
it declares, " She [Lola] lived with the King of Bavaria, a
man of eighty-seven. The nature of that intimacy can best
be surmised by reading the second and third verses of the First
Book of Kings, Chapter i. It is evident to any reflecting mind
that it was a sort of King David arrangement." As for the
rest of the pamphlet, it was chiefly taken up with an elaborate
argument that, all said and done, its subject was no worse
than other ladies, and much better than many of them.

Among extracts from this well intentioned effort, the
following are the more important :

> A certain Marquis Auguste Papon, a quondam pan-
> derer to the natural desires and affections which are
> common to the whole human race, published and cir-
> culated throughout Europe a volume which stamps his
> own infamy (as we shall have occasion to show in the
> course of this reply) in far more ineffaceable characters
> than that of those whom, in his vindictiveness, he
> gloatingly sought to destroy.

> But, before we proceed to dissect his book, it may be
> permitted us to ask the impartial reader what there is so
> very remarkable in the conduct of the King of Bavaria

and Lola Montez as to distinguish them unfavourably from the monarchs and women celebrated for their talent, originality, and beauty who have gone before. Where are Henry IV of France, Henry V, Louis XIV, and Louis XV, with their respective mistresses ? Who of their people ever presumed to interfere on the score of morality with the favours and honours conferred on those distinguished women ? Nay, to come down to a later period, has the Marquis Auguste Papon ever heard of the loves of Louis XVIII and Madame de Cuyla, and that after the monarch's restoration in 1814 ? Is he ignorant of those of Napoleon himself and Mademoiselle Georges ? Have not almost all the royal family of England—even those of the House of Hanover—been notorious for their connection with celebrated women ? Has he never heard of Mrs. Walkinshaw, ostensible mistress of Charles Edward the Pretender, of Lucy Barlow, mistress of Charles II, mother of the Duke of Monmouth ? Of Arabella Churchill and Katherine Sedley, mistresses of James II ? Of the Countess of Kendal, mistress of George II, who was received everywhere in English society ? Or of George IV and the Marchioness of C——? Of the Duke of York and Mary Anne Clark ? Of the Duke of Clarence and the amiable and respected Mrs. J——? And last, not least, of the present King of Hanover and late Duke of Cumberland, who labours even unto this hour under suspicion of having murdered his valet Sellis, to conceal his adultery with his wife ? In what differs the King of Bavaria from these ?

But even to descend lower into the social scale of those who have occupied the attention of the world without incurring its marked and impertinent censure, has the Marquis Auguste Papon ever heard of the beautiful Miss Foote, who, first the favourite of the celebrated Colonel Berkeley (a natural brother of the Duke of Devonshire) and secondly of a personal friend of the writer of this reply—the celebrated Pea Green Hayne—became finally the charming and amiable Countess of Harrington, one of the sweetest women that ever were placed at the head of the Stanhope family or graced a peerage ?

Who, that ever once enjoyed the pleasure of knowing this fairest flower in the parterre of England's aristocracy of beauty, would, in a spirit of revenge and disappointed avarice, have had the grossness to insult *her* as the Marquis of Papon—the depository of all her secrets— has insulted the Countess of Landsfeld with the loath- some name of " courtesan," because, yielding to the confidence of her woman's heart, she had been the adored of two previous lovers ? Never did Lord Petersham, afterwards the Earl of Harrington, take a more sensible course than when he elevated in a holy and irreproach- able love—a love that strangled scandal in its bloated fullness—the fascinating Maria Foote to the position she was made to adorn, being twin sister in beauty as well as in law to the charming Miss Green, whose ripe red lips and long dark-lashed blue and laughing eyes were, before her marriage with Colonel Stanhope, the admiration and subject of homage of all London. Should her eye ever rest on this page, she will perceive that we have not forgotten its power and expression.

To descend still lower in the scale of social life, has the Marquis Auguste Papon ever heard of the celebrated Madame Vestris, now Mrs. Mathews ? Is he ignorant that her theatre—the Olympic—was ever a resort of the most fashionable and aristocratic people of London ? Did her moral life in any way detract from her popularity as a woman of talent and of beauty, and an artiste of exceeding fascination and merit ? And yet she had more lovers than the Marquis Auguste Papon can, with all his ingenuity, raise up in evidence against the remarkable woman he, in his not very creditable spirit of vengeance, has sworn to destroy.

Let us enumerate those we know to have been the lovers of Madame Vestris, who, after having passed her youth in all the variety of enjoyment, at length became the wife of a man, not without talent himself, and whose father stood first among the names celebrated in the comic art.

First was a personal friend of the writer of this reply to the unmanly attack of the Marquis Auguste Papon. And we have reason to remember it, for the connection of Henry Cole with the most fascinating woman of her day led to a duel in Hyde Park, of which that lady was the immediate cause, between the writer and a British officer who was so ungallant as to seek to check the enthusiasm created by her scarcely paralleled acting. To him succeeded Sir John Anstruther, and after Sir John the celebrated Horace Claggett. In what order their successors came we do not recollect, but of those who knew Madame Vestris in all the intimacy of the most tender friendship were Handsome Jack, Captain Best, Lord Edward Thynne, and Lord Castlereagh. These things were no secrets to the thousands who, fascinated by her beauty and the perfection of her acting, nevertheless thronged the theatre she was admitted to have conducted with the most amiable propriety and skill. On the contrary, they were as much matters of general knowledge among people of the first rank and fashion as the sun at noon-day. And yet what gentleman ever presumed to affix to the name of this gifted woman, whose very disregard of the opinion of those who hypocritically and *sub rosa* pursued in nearly ninety-nine cases out of a hundred the same course—what gentleman, we ask, ever dared to commit himself so far as to term her a " courtesan " ?

There was a good deal more of it, for the " Reply " ran to seventy-six pages.

The title-page of this counterblast ran :

LOLA MONTEZ

or

A REPLY TO THE

" PRIVATE HISTORY AND MEMOIRS "

of

THAT CELEBRATED LADY

RECENTLY PUBLISHED

By

THE MARQUIS PAPON

FORMERLY SECRETARY TO

THE KING OF BAVARIA

AND FOR A PERIOD

THE PROFESSED FRIEND AND ATTENDANT

of

THE COUNTESS OF LANDSFELD

Stet Nomnis Umbra—Junius

NEW YORK

1851

IV

Bavaria was the key position in the sphere of European politics just then. Ludwig, however, had dallied with the situation too long. Nothing that he could do now would save him. Unrest was in the air. All over Europe the tide of democracy was rising, and fast threatening to engulf the entrenched positions of the autocrats. Metternich, reading the portents, was planning to leave a mob-ridden Vienna for the more tranquil atmosphere of Brighton ; Louis Philippe, setting him an example, had already fled from Paris ; and Prince William of Prussia, shaving off his moustache (and travelling on a false passport), was hurrying to England while the going was still good. With these examples to guide them, the Bavarians, tired of soft promises and smooth words, were clamouring for a fresh hand at the helm. Realising that the choice lay between this and a republic, Ludwig bowed to the inevitable ; and, with crocodile tears and hypocritical pro- testations of good faith, surrendered his sceptre.

To give the decision full effect, he issued a Proclamation :

" Bavarians ! A new condition has arisen. This differs substantially from the one under which I have governed you for twenty-three years. Accordingly, I lay down my sceptre in favour of my beloved son, Prince Maximilian. I have always governed you with full regard for your welfare. Had I been a mere clerk, I could not have worked more strenu- ously ; had I been a Minister of Finance, I could not have devoted more attention to the requirements of my country. I thank God that I can look the whole world fearlessly in the face and there confront the most scrutinising eye. Although I now relinquish my crown, I can assure you that my heart still beats as warmly as ever for Bavaria.

" MUNICH,
    March 21, 1848."

Ludwig's signature to this mixture of rigmarole and bom- bast was followed by those of his sons, the Princes Maximilian Luitpold, Adalbert, and Carl. As for Maximilian, the new sovereign, he, rather than risk being thrown out of the saddle, was prepared to make a clean sweep of a number of existing grievances. As an earnest of his intentions, he promised, in the course of a frothy oration, to grant an amnesty to political prisoners, liberty of the press, the abolition of certain taxes, the institution of trial by jury, and a long delayed reform of the franchise.

With the idea, no doubt, of filling the vacancy in his

affections caused by the abrupt departure of Lola Montez, Fräulein Schroder, a young actress at the Hof Theatre, endeavoured to comfort Ludwig in his retirement. He, however, was beyond forming any fresh contacts.

"My happiness is gone from me," he murmured sadly. "I cannot stop in a capital to which I have long given a father's loving care."

Firm in this resolve, he left Munich for the Riviera and took a villa among the olives and oranges of Nice. There he turned over a fresh leaf. But he did not stop writing poetry. Nor did he stop writing to the woman who was still in his thoughts. One ardent epistle that followed her into exile ran in this fashion :

> Oh, my Lolita ! A ray of sunshine at the break of day ! A stream of light in an obscured sky ! Hope ever causes chords long forgotten to resound, and existence becomes once again pleasant as of yore. Such were the feelings which animated me during that night of happiness when, thanks to you alone, everything was sheer joy. Thy spirit lifted up mine out of sadness ; never did an intoxication equal the one I then felt !
>
> Thou hast lost thy gaiety ; persecution has stripped you of it ; and has robbed you of your health. The happiness of your life is already disturbed. But now, and more solidly than ever, are you attached to me. Nobody will ever be able to separate us. You have suffered because you love me.

When accounts of what was happening in Bavaria reached England a well pickled rod was applied to Lola's back :

"The sanguinary and destructive conduct of the Munich mob," began a furious leading article, "was caused by the supposed return of Bavaria's famous strumpet, Lola Montez. This heroine was once familiar to the eyes of all Paris, and notorious as a courtesan. When she was invested with a title, the Bavarians shuddered at their degradation. It was nothing

less than an outrage on the part of royalty, never to be forgotten or forgiven."

The columns of *Maga* also wielded the rod in vigorous
fashion :

" The late King, one of the most accomplished of dilettanti,
worst of poets, and silliest of men, had latterly put the coping-
stone to a life of folly by engaging in a most bare-faced
intrigue with the notorious Lola Montez. The indecency and
infatuation of this last *liaison*—far more openly conducted
than any of his former numerous amours—had given intense
umbrage to the nobility whom he had insulted by elevating
the ci-devant opera-dancer to their ranks."

Yet, with all his faults heavy upon him, Ludwig, none the
less, had his points. Thus, in addition to converting Munich
from a second-rate town to a really important capital, he did
much to encourage the development of art and letters and
science and education throughout his kingdom. Ignaz
Döllinger, the theologian, Joseph Görres, the historian, Jean
Paul Richter, the poet, Franz Schwanthaler, the sculptor, and
Wilhelm Thirsch, the philosopher, with Richard Wagner and
a host of others basked in his patronage. When he died,
twenty years later, these facts were remembered and his little
slips forgotten. The Müncheners gave him burial in the
Basilica ; and an equestrian statue, bearing the inscription,
" Just and Persevering," was set up in the Odeon-Platz.

It is the fashion among certain historians to charge Lola
Montez with responsibility for the revolution in Bavaria. But
this charge is not justified. The fact is, the kingdom was ripe
for revolution ; and the equilibrium of the government was
so unstable that Ludwig would have lost his crown, whether
she was in the country or not.

It is just as well to remember this.

V

After a few months among them, Lola, tiring of the Swiss
cantons, thought she might as well discover if England, which

she had not visited for six years, could offer any fresh attractions. Accordingly, resolved to make the experiment, on December 30, 1848, she arrived in London.

The *Satirist*, hearing the news, suggested that the managers of Drury Lane and Covent Garden should engage her as a " draw." But she did not stop in England very long, as she returned to the Continent almost at once.

In the following spring, she made a second journey to London, and sailed from Rotterdam. Unknown to her, the passenger list was to have included another fallen star. This was Metternich, who, with the riff-raff of Vienna thundering at the doors of his palace, was preparing to seek sanctuary in England. Thinking, however, that the times were not altogether propitious, he decided to postpone the expedition.

" If," he wrote, " the Chartist troubles had not prevented me embarking yesterday at Rotterdam, I should have reached London this morning in the company of the Countess of Landsfeld. She sailed by the steamer in which I was to have travelled. I thank heaven for having preserved me from such contact ! "

All things considered, it is perhaps just as well that the two refugees did not cross the Channel together. Had they done so, it is probable that one of them would have found a watery grave.

Metternich had worsted Napoleon, but he found himself worsted by Lola Montez. On April 9, he wrote from The Hague :

" I have put off my departure for England, because I wished to know first what was happening in that country as a result of the Chartists' disturbance. I consider that, for me who must have absolute rest, it would have been ridiculous to have arrived in the middle of the agitation."

Louis Napoleon, however, was made of sterner stuff ; and it is to his credit that, as a return for the hospitality extended him, he was sworn in as a special constable.

CHAPTER XII

A " LEFT-HANDED " MARRIAGE

I

ON arriving in London, and (thanks to the bounty of Ludwig) being well provided with funds, Lola took a house in Half Moon Street, Piccadilly. There she established something of a *salon*, where she gave a series of evening receptions. They were not, perhaps, up to the old Barerstrasse standard ; still, they brought together a number of the less important " lions," all of whom were only too pleased to accept invitations.

Among the hangers-on was Frederick Leveson-Gower, a son of Earl Granville. He had met the great Rachel in Paris and was ecstatic about her. " Not long after," he says, " I got to know another much less gifted individual, but who having captivated a King, upset two Ministries, and brought about a revolution in Bavaria, was entitled to be looked upon as celebrated. This was Lola Montez."

In his character of what is still oddly dubbed a " man-about-town," Serjeant Ballantine was also among those who attended these Half Moon Street gatherings. " His hostess," he says, " had certain claims to celebrity. She was, I believe, of Spanish origin, and certainly possessed that country's style of beauty, with much dash of manner and an extremely *outré* fashion of dress." Another occasional visitor was George Augustus Sala, a mid-Victorian journalist who was responsible for printing more slipshod inaccuracies than any two members of his craft put together. He says that he once contemplated writing Lola's memoirs. He did not, however, get beyond " contemplating."

This, perhaps, was just as well, since he was so ill-equipped for the task that he imagined she was a sister of Adah Isaacs Menken.

" About this time," he says, " I made the acquaintance, at a little cigar shop under the pillars in Norreys Street, Regent Street, of an extremely handsome lady, originally the wife of a solicitor, but who had been known in London and Paris as a ballet-dancer under the name of Lola Montez. When I knew her, she had just escaped from Munich, where she had been too notorious as Countess of Landsfeld. She had obtained for a time complete mastery over old King Ludwig of Bavaria ; and something like a revolution had been necessary to induce her to quit the Bavarian capital."

A ridiculous story spread that Lord Brougham (who had witnessed her ill-starred début in 1843) wanted to marry her. The fact that there was already a Lady Brougham in existence did not curb the tongues of the gossipers. " She refused the honourable Lord," says a French journalist, " in a manner that redounded to her credit."

Journalists, anxious for " copy," haunted Half Moon Street all day long. They were never off her doorstep. " Town gossip," declared one of them, " is in full swing ; and the general public are all agog to catch a glimpse of the latest ' lioness.' Lola Montez is on every lip and in everybody's eye. She is causing an even bigger sensation than that inspired by the Swedish Nightingale, Madame Jenny Lind."

Notwithstanding the ill-success of a former attempt to exploit her personality behind the footlights, Mrs. Keeley produced a sketch at the Haymarket written " round " Lola Montez. This, slung together by Stirling Coyne, was called : *Pas de Fascination.* The scene was laid in " Neverask-*where* " ; and among the characters were " Prince Dun-brownski," " Count Muffenuff," and " General von Bolte."

It scarcely sounds rib-rending.

Mrs. Charles Kean, who attended the first performance, described *Pas de Fascination* as " the most daring play I ever witnessed." Lola Montez herself took it in good part. She sat in a box, " and, when the curtain fell, threw a magnificent bouquet at the principal actress." Coals of fire.

Not to be behindhand in offering tit-bits of " news," an American correspondent informed his readers that : " During the early part of 1849, Lola Montez, arrayed in the Royal Bavarian jewels, crashed into one of the Court balls at Buckingham Palace. Needless to remark," he added, " the audacity has not been repeated." From this, it would appear that the Lord Chamberlain had been aroused from his temporary slumbers.

The *Satirist* had assured his readers " the public will soon be hearing more of Madame Montez." They did. What they heard was something quite unexpected. This was that she had made a second experiment in matrimony, and that her choice had fallen on a Mr. George Heald, a callow lad of twenty, for whom a commission as Cornet in the Life Guards had been purchased by his family.

II

The precise reasons actuating Lola in adopting this step were not divulged. Several, however, suggested themselves. Perhaps she was attracted by the Cornet's glittering cuirass and plumed helmet ; perhaps by his substantial income ; and perhaps she tired of being a homeless wanderer, and felt that here at last was a prospect of settling down and experimenting with domesticity.

When the announcement appeared in print there was much fluttering among the Mayfair dovecotes. As the bridegroom had an income of approximately £10,000 a year, the débutantes —chagrined to discover that such an " eligible " had been snatched from their grasp—felt inclined to call an indignation meeting.

" Preposterous," they said, " that such a woman should have snapped him up ! Something ought to be done about it."

But, for the moment, nothing was " done about it," and

Berrymead Priory, Acton, where Lola Montez lived with Cornet Heald

Lola Montez in London.   Aged thirty
(*Engraved by Auguste Hüssner*)

the knot was tied on July 14. Lola saw that the knot should be a double one ; and the ceremony took place, first, at the French Catholic Chapel in King Street, and afterwards at St. George's, Hanover Square.

A press representative, happening to be among the congregation, rushed off to Grub Street. There he was rewarded with a welcome five shillings by his editor, who, in high glee at securing such a piece of news before any other journal, had a characteristic paragraph on the subject :

> Lola Montez, Countess of Landsfeld, the ex-danseuse and ex-favourite of the imbecile old King of Bavaria, is, we are able to inform our readers, at last married legitimately. *On dit* that her young husband, Mr. George Trafford Heald, has been dragged into the match somewhat hurriedly. It will be curious to mark the progress of the Countess in this novel position. A sudden change from a career of furious excitement to one in which prudence and a regard for the rules of good society are the very opposite to those observed by loose foreigners must prove a trial to her. Whipping commissaries of police, and setting ferocious dogs at inoffensive civilians, may do very well for Munich. In England, however, we are scarcely prepared for these activities, even if they be deemed the privilege of a countess.

Disraeli, who had a hearty appetite for all the tit-bits of gossip discussed in Mayfair drawing-rooms, heard of the match and mentioned it in a letter to his sister, Sarah :

July, 1849.

The Lola Montez marriage makes a sensation. I believe he [Heald] has only £3,000 per annum, not £13,000. It was an affair of a few days. She sent to ask the refusal of his dog, which she understood was for sale —of course it wasn't, being very beautiful. But he sent it as a present. She rejoined ; he called ; and they were

married in a week. He is only twenty-one, and wished to
be distinguished. Their dinner invitations are already
out, I am told. She quite convinced him previously that
she was not Mrs. James ; and, as for the King of Bavaria,
who, by the by, allows her £1500 a year, and to whom she
writes every day—that was only a *malheureuse* passion.

Apropos of this union, a popular riddle went the round of
the clubs : " Why does a certain young officer of the Life
Guards resemble a much mended pair of shoes ? " The answer
was, " Because he has been heeled [Heald] and soled [sold]."

The honeymoon was spent at Berrymead Priory, a house
that the bridegroom owned at Acton. This was a substantial
Gothic building, with several acres of well timbered ground
and gardens. Some distance, perhaps, from the Cornet's
barracks. Still, one imagines he did not take his military
duties very seriously ; and leave of absence " on urgent
private affairs " was, no doubt, granted in liberal fashion.
Also, he possessed a phæton, in which, with a spanking
chestnut between the shafts, the miles would soon be
covered.

The Priory had a history stretching back to the far off days
of Henry III, when it belonged to the Chapter of St. Paul's
Cathedral. Henry VII, in high-handed fashion, presented it
to the Earl of Bedford ; and a subsequent occupant was the
notorious Elizabeth Chudleigh, the bigamous spouse of the
Duke of Kingston. Another light lady, Nancy Dawson, is
also said to have lived there as its châtelaine, under the
" protection " of the Duke of Newcastle.

At the beginning of the last century the property was
acquired by a Colonel Clutton. He was followed by Edward
Bulwer, afterwards Lord Lytton, who lived there on and off
(chiefly off) with his wife, until their separation in 1836. On
one occasion he gave a dinner-party, among the guests being
John Forster, " to meet Miss Landon, Fontblanque, and
Hayward." To the invitation was added the warning, " We

dine at half-past five, to allow time for return, and regret much having no spare beds as yet." A spare bed, however, was available for Lord Beaconsfield, when he dined there in the following year.

On the departure of Bulwer, the house had a succession of tenants ; and for a short period it even sheltered a bevy of Nuns of the Sacred Heart. It was when they left that the estate was purchased by Mr. George Heald, a barrister with a flourishing practice. He left it to his booby son, the Cornet : and it was thus that Lola Montez established her connection with Berrymead Priory.

While the original house still stands, the garden in which it stood has gone ; and the building itself now serves as the premises of the Acton Constitutional Club. But the committee have been careful to preserve some evidence of Cornet Heald's occupancy. Thus, his crest and family motto, *Nemo sibi Nascitur*, are let into the mosaic flooring of the hall, and the drawing-room ceiling is embellished with his initials picked out in gold.

III

Prejudice, perhaps, but unions between the sons of Mars and the daughters of Terpsichore were in those days frowned upon by the military big-wigs at the Horse Guards. Hence, it was not long before an inspired note on the subject of this one appeared in the *Standard* :

> We learn from undoubted authority that, immediately on the marriage of Lieutenant Heald with the Countess of Landsfeld, the Marquess of Londonderry, Colonel of the 2nd Life Guards, took the most decisive steps to recommend to Her Majesty that this officer's resignation of his commission should be insisted on ; and that he should at once leave the regiment, which this unfortunate and extraordinary act might possibly prejudice.

Her Majesty, having consulted the Prince Consort and the Duke of Wellington, shared this view. Instead, however, of being summarily " gazetted out," the love-sick young warrior was permitted to " send in his papers."

Thinking that he had acted precipitately in resigning, Cornet Heald (egged on, doubtless, by Lola) endeavoured to get his resignation cancelled. The authorities, however, were adamant. " Much curiosity," says a journalistic comment, " has been aroused among the Household Troops by the efforts of this officer to regain his commission after having voluntarily relinquished it. Notwithstanding his youth and the fact that he had given way to a sudden impulse, Lord Londonderry was positively inflexible. Yet the influence and eloquence of a certain ex-Chancellor, well known to the bride, was brought to bear on him."

The " certain ex-Chancellor " was none other than Lord Brougham.

Much criticism followed in other circles. Everybody had an opinion to advance. Most of them were far from complimentary, and there were allusions by the dozen to " licentious soldiery " and " gilded popinjays." The rigid editor of *The Black Book of the British Aristocracy* was particularly indignant. " The Army," he declared, in a fierce outburst, " is the especial favourite of the aristocratic section. Any brainless young puppy with a commission is free to lounge away his time in dandyism and embryo moustaches at the public expense."

The *Satirist*, living up to its name, also had its customary sting :

Of course, the gallant Colonel of the Household Troops could not do less. That distinguished corps is immaculate ; and no breath of wind must come between it and its propriety. There is but one black sheep in the 2nd Life Guards, and that, in the eyes of the coal black colonel (him of the collieries), is the soft, enchanted, and enchained Mr. Heald. Poor Heald ! Indignant Londonderry ! How subservient, in truth, must be the lean subaltern to his fat colonel.

A Sunday organ followed suit. " What," it demanded,
" may be the precise article of the military code against which
Mr. Heald is thought to have offended ? One could scarcely
have supposed that officers in Her Majesty's service were
living under such a despotism that they should be compelled
to solicit permission to get married, or their colonel's
approbation of their choice."

In addition to thus disapproving of marriages between his
officers and ladies of the stage, Lord Londonderry (a veteran
of fifty-five years' service) disapproved with equal vigour of
tobacco. " What," he once wrote to Lord Combermere,
" are the Gold Sticks to do with that sink of smoking, the
Horse Guards' guard and mess-rooms ? Whenever I have
visited them, I have found them *worse* than any pot-house, and
this actually opposite the Adjutant-General's and under his
Grace's very nose ! "

The example set by Cornet Heald seems to have been
catching. " Another young officer of this regiment," announced the *Globe*, " has just run off with a frail lady belonging
to the Theatre and actually married her at Brighton." He,
too, was required to " send in his papers."

Besides losing his commission, Cornet Heald had, in his
marriage, all unwittingly laid up a peck of fresh trouble for
himself. This was brought to a head by the action of his
spinster aunt, Miss Susannah Heald, who, until he came of
age, had been his guardian. Suspecting Lola of a " past,"
she set herself to pry into it. Gathering that her nephew's
inamorata had already been married, she employed enquiry
agents to look into this previous union and discover just how
and when it had been dissolved. They did their work well,
and reported that the divorce decree of seven years earlier
had not been made absolute, and that Lola's first husband,
Captain James, was still alive. Armed with this knowledge,
Miss Heald hurried off to the authorities, and, having " laid
an information," had Lola Montez arrested for bigamy.

The case was heard at Marlborough Street police court,

with Mr. Bingham sitting as Magistrate.   Mr. Clarkson conducted the prosecution, and Mr. Bodkin appeared for the
defence.

" The proceedings of a London police court," declared
John Bull, " have seldom presented a case more fruitful of
matter for public gossip than was exhibited in the investigation
at Marlborough Street, where the mediated wife of a British
officer (and one invested with the distinction of Royal favouri-
tism) answered a charge of imputed bigamy. . . . It will
readily be inferred that we allude to that extraordinary per-
sonage known as Lola Montez, *alias* the Countess of
Landsfeld."

Lola had, as the theatrical world would put it, dressed for
the part.   She had probably rehearsed it, too.   She wore, we
learn, " a black silk costume, under a velvet jacket, and a
plain white straw bonnet trimmed with blue ribbons."   As
became a countess, she was not required to sit in the dock, but
was given a chair in front of it.   " There," said a reporter,
" she appeared quite unembarrassed, and smiled frequently
as she made a remark to her husband.   She was described on
the charge sheet as being twenty-four years of age, but in our
opinion she has the look of a woman of at least thirty."

" In figure," added a second occupant of the press box,
" madam is rather plump, and of middle height, with pale complexion, unusually large blue eyes and long black lashes.   Her
reputed husband, Mr. Heald, is a tall young man of boyish
aspect, fair hair and small brown moustachios and whiskers.
During the whole of the proceedings he sat with the Countess's
hand clasped in his, occasionally giving it a fervent squeeze,
and murmuring fondly in her ear."

All being ready, Mr. Clarkson opened the case for the
prosecution.

" The offence imputed to the lady at the bar," he said, " is
that, well knowing her husband, Captain Thomas James, was
still alive, she contracted another marriage with this young
gentleman, Mr. George Trafford Heald.   If this be established,

serious consequences must follow, as I shall prove that the
Ecclesiastical Court merely granted a decree *a mensa et thoro*."
He then put in a copy of this document, and pointed out that,
by its provisions, neither party was free to re-marry during the
life-time of the other.   Counsel also submitted an extract from
the register of the Hanover Square church, showing that, on
July 19, the defendant had, under the name of " Maria Torres
de Landsfeld," gone through a ceremony of marriage with
Cornet Heald.

Police-sergeant Gray, who had executed the warrant,
described the arrest.

" When I told her she must come along with me, the lady up
and said : ' This is all rubbish.   I was properly divorced from
Captain James by Act of Parliament.   Lord Brougham was
present when the divorce was granted.   I don't know if Captain
James is still alive or not, and I don't care a little bit.   I was
married to him in the wrong name, and that made the whole
thing illegal.' "

" Did she say anything else ? " enquired the magistrate.

" Yes, Your Worship," returned the sergeant, consulting
his note-book.   " She said : ' What on earth will the Royal
Family say when they hear of this ?   There's bound to be the
devil of a fuss.' "

" Laughter in Court ! " chronicled the pressmen.

" And what did you say to that ? " enquired Mr. Bingham.

" I said that anything she said would be taken down by
myself and used in evidence against her," was the glib
response.

The execution of the warrant would appear to have been
carried out in dramatic fashion.

Having evidently got wind of what was awaiting her, Lola
and the Cornet had packed their luggage and arranged to
leave England.   Just as they were stepping into their carriage,
Miss Susannah Heald and her solicitor, accompanied by a
couple of police officers, drove up in a cab to Half Moon
Street.   When the latter announced that they had a warrant

for her arrest, there was something of a scene. " The Countess," declared an imaginative reporter (who must have been hovering on the doorstep), " exhibited all the appearance of excessive passion. She used very strong language, pushed the elderly Miss Heald aside, and bustled her husband in vigorous fashion. However, she soon cooled down, and, on being escorted to Vine Street police station, where the charge of bigamy was booked, she graciously apologised for any trouble she had given the representatives of the law. She then begged permission to light a cigar, and suggested that the constables on duty there should join her in a social whiff."

Miss Susannah Heald, described as " an aged lady," deposed that she was Cornet Heald's aunt, and that she had been appointed his guardian during his minority, which had only just expired. She was bringing the action, she insisted, " from a sense of duty."

Another witness was Captain Charles Ingram, a mariner in the service of the East India Company. He identified the accused as the Mrs. James who had sailed in a ship under his command from Calcutta to London in the year 1842.

While an official return, prepared by the military authorities, showed Captain James to have been alive on June 13, there was none to show that he was still in the land of the living on July 19, the date of the alleged bigamous marriage. The prosecution affected to consider this point unimportant. The magistrate, however (on whom Lola's bright eyes had done their work), did not agree.

" The point," he said, " is, to my mind, very important. During the interval that elapsed between these two dates many things may have happened which would render this second marriage quite legal. It is possible, for instance, that Captain James may have been snatched from this world to another one by any of those numerous casualties—such as wounds in action or cholera—that are apt to befall members of the military profession serving in a tropical climate. What do you say to that, Mr. Clarkson ? "

Mr. Clarkson had nothing to say. Mr. Bodkin, however, when it came to his turn, had a good deal to say. The charge against his client was, he declared, " in all his professional experience, absolutely unparalleled." Neither the first nor the second husband, he pointed out, had advanced any complaint ; and the offence, if any, had been committed under circumstances that fully justified it. He did not wish to hint at improper motives on the part of Miss Heald, but it was clear, he protested, that her attitude was governed by private, and not by public, ends. None the less, he concluded, " I am willing to admit that enough has been put before the Court to justify further enquiry."

Such an admission was a slip which even the very rawest of counsel should have avoided. It forced the hand of the magistrate.

" I am asked," he said, " to act on a presumption of guilt. As proof of guilt is wanting, I am reluctant to act on such presumption, even to the extent of granting a remand, unless the prosecution can assure me that more evidence will be offered at another hearing. Since, however, the defendant's own advocate has voluntarily admitted that there is ground for further enquiry, I am compelled to order a remand. But the accused will be released from custody on providing two sureties of £500 each, and herself in one of £1000."

The adjourned proceedings began a week later, and were heard by another magistrate, Mr. Hardwick. This time, however, there was no defendant, for, on her name being called by the usher, Mr. Bodkin pulled a long face and announced that his client had left England. " I cannot," he said, " offer any reason for her absence." Still, he had a suggestion. " It is possible," he said, " that she has gone abroad for the benefit of her health." The question of estreating the recognizances then arose. While not prepared to abandon them altogether, counsel for the prosecution was sufficiently generous to say that so far as he was concerned no objection would be offered to extending them.

When, after two more adjournments, the defendant still failed to surrender to her bail, the magistrate and counsel for the prosecution altered their tone.

" Your Worship," said Mr. Clarkson, " it has come to my knowledge that the person whose real name is Mrs. James, and who is charged with the felonious crime of bigamy, is now some hundreds of miles beyond your jurisdiction, and does not mean to appear. Accordingly, on behalf of the highly respectable Miss Heald, I now ask that the recognizances be forfeited. My client has been actuated all through by none but the purest motives, her one object being to remove the only son of a beloved brother from a marriage that was as illegal as it was disgraceful. If we secure evidence from India that Captain James is still alive, we shall then adopt the necessary steps to remove this deluded lad from the fangs of this scheming woman."

" Let the recognizances be estreated," was the magisterial comment.

" Sensation ! " scribbled the reporters.

Serjeant Ballantine, who liked to have a hand in all *causes célèbres*, declares that he was consulted by Lola's solicitors, with a view to undertaking her defence. If so, he would seem to have read his instructions very casually, since he adds : " I forget whether the prosecution was ultimately dropped, or whether she left England before any result was arrived at. My impression is that the charge could not have been substantiated."

Ignoring the fact that the case was still *sub judice*, the *Observer* offered its readers some severe comments :

" The Helen of the age is most assuredly Lola Montez, *alias* Betsy James, *alias* the Gräfin von Lansfelt, *alias* Mrs. Heald. As far as can be gathered from her dark history, her first public act was alleged adultery, as her last is alleged bigamy. . . . The evidence produced before the Consistory Court is of the most clear and convincing nature, and proves that the character of this lady (whose fame has become so

disgustingly notorious) has been from an early date that of a
mere wanton, alike unmindful of the sacred ties of matrimony
and utterly careless of the opinion of the world upon morality
or religion."

By the way, during the police court proceedings, fresh light
on the subject of Lola's parentage was furnished by an odd
entry in an Irish paper :

" Lola Montez, Countess of Landsfeld, is the daughter of a
Cork lady. Her mother was at one time employed as a member of a millinery establishment in this city ; and was married
here to Lieutenant Gilbert, an officer in the army. Soon after
the marriage, he sailed with his wife and child to join his
regiment in India. At the end of last year, Lola's mother,
who is now in delicate health, visited her sister in Cork."

IV

Thanks to the bright eyes of Lola (or perhaps to the musical
jingle of the Cornet's cash bags), a very loose watch was kept
on the pair. Hence the reason why the Countess of Landsfeld
(as she still insisted on being called) had not kept her second
appointment at Marlborough Street was because, together
with the dashing ex-Life Guardsman, she had left England
early that morning. Travelling as Mr. and Mrs. Heald, the
pair went, first, to Paris, and then to Italy.

A British tourist who happened to be in Naples wrote to
The Times, giving an account of a glimpse he had of them.
According to him, the couple, " a youthful bridegroom and a
fair lady," accompanied by a courier, a *femme de chambre*, and a
carriage, took rooms at the Hotel Vittoria. After one night
there, they left the next morning, hiring a special steamer, at a
cost of £400, to take them to Marseilles. The hurried departure was said to be due to a lawyer's letters that was waiting
for the bridegroom at his banker's. " I am told," adds the
correspondent, " that Mr. and Mrs. Heald were bound on an
excursion to the Pyramids ; and that, when the little business
for which the lady is wanted at home has been settled, they

mean to prosecute their intention. Pray, sir, help Mrs. Heald out of her present affliction. Is this the first time that a lady has had two husbands ? And is she not bound for the East, where every man has four wives ? "

The booby Cornet, with his ideas limited to fox-hunting and a study of *Ruff's Guide*, was no mate for a brilliant woman like Lola. Hence disagreements soon manifested themselves. A specially serious one would seem to have arisen at Barcelona, for, says a letter from a mutual acquaintance, " the Countess and her husband had a warm discussion, which ended in an attempt by her to stab him. Mr. Heald, objecting to such a display of conjugal affection, promptly quitted the town."

Further particulars were supplied by another correspondent : " I saw Mr. Heald," says this authority. " He is a tall, thin young man, with a fair complexion, and often uses rouge hide his pallor. Many pity him for what has happened. Others, however, pity the lovely Lola. Before he left this district, Mr. Heald called on the English Consul. ' I have come,' he said, ' to ask your advice. Some of my friends here suggest that I should leave my wife. What ought I to do about it ? If I stop with her, I am afraid of being assassinated or poisoned.' He then exhibited a garment covered with blood. The Consul replied : ' I am positively astonished that, after the attack of which you speak, you did not complain to the police, and that you have since lived with your wife on terms of intimacy. If you want to abandon her, you must do as you think best. I cannot advise you.' "

H.B.M. Consul, however, did stretch a point, since he (perhaps fearing further bloodshed) offered to *viser* the applicant's passport for any other country. Thereupon, Mr. Heald betook himself to Mataro. But, becoming conscience-smitten, he promptly sat down and wrote an apologetic letter to the lady he left behind him, begging her forgiveness. " If you should ever have reason to complain of me again," he said, " this letter will always act as a talisman."

Apparently it had the effect, for Lola returned to her penitent spouse.

The Barcelona correspondent of *L'Assemblée Nationale* managed to interview the Cornet.

" He says," announced this authority, " that others persuaded him to depart, against his real wishes. On rejoining him, Mrs. Heald was most indignant. Her eyes positively flashed fire ; and, if she should chance to encounter the men who took her husband from her, I quite tremble to think what will happen ! "

Something obviously did happen, for, according to de Mirecourt, " during their sojourn in Sunny Spain, the admirable English husband made his wife the gratified mother of two beautiful offspring." Parenthood, however, would appear to have had an odd effect upon this couple, for, continues de Mirecourt : " *Mais, en dépit de ces gages d'amour, leur bonheur est troublé par des querelles intestines.*"

It was from Spain that, having adjusted their differences temporarily, the couple went back to Paris. As a peace offering, a rising young artist, Claudius Jacquand, was commissioned to paint both their portraits on a single canvas. During, however, another domestic rupture, Heald demanded that Lola's features should be painted out. " I want nothing," he said, " to remind me of that woman." Unfortunately, Lola had just made a similar demand where the Cornet was concerned. Jacquand was a man of talent, but he could not do impossibilities. Thereupon, Lola, breathing fire and fury, took the canvas away and hung it with its back to the front in her bedroom. " To allow my husband to watch me always would," she said, " be indelicate ! "

There is a theory that, within the next twelve months, the ill-assorted union was dissolved by Heald getting upset in a rowing-boat and drowned in Lisbon harbour. The theory, however, is a little difficult to reconcile with the fact that, on the close of the Great Exhibition at the end of 1851, he attended an auction of the effects, where he bought a parquet floor and had it laid down in his drawing-room at Berrymead Priory. After this he had a number of structural alterations added ; fitted the windows with some stained glass, bearing his crest and initials ; and, finally, did not give up the lease until 1855. Pretty good work, this, for a man said to have met with a watery grave six years earlier.

As a matter of strict fact, Cornet Heald was not drowned, either at Lisbon or anywhere else. He died in his bed at Folkestone, in 1856. The medical certificate attributed the cause of death to consumption. In the *Gentleman's Magazine*, however, the diagnosis was different, viz., " broken heart."

All things pass. In 1859 the executors of the dashing Cornet sold the Berrymead property for £7000, to be re-purchased soon afterwards for £23,000 by a land-development company. The house now serves as the premises of the Priory Constitutional Club, Acton. A certain amount of evidence of Cornet Heald's one-time occupancy still exists. Thus his crest and motto, *Nemo sibi Nascitur*, are let into the mosaic flooring of the hall, and the drawing-room ceiling is embellished with his initials picked out in gold.

CHAPTER XIII

ODYSSEY

I

NOTWITHSTANDING the tie of alleged parent-hood, domestic relations between them did not improve, and the couple soon parted. The knowledge that she was still " wanted " there kept Lola out of England. Instead, she went to Paris, where such unpleasantnesses as warrants could not touch her. There she was given a warm welcome, by old friends and new.

During this visit to Paris an unaccustomed set-back was experienced. She received it from Émile de Girardin, of whom she endeavoured to make a conquest. But this " wild-eyed, pale-faced man of letters," as she called him, would have none of her. Perhaps he remembered what had befallen Dujarier.

As was to be expected, the coming among them of Lola Montez attracted the attention of the *courrierists*, who earned many welcome francs by filling columns with details of her career. What they did not know about it they invented. They knew very little. Thus, one such article (appropriately signed " Fantasio ") read as follows :

" Madame Lola Montez, who is now happily returned to us, is the legitimate spouse of Sir Thomas James, an officer of the English Army. Milord Sir James loved to drink and the beautiful Lola loved to flirt. A wealthy Prince of Kabul was willing to possess her for her weight in gold and gems. Up till now, her principal love affairs have been with Don Enriquez, a Spaniard, Brûle-Tout, a well-developed French mariner, and

John, a phlegmatic Englishman. One day Sir James bet that he could drink three bottles of brandy in twenty minutes. While he was thus occupied, the amorous Lola made love to three separate gallants."

" It will doubtless," added a second, " be gratifying to her pride to queen it again in Paris, where she was once hissed off the stage. There she will at any rate now be received at the Bavarian Embassy, and exhibit the Order of Maria Theresa. She was invested with this to the considerable scandal of the Munich nobility, who cannot swallow the idea of such a distinction being bestowed on a dancer."

This sort of thing and a great deal more in a similar strain, was accepted as gospel by its readers. But for those who wished her ill, any lie was acceptable. Thus, although there was not a scrap of evidence to connect her with the incident, a paragraph, headed " Lola Again ? " was published in the London papers :

> Yesterday afternoon an extraordinary scene was witnessed by the promenaders in the Champs Elysées. Two fashionably attired ladies, driving in an elegant equipage, were heard to be employing language that was anything but refined. From words to blows, for suddenly they began to assault one another with vigorous smacks. The toilettes and faces of the fair contestants were soon damaged ; and, loud cries of distress being uttered, the carriage was stopped, and, attracted by the fracas, some gentlemen hurried to render assistance. As a result of their interference, one of the damsels was expelled from the vehicle, and the other ordered the coachman to drive her to her hotel. This second lady is familiar to the public by reason of her adventures in Bavaria.

Albert Vandam, a singularly objectionable type of journalist, who professed to be on intimate terms with everybody in Paris worth knowing, has a number of offensive and unjustifiable allusions to Lola Montez at this period of her career. He talks of her " consummate impudence," of her " pot-house wit," and of her " grammatical errors," and dubs her, among other things, " this almost illiterate schemer."

" Lola Montez," says the egregious Vandam, " could not make friends." He was wrong. This was just what she could do. She made many staunch and warm-hearted friends. It was because she snubbed him on account of his pushfulness that Vandam elected to belittle her.

Lola Montez chose her friends for their disposition, not for their virtue. One of them was George Sand, " the possessor of the largest mind and the smallest foot in Paris." She also became intimate with Alphonsine Plessis, and constantly visited the future " Lady of the Camelias " in her *appartement* on the Boulevard de la Madeleine. Another *habitué* there at this period was Lola's old Dresden flame, the Abbé Liszt, who, not confining his attentions to the romanticists, had no compunction about poaching on the preserves of Dumas *fils*, or, for that matter, of anybody else. As for the fair, but frail, Alphonsine, she said quite candidly that she was " perfectly willing to become his mistress, if he wanted it, but was not prepared to share the position." As Liszt had other ideas on the subject, the suggestion came to nothing.

Some years afterwards, one of his pupils, an American young woman, Amy Fay, took his measure in a book, *Music-study in Germany* :

" Liszt," she wrote, " is the most interesting and striking-looking man imaginable. Tall and slight, with deep-set eyes, shaggy eyebrows and long iron-grey hair which he wears parted in the middle. His mouth turns up at the corners, which gives him a most crafty and Mephistophelean expression when he smiles, and his whole appearance and manner have a sort of Jesuitical elegance and ease."

Before she set out on this journey, Lola wrote to an acquaintance : " What makes men and women distinguished is their individuality ; and it is for that I will conquer or die ! " Of this quality, she had enough and to spare. Her Paris life was hectic ; or, as the Boulevardiers put it, *elle faisait la bombe.*

Among the tit-bits of gossip served up by a reporter was the following :

" Lola is constantly giving tea-parties in her Paris flat. A gentleman who is frequently bidden to them tells us that her masculine guests are restricted to such as have left their wives, and that the feminine guests consist of ladies who have left their husbands."

An Englishman whom she met at this time was Savile Morton, a friend of Thackeray and Tennyson. One night when she was giving a supper-party, a fellow-guest, Roger de Beauvoir, happened to read to the company some verses he had written. The hostess, on the grounds of their alleged " coarseness," complained to Morton that she had been insulted. As a result, Morton, being head over ears in love with her, sent de Beavoir a challenge. Lola, however, having had enough of duels, took care that nothing should come of it ; and insisted that an apology should be given and accepted.

At one time she was optimistic enough to take a villa at Beaujon on a fifteen years' lease, and had it refurnished in sumptuous fashion on credit. The first two instalments of the rent were met. When, however, the landlord called to collect the third one, he was put off with the excuse that : " Mr. Heald was away and had forgotten to send the money, but would be back in a week." This story might have been accepted, had not the landlord discovered that his tenant was planning to leave surreptitiously and that some of the furniture had already been removed. As a result, a body of indignant tradesmen, accompanied by the Maire of the district, in tricoloured sash and wand of office complete, betook themselves to the villa and demanded a settlement of accounts for goods delivered. This time they were told that the money had arrived, but that the key of the box in which it had been deposited for safety was lost. Assuring them that she would fetch a locksmith, Lola slipped out of the house, and, stepping into a waiting cab, drove off to a new address near the Étoile. This was the last that the creditors saw of her.

In January, 1851, Lola, setting an example that has since then become much more common among theatrical ladies, compiled her " memoirs." When the editor of *Le Pays* undertook to publish them in his columns, a rival editor, jealous of the " scoop," referred to their author as " Madame James, once Madame Heald, formerly Mlle Lola Montez, and for nearly a quarter of an hour the Countess of Landsfeld."

The work was dedicated to her old patron, King Ludwig, with a florid *avant-propos* :

> Sire : In publishing my memoirs, my purpose is to reveal to a world still engulfed in a vulgar materialism Your Majesty's lofty thoughts about art, poetry, and philosophy. The inspiration of this book, Sire, is due to yourself, and to those other remarkable men whom Fortune—always the protector of my younger years—has given me as councillors and friends."

Lola must have written with more candour than tact. At any rate, after the first three chapters had appeared, the editor of *Le Pays*, on the grounds that they would " shock his purer readers," refused to continue the series. " We positively decline," he announced, " to sully our columns further."

II

Authorship having thus proved a failure, Lola, swallowing her disappointment, directed her thoughts to her old love, the ballet. To this end, she placed herself in the hands of a M. Roux ; and, a number of engagements having been secured by him, she began a provincial tour at Bordeaux. By the time it was completed the star and her manager were on such bad terms that, when they got back to Paris, the latter was dismissed. Thereupon, he hurried off to a notary, and brought an action against his employer, claiming heavy damages.

According to Maître Desmaret, his client, M. Roux, had been engaged in the capacity of *pilote intermédiare* during a prospective tour in Europe and America. For his services he was to have 25 per cent of the box-office receipts. On this understanding he had accompanied his principal to a number of towns. He then returned to Paris ; and while he was negotiating there for the defendant's appearance at the Vaudeville, he suddenly discovered that she was planning to go to America without him. As a result, he was now claiming damages for breach of contract. These he laid at the modest figure of 10,000 francs.

M. Blot-Lequesne, on behalf of Lola Montez, had a somewhat different story to tell. The plaintiff himself, he declared, wanted to get out of the contract and had deliberately disregarded its terms. His client, he said, had authorised him to accept an engagement for her to dance six times a week ; but, in his anxiety to make additional profit for himself, he had compelled her to dance six times a day. Apart from this, he had " signally failed to respect her dignity as a woman, and had invented ridiculous stories about her career." He had even done worse, for, " without her knowledge or sanction, he had compiled and distributed among the audiences where she appeared an utterly preposterous biography of his employer." This, among other matters, asserted that she had " lived and danced for eleven years in China and Persia ; and that she had been befriended by the dusky King of Nepaul, as well as by numerous rajahs."

The concluding passage from this effort was read to the judge :

" Ten substantial volumes would be filled with the chronicle of the eccentricities of Mlle Lola Montez, and much of them would still be left unsaid. In the year 1847 a great English lord married her in London. Unfortunately, they found themselves not in sympathy, and in 1850 she returned to the dreams of her spring-time. The Countess has now completed one half of her projected tour. In November she leaves France for

A " Belle of the Boulevards."   Lola Montez in Paris

The " Spider Dance."   Cause of much criticism

America and—well—God only knows what will happen then ! "

" As long," said counsel, " as the amiable Mlle Montez was treated by M. Roux like a wild animal exhibited at a country fair, she merely shrugged her shoulders in disgust. When, however, she saw how this abominable pamphlet lifted the curtain from her private life, it was another thing altogether. She expressed womanly indignation, and made a spirited response.

" What was that ? " enquired the judge, with interest.

" She said : ' It is lucky for you, sir, that my husband is not here to protect me. If he were, he would certainly pull your nose ! ' "

As was inevitable, this expression of opinion shattered the *entente*, and the manager returned to Paris by himself. Hearing nothing from him, Lola Montez thought that she was at liberty to make her own plans, and had accordingly arranged the American tour without his help.

On November 6, 1851, continued counsel, Lola Montez arrived in Paris, telling M. Roux that she would leave for America on November 20, but that she would fulfil any engagement he secured during the interval. Just before she was ready to start he said he had got her one, but he would not tell her where it was or produce any written contract.

Accepting this version as the correct one, the Court pronounced judgment in favour of Lola Montez.

III

M. Roux having thus been dismissed with a flea in his ear, Lola, on the advice of Peter Goodrich, the American consul in Paris, next engaged Richard Storrs Willis (a brother of N. P. Willis, the American poet) to look after her business affairs, and left Europe for America. As the good ship *Humbolt*, by which she was sailing, warped into harbour at New York, a salute of twenty-one guns thundered from the Battery. Lola, mightily pleased, took this expenditure of ammunition as a

tribute to herself. When, however, she discovered that it
was really to herald the coming of Louis Kossuth, who also
happened to be on board, she registered annoyance and
retired to her cabin, to nurse her wrath. A Magyar patriot
to be more honoured than an English ex-favourite of a King !
What next ?

" A gentleman travelling with her informed our representative," said the *New York Herald*, " that Madame had
declared Kossuth to be a great humbug. The Countess was a
prodigious favourite among the masculine passengers during
the voyage, and continually kept them in roars of laughter."

But, if disappointed in one respect, Lola derived a measure
of compensation from the fact that the bevy of reporters who
met the vessel found her much more interesting than the
stranger from Hungary.

" Madame Lola Montez," remarked one of them, who had
gone off with a bulging note-book, crammed with enough
" copy " to fill a column, " says that a number of shocking
falsehoods about her have been published in our journals. Yet
she insists she is not the woman she is credited (or discredited)
with being. If she were, her admirers, she thinks, would be
still more plentiful than they are. She expresses herself as
fearful that she will not have proper consideration in New
York ; but she trusts that the great American public will
suspend judgment until they have made her acquaintance."

" The Countess of Landsfeld, who is now among us," adds
a second scribe, " owes more to the brilliancy of intellect with
which Heaven has gifted her than to her world-wide celebrity
as an artiste. Her person and bearing are unmistakably
aristocratic. If we may credit the stories which from time to
time have reached us, she can, if necessary, use her riding-
whip in vigorous fashion about the ears of any offending biped
or quadruped. In America she is somewhat out of her
latitude. Paris should be her real home."

For the present, however, Lola decided to stop where she was.
While she was in America on this tour, Barnum wanted to

be her impresario, and promised " special terms." Despite, however, the lure of " having her path garlanded with flowers and her carriage drawn by human hands from hotel to theatre," the offer was not accepted.

The New York début of Lola Montez was made on December 29, 1851, in a ballet : *Betly, the Tyrolean*. Public excitement ran high, for appetites had been whetted by the sensational accounts of her " past " with which the papers were filled.

" Scandal does not necessarily create a great dancer," declared one rigid critic ; and a second had a long column, headed : " MONTEZ *v.* RESEPCTABILITY," in which he observed (thoughtfully supplying a translation) : " *Parturiunt* MONTEZ, *nascitur ridiculus mus.*" All the same, the box-office reported record business. As a result, prices were doubled, and the seats put up to auction.

If she had her enemies in the press, Lola also had her champions there. Just before she arrived, one of them, a New York paper, took up the cudgels on her behalf in vigorous fashion :

The most funny proceeding that is going on in this town is the terrible to-do that is being made about Lola Montez. If this state of things continues we will guarantee a continuance of the fun after Lola makes her advent among us, for if she doesn't properly horse-whip those squeamish gentlemen we are much mistaken in her character.

Now we want to call the attention of our fair-minded readers to a few other matters that are sure to occur. Here are the various papers pouring out a torrent of abuse on Lola. What will it all amount to ? In a few weeks she will land. In a few weeks a popular theatre will be occupied by her, and tens of thousands will throng that theatre. The manager will reap a fortune, and so will Lola Montez ; and those short-sighted conductors· of the Press will be begging for tickets and quarrelling among themselves as to who

can say the most extravagant things in her favour.
Public curiosity will be gratified at any price ; and if
Lola Montez is a capital dancer she will soon dance down
all opposition. With what grace can the public talk about
virtue in a public actress, when they have followed in the
wake of an ELSSLER ? If the private character of a public
actress is to be the criterion by which to judge of her
professional merit, then half the theatres would be compelled to shut their doors.

We are as independently correct as any other paper
that exists. We don't care a straw whether we go on with
or without the other newspapers. We will do justice and
say what is true, regardless of popularity. We detest
hypocrisy ; and we have no disposition to make a mountain out of a molehill, or to see a mote in the eye of Lola
Montez, and not discover a beam in the eye of Fanny
Elssler, or of any of the other great dancers or actresses.

" What is Lola Montez ? " enquire the public. A
good dancer, says the manager of a theatre. She is also
notorious. The public will crowd the theatre to see her
and to judge whether she is not also a good actress ; and
if they get their money's worth, they are satisfied. They
do not pay to judge of the former history of Lola Montez.
. . . A few squeamish people cannot prevent Lola
Montez from creating a sensation here, or from crowding
from pit to dome any house where she may appear ; and,
as they will be the first to endorse her success, they would
be more consistent were they to let her alone until she
secures it.

None the less, there was competition to meet. A great deal
of competition, for counter-attractions were being offered in
all directions. Thus, " Professor " Anderson was conjuring
rabbits out of borrowed top hats ; Thackeray was lecturing
on " The English Humourists " ; Macready was bellowing
and posturing in Shakespeare ; General Tom Thumb was

exhibiting his lack of inches ; and Mrs. Bloomer was advancing the cause of " Trousers for Women ! " Still, Lola more
than held her own as a " draw."

In January the bill was changed to *Diana and the
Nymphs*. The fact that some of the " Nymphs " supporting
the star adopted a costume a little suggestive of modern nudism
appears to have upset a feminine critic.

" When," was her considered opinion, " a certain piece first
presented a partly unclothed woman to the gaze of a crowded
auditory, she was met with a gasp of astonishment at the
effrontery which dared so much. Men actually grew pale at
the boldness of the thing ; young girls hung their heads ;
a death-like silence fell over the house. But it passed ; and,
in view of the fact that these women were French ballet-
dancers, they were tolerated."

To show that she was properly qualified to express her views
on such a delicate matter, this censor added : " Belonging, root
and branch, to a theatrical family, I have not on that account
been deemed unworthy to break bread at an imperial table,
nor to grasp the hand of friendship extended to me by an
English lordly divine."

By the way, on this subject of feminine attire (or the lack of
it) a rigid standard was also applicable to the audience's side
of the curtain, and any departure from it met with reprisals.
This is made clear by a shocked paragraph chronicling one
such happening at another theatre :

" During the evening of our visit there transpired an
occurrence to which we naturally have some delicacy in alluding.
Since, however, it indicates a censorship in a quarter where
refinement is perhaps least to be expected, it should not be
suffered by us to pass unnoticed. In the stalls, which were
occupied by a number of ladies and gentlemen in full evening
costume, and of established social position, there was to be
observed a woman whose remarkable lowness of corsage
attracted much criticism. Indeed, it obviously scandalised
the audience, among the feminine portion of which a painful

sensation was abundantly perceptible. At last, their indignation found tangible expression ; and a voice from the pit was heard to utter in measured accents a stern injunction that could apply to but one individual. Blushing with embarrassment, the offender drew her shawl across her uncovered shoulders. A few minutes later, she rose and left the house, amid well merited hisses from the gallery, and significant silence from the outraged occupants of the stalls and boxes."

Decorum was one thing ; *décolletage* was another. In the considered opinion of 1851 the two did not blend.

A certain Dr. Judd, who, in the intervals of his medical practice, was managing a Christy Minstrels entertainment at this period, has some recollections of Lola Montez. " Many a long chat," he says, " I had with her in our little bandbox of a ticket-office. Thackeray's *Vanity Fair* was being read in America just then, and Lola expressed to me great anger that the novelist should have put her into it as Becky Sharp. ' If he had only told the truth about me,' she said, ' I should not have cared, but he derived his inspiration from my enemies in England.' "

This item appears to have been unaccountably missed by Thackeray's other historians.

IV

Lola's tastes were distinctly " Bohemian," and led her, while in New York, to be a constant visitor at Pfaff's underground *delicatessen* café, then a favourite haunt of the literary and artistic worlds of the metropolis. There she mingled with such accepted celebrities as Walt Whitman, W. Dean Howells, Commodore Vanderbilt, and that other flashing figure, Adah Isaacs Menken. She probably found in Pfaff's a certain resemblance to the Munich beer-halls with which she had been familiar. A bit of the Fatherland, as it were, carried across the broad Atlantic. German solids and German liquids ; talk and laughter and jests among the company of actors and actresses and artists and journalists gathered night

after night at the tables ; everybody in a good temper and
high spirits.

Walt Whitman, inspired, doubtless, by beer, once described
the place in characteristic rugged verse :

> The vaults at Pfaff's, where the drinkers and laughers meet
> to eat and drink and carouse,
> While on the walk immediately overhead pass the myriad feet
> of Broadway.

There was a good deal more of it, for, when he had been
furnished with plenty of liquid refreshment, the Muse of
Walt ran to length.

From New York Lola set out on a tour to Philadelphia,
St. Louis, and Boston. While in this last town, she " paid a
visit of ceremony " to one of the public schools. Although
the children there " expressed surprise and delight at the
honour accorded them," the *Boston Transcript* shook its
editorial head ; and " referred to the visit in a fashion that
aroused the just indignation of the lady and her friends."

The cudgels were promptly taken up on her behalf by a
New York journalist :

" Lola Montez," he declared, " owes less of her strange
fascination and world-wide celebrity to her powers as an
artiste than to the extraordinary mind and brilliancy of
intellect with which Heaven has thought fit to endow her.
At one moment ruling a kingdom, through an imbecile
monarch ; and the next, the wife of a dashing young English
lord. . . . Her person and bearing are unmistakably aristocratic. In her recent visit to one of our public schools she
surprised and delighted the scholars by addressing them in
the Latin language with remarkable facility."

It would be of interest to learn the name of the " dashing
young English lord." This, however, was probably a brevet
rank conferred by the pressman on Cornet Heald.

On April 27, 1852, Lola Montez appeared at the Albany
Museum in selections from her repertoire. On this occasion
she brought with her a " troupe of twelve dancing girls."

As an additional lure, the bills described these damsels as
" all of them unmarried, and most of them under sixteen."

But the attraction which proved the biggest success in her
repertoire was a drama called *Lola in Bavaria*. This was said
to be written by " a young literary gentleman of New England,
the son of a somewhat celebrated poetess." The heroine,
who was never off the stage for more than five minutes, was
depicted in turns as a dancer, a politician, a countess, a
revolutionary, and a fugitive ; and among the other characters
were Ludwig I, Eugéne Sue, Dujarier, and Cornet Heald,
while the setting offered " a correct representation of the Lola
Montez palace at Munich." It seemed good value. At any
rate, the public thought it was, and full houses were secured.
But the critics restrained their raptures. " I sympathise," was
the acid comment of one of them, " with the actresses who were
forced to take part in such stuff "; and Joseph Daly described
the heroine as " deserting a royal admirer to court the
sovereign public." The author of this balderdash was one
C. P. T. Ware, " a poor little hack playwright, who wrote
anything for anybody."

March of 1853 found Lola Montez fulfilling an engagement
at the Variétés Theatre, St. Louis. Kate Field, the daughter
of the proprietor, wrote a letter on the subject to her aunt.

" Well, Lola Montez appeared at father's theatre last night
for the first time. The theatre was crowded from parquet to
doors. She had the most beautiful eyes I ever saw. I liked
her very much ; but she performed a dumb girl, so I cannot
say what she would do in speaking characters."

During this engagement Lola apparently proved a little
difficile, for her critic adds : " She is trying to trouble father
as much as possible."

Lola certainly was apt to " trouble " people with whom she
came into contact. As an accepted " star," she had a high
sense of her own importance and considered herself above
mere rules. Once, when travelling from Niagara to Buffalo
by train, she elected to sit in the baggage car and puff a

cigarette. " While," says a report, " thus cosily ensconced, she was discovered by the conductor and promptly informed by him that such behaviour was not permitted. Thereupon, Madame replied that it was her custom to travel where and how she pleased, and that she had frequently horse-whipped much bigger men than the conductor. This settled the matter, for the company's officer did not care to challenge the tigress."

The visit to Buffalo was crowned with success. " Lola Montez," declared the *Troy Budget*, " has done what Mrs. McMahon failed to accomplish—she positively charmed the Buffaloes. This can perhaps be attributed to her judicious choice of the ex-Reverend Chauncey Burr, by whom she is accompanied on her tour in the capacity of business-manager."

The choice of an " ex-Reverend " to conduct a theatrical tour seems, perhaps, a little odd. Still, as Lola once remarked : " It is a common enough thing in America for a bankrupt tradesman or broken-down jockey to become a lawyer, a doctor, or even a parson." Hence, from the pulpit to the footlights was no great step.

CHAPTER XIV

THE " GOLDEN WEST "

I

AS this was before the days when actresses in search of
publicity announce that they are *not* going to Hollywood, Lola had to hit on a fresh expedient to keep
her name in the news. Ever fertile of resource, the one she
now adopted was to give out that this would be her "positively
last appearance, as she was abandoning the stage and becoming
a nun." The scheme worked, and the box-office coffers were
filled afresh. But Lola did not take the veil. Instead, she
took a trip to California, sailing by the Isthmus route in the
summer of 1853.

A ridiculous book, *The Wonderful Adventures of Mrs.
Seacole*, with an introductory puff by a windbag, W. H. Russell,
has a reference to this project :

> Came one day Lola Montez, in the full zenith of her
> evil fame, bound for California, with a strange suite. A
> good-looking, bold woman, with fine, bad eyes and a
> determined bearing ; dressed ostentatiously in perfect
> male attire, with shirt collar turned down over a lapelled
> coat, richly worked shirt front, black hat, French un-
> mentionables, and natty polished boots with spurs. She
> carried in her hand a riding-whip. . . . An impertinent
> American, presuming—perhaps not unnaturally—upon
> her reputation, laid hold jestingly of the tails of her long
> coat ; and, as a lesson, received a cut across his face that
> must have marked him for some days. I did not wait to
> see the row that followed, and was glad when the wretched
> woman rode off on the following morning.

Russell was not a fellow-passenger in the ship by which Lola travelled. Somebody else, however, who did happen to be one, gives a very different description of her conduct on the journey :

" We had not been at sea one day," says Mrs. Knapp, " before all the saloon occupants were charmed by this lovely young woman. Her vivacity was infectious, and her *abandon* was always of a specially airy refinement."

The arrival of Lola Montez at San Francisco would have eclipsed that of any Hollywood heroine of the present era. A vast crowd, headed by the City Fathers, " in full regalia," gathered at the quay. Flags decked the public buildings ; guns fired a salute ; bands played ; and the schoolchildren were assembled to strew her path with flowers as she stepped down the gangway ; and, " to the accompaniment of ringing cheers," the horses were taken from her carriage, which was dragged by eager hands through the streets to her hotel. "The Countess acknowledged the reception accorded her with a graceful inclination."

" What if Europe has exiled her ? " demanded an editorial. " This is of no consequence. After all, she is Lola Montez, acknowledged Mistress of Kings ! She is beautiful above other women ; she is gorgeous ; she is irresistible ; and we are genuinely proud to welcome her."

Enveloped in legend, the reputation of the newcomer for " eccentricity " had preceded her. She lived up to this reputation, too, for, when the spirit moved her (and it did so quite often), she would dance in the beer gardens " for fun " ; she had her hair cut short, when other women were affecting chignons ; and—wonder of wonders—she would " actually smoke cigarettes in public." Clearly, a trifle ahead of her period.

By the way, while she was in San Francisco, Lola is said to have renewed her acquaintance with the mysterious Jean François Montez, who, during the interval since they last met, had turned over a fresh leaf and was now married. But according to a chronicler : " The family felicity very soon succumbed to the lure of the lovely Lola." Without, too, any support for the assertion, a contributor of theatrical gossip dashed off an imaginative column, in which he declared her, among other things, to have been " the petted companion of Louis Napoleon "; and also " the idolised dancer of the swells and wits of the capitals of the Old World, with the near relatives of royalty and the beaux of Paris for her intimates."

This was going too far. Lola, much incensed, shook her dog-whip and threatened reprisals.

" What's the matter with you ? " demanded the journalist, astonished at the outburst, " it's good publicity, isn't it ? "

" Yes, but not the sort I want," was the response.

Still, whether she wanted it, or not, Lola was soon to have a good deal more " publicity." This was because she suddenly appeared with a husband on her arm.

Although the bridegroom, Patrick Purdy Hull, was a fellow-editor, the *Daily Alta*, of California, considered that the news value of the event was not worth more than a couple of lines :

" On the 2nd inst. Lola Montez and P. P. Hull, Esq., of this city (and late of the *San Francisco Whig*) were married at the Mission Dolores."

Obviously regarding this as a somewhat meagre allowance, a New York journal furnished fuller details :

Among the recent domestic happenings of the times in California, the marriage of the celebrated Lola Montez will attract most attention. This distinguished lady has again united herself in the bonds of wedlock, the happy young man being Patrick Purdy Hull, Esq., formerly of Ohio, and for the past four years employed in the newspaper business in San Francisco.

Mr. Hull was a fellow-passenger with the fascinating Countess on her trip to California ; and the acquaintance then formed fast ripened into an attachment which terminated fatally to his bachelorhood. The nuptials were consummated [*sic*] at the Holy Church of the Mission Dolores in the presence of a highly respectable gathering of prominent citizens.

The " prominent citizens " included " Governor Wainwright, Judge Wills, Captain McMichael, Mr. and Mrs. Clayton, and Beverley Saunders, Esq." An attempt was made to keep the ceremony secret ; and, with this end in view, the invited guests were pledged not to divulge it beforehand. On the previous evening Captain McMichael, being something of a tactician, announced to them : " We do not yet know for certain that the affair will ever come off, and we may all be jolly well sold." When they assembled at the Mission Church, it looked as if this would happen, as neither of the couple appeared. Suddenly, however, they drove up in a carriage and entered the church. The " blushing bride," says a reporter who had hidden behind a pillar, "carried a bouquet of orange blossoms, and the organ played ' The Voice that breathed o'er Eden ' " ; and another chronicler adds : " On the conclusion of the ceremony, all adjourned to partake of a splendid spread, with wine and cigars *ad lib*." But this was not all, for : " Governor Wainwright, giving a significant wink, kissed the new-made bride, Mrs. Hull. His example was promptly followed by Mr. Henry Clayton, ' just to make the occasion memorable,' he said. ' Such is the custom of my country,' remarked Madame Lola. She was not kissed by anybody else, but she none the less had a pleasant word for all."

II

It was at Sacramento that Lola and her new husband began their married life. The conditions of the town were a little primitive just then ; and even in the principal hotel the single guests were expected to sleep in dormitories. The cost of board and lodging (with bed in a bunk) was 150 dollars a week. As for the " board," standing items on the daily menu would be boiled leg of grizzly bear, donkey steak, and jack-rabbit. " No kickshaws " was the proud boast of every chef.

In addition to his editorial labours (which were not unduly exacting), Hull was employed by the Government on census work, preparing statistics of the rapidly increasing population. But Lola, much to his annoyance, did not add to his figures for the Registrar-General's return. The footlights proved a stronger lure than maternity ; and, almost immediately after her marriage, she accepted an engagement at one of the theatres, where she appeared as Lady Teazle. A countess in that part of the world being a novelty, the public rallied to the box-office in full force and " business " was phenomenal. Still, competition there, as elsewhere. Some of it, too, of a description that could not be ignored. Thus, Ole Bull was giving concerts at the Opera House, and causing hardened diggers to shed tears when he played " Home Sweet Home " to them on his violin ; Edwin Booth, " supported by a power-ful company," was mouthing Shakespeare, and tearing passion to tatters in the process ; and a curious freak, billed as " Zoyara, the Hermaphrodite " (with a " certificate of genuine-ness, as to her equestrian skill and her virtues as a lady, from H.M. the King of Sardinia ") was cramming the circus to capacity every afternoon and evening. Yet, notwithstanding His Majesty's " certificate," it is a fact that its recipient " married " a woman member of the troupe. " The long sustained deception has been dropped," says a paragraphist, " and the young man who assumed the name of ' Madame Zoyara ' is now to be seen in correct masculine attire."

Still, despite all this, Lola kept her public. After all, a countess was a countess. But, before long, there was a differ-ence of opinion with the manager of the theatre in which she was appearing. Lola, who never brooked criticism, had " words " with him. High words, as it happened ; and, flourishing her whip in his face, she tore up her contract and walked out of the building.

" Get somebody else," she said. " I'm through."

The difference of opinion appears to have arisen because
Lola elected to consider herself " insulted " by a member of
the audience while she was dancing, and the manager had not
taken her part. The next evening, accordingly, she made a
speech in public, giving him a " bit of her mind." The result
was, declared the *San Francisco Alta*, " the Countess came off
the victor, bearing away the *bravas* and bouquets. At the
conclusion of her address she was hailed by thunderous cheers,
amid which she smiled sweetly, dropped a curtsey, and retired
gracefully."

Much to their surprise, those who imagined that the
honours of the evening went to Lola read in the next issue of
the *Californian* that " the applause was all sham, the paid
enthusiasm of a hired house." This was more than flesh and
blood could stand. At any rate, it was more than Lola could
stand ; and she sent the editor a fierce letter, challenging him
to a duel. " I must request," was its last passage, " that this
affair of honour be arranged by your seconds as soon as
possible, as my time is quite as valuable as your own : MARIE
DE LANDSFELD-HULL (LOLA MONTEZ)."

The editor of the *Californian* did not accept the suggestion.
Instead, he applied the necessary balm, and the pistols-for-
two-and-coffee-for-one order was countermanded.

III

A woman of moods, when Lola made a change, it was a
complete one. She made one now. The artificiality of the
towns, with their false standards and atmosphere of pretence,
had begun to pall. She wanted to try a fresh *milieu*. Everybody was talking just then of Grass Valley, a newly opened-up
district, set amid a background of the rugged Sierras, where
gangs of miners were delving for gold in the bowels of Mother
Earth, and, if half the accounts were true, amassing fortunes.
Why not go there and see for herself ? It would at least be a
novel experience.

No sooner said than done. Hiring a mule team and wagon,

and accompanied by Patrick Hull, she started off on a preliminary tour of inspection of the district.

Travelling was unhurried in those leisurely days. There
were several stoppages ; and the roads were rough, and long
detours had to be made to avoid yawning canyons. " At the
end of two weeks from the time they left Sacramento behind
them, Pat Hull and his charming bride wheeled across the
mountains into Grass Valley."

" There were about 1600 people in the township of Marysville at this period," says a chronicler, " and 1400 of them were
of the masculine sex. The prospect of sudden riches was the
attraction that drew them. England and the Continent were
represented by some of the first families. A dozen were
graduates of Oxford and Cambridge ; there were two young
relatives of Victor Hugo ; there were a number of scions of
the impoverished nobility of Bohemia ; and several hundred
Americans. Among the latter was William Morris Stewart,
a Marysville lawyer, who was afterwards to become a
senator and attorney-general."

Grass Valley at this period (the autumn of 1853) was little
more than a wilderness. The nearest town of any size was
Nevada City, fringed by the shadows of the lofty Sierras.
Between the gulches had sprung up as if by magic a forest of
tented camps and tin-roofed shanties, with gambling-booths
and liquor saloons by the hundred, in which bearded men
dug hard by day, and played faro and monte and drank deep
by night. Fortunes were made—and spent—and nuggets
were common currency. The cost of living was very high.
But it cost still more to be ill, since a grain of gold was the
accepted tariff for a grain of quinine.

The whole district was a melting-pot. Attracted by the prospect of the precious metal that was to be wrung from it, there
had drifted into the Valley a flotsam and jetsam, representatives
of all nations and of all callings. As was natural, Americans in
the majority ; but, with them, Englishmen and Frenchmen
and Germans and Italians, plus an admixture of Chinamen

and Kanakas ; also an undesirable element of deserters from ships and convicts escaped from Australia. To keep them in some sort of order, rough justice was the rule. Mayors and sheriffs had arbitrary powers, and did not hesitate to employ them. Judge Lynch was supreme; and a length of hemp dangling from a branch was part of the equipment of every camp.

With a full knowledge of all these possible drawbacks, Lola Montez looked upon Grass Valley and saw that it was good. Perhaps the Bret Harte atmosphere appealed to her. At any rate, she decided to settle down there temporarily ; and, with this end in view, she persuaded Hull to buy a six-roomed cottage just above Marysville.

When Lola Montez—for all that she had a wedding-ring on her finger, she still stuck to the name—arrived there with her new husband, the conditions of life in Grass Valley were a little primitive. A telegraph service did not exist ; and letters were collected and delivered irregularly. Transport with the outer world was by stage coach and mule and pony express. Whisky had to come round by Cape Horn ; sugar from China ; and meat and vegetables from Australia. The fact was, the early settlers were much too busily employed extracting nuggets and gold dust to concern themselves with the production of any other commodity.

Mrs. Dora Knapp, a neighbour of Lola Montez in Grass Valley at this period, has contributed some reminiscences of her life there :

" We, who knew of her gay career among the royalty and nabobs, were astonished that she should have gone to the camp. She frequently had letters from titled gentlemen in Europe, begging her to come back and live on their rich bounty. It was simply because she was weary of splendour and fast living that the Countess turned with such fondness to life in a mining camp."

To Patrick Hull, however, the attractions of the district were not so obvious. Ink was in his blood. He wanted to get back to his editorial desk, preferring the throbbing of printing presses to the rattle of spades and picks and the clanking of drills. Nor did " love in a cottage " appeal to him. When Lola refused to give up Grass Valley, he developed a fit of sulks and turned to the whisky bottle for consolation.

Under the circumstances, matrimonial bliss was impossible. Such a life was a cat and dog one. Its end arrived very soon.

" Lola Montez and her new husband," says the knowledgeable Mrs. Knapp, " had not lived together more than a few months before trouble began. When two such spirits came together, there was bound to be a clash. The upshot was that one day Lola pushed Patrick down the stairs, heaved his grip out of the window and ordered him to quit."

Mr. Hull, who could take a hint as well as any man, did " quit." He did more. He took to his bed and expired. " In his native state," says a tearful obituary, " he was respected and loved by a large circle. The family of Manuel Guillen (in whose house he lay), inspired by a sentiment of genuine benevolence, bestowed upon him all the tender watchfulness due to a beloved son and brother ; and nothing was omitted that promised cure or promoted comfort."

But this was not until some time after he had received his abrupt *congé* from Lola Montez.

Once more, Lola had drawn a blank in the matrimonial market.

IV

With Adrienne Lecouvreur, Lola Montez must often have asked herself, *Que faire au monde sans aimer?* " Living without loving " had no appeal for her. Hence, she was soon credited (or discredited) with a fresh *liaison*. This time her choice fell on a German baron, named Kirke, who also happened to be a doctor. There was a special bond between them, for he had come from Munich, and could thus awaken memories and tell her of Ludwig, of Fritz Peissner and the other good comrades of the *Alemannia*, and of the house in the Barerstrasse where she had once queened it.

" This fourth adventure in matrimony was," says a

chronicler, " copiously consummated." An odd choice of
words. But, successful or not, it was short-lived. One fine
day the baron took his gun with him into the forest. He did
not return. " Killed in a shooting accident " (a fairly common occurrence in the Wild West at that period) was the
coroner's verdict. As a result, Lola was once more without a
masculine protector.

The position was not devoid of an element of danger, for
the district swarmed with lawless gangs, to whom a woman
living by herself was looked upon as fair prey. But Lola was
not disturbed. She had plenty of courage. She knew, too,
that the miners had formed themselves into a " guard of
honour," and that it would have gone ill with anybody
attempting to molest her. If the diggers were rough, they
were chivalrous.

In response to a general invitation from the camp, Lola
more than once gave an exhibition of her quality as a
danseuse. Although the charge for admission was a hundred
dollars, the hall where she appeared was always crammed
to the doors. She expanded out, too, in other directions ;
and a picturesque account of her life at this period says
that she slept under the stars ("canopy of heaven"
was the writer's more poetical way of putting it) and wore
woollen underclothing knitted by herself. Another detail
declares that she held a " weekly soirée in her cottage, attended
by the upper circles of the camp, a court of littérateurs and
actors and wanderers " ; and that among the regular guests
were " two nephews of Victor Hugo, a quartet of cashiered
German barons, and a couple of shady French counts."
Obviously, a somewhat mixed gathering. For all this, however, the receptions were " merely convivial assemblies,
with champagne and other wine, served with cake and fruit
ad lib, and everyone smoked. The two Hugo neighbours were
always there, as well as a son of Preston Brooks, the South
Carolina congressman. A dozen of us looked forward to
attending these *salons*, which we called ' experience-meetings.'

Senator William M. Stewart, then a young lawyer in Nevada, said he used to count the days between each. Every song, every story, every scrap of humour or pathos that any of the young men came across would be preserved for the next gathering. Occasionally, our charming hostess would have a little fancy-dress affair at the cottage, and, clad in the fluffy and abbreviated garments she had once worn on the stage, show us that she still remembered her dancing-steps."

When not engaged in these innocent relaxations, Lola would give herself up to other pursuits. Thus, she hunted and fished and shot, and often made long trips on horseback through the forests and sage bush. Having a fondness for all sorts of animals, on one such expedition she captured a bear cub, with which she returned to her cabin and set herself to tame. While thus employed, she was visited by a wandering violinist, who, falling a victim to her charms, begged a lock of her hair as a souvenir of the occasion. Thereupon, Lola, always anxious to oblige, struck a bargain with him. " I have," she said, " a pet grizzly in my orchard. If you will wrestle with him for three minutes, you shall have enough of my hair to make a bow for your fiddle. Let me see what you can do." The challenge was accepted ; and the amorous violinist, merely stipulating that the animal should be muzzled, set to work and secured the coveted guerdon.

Something of a risk, perhaps. Still, it would have been a more serious one if Lola had kept a rattlesnake.

Appearances are deceptive, and Bruin was less domesticated than Lola imagined. One day, pining perhaps for fresh diet, he grappled with his mistress and bit her hand. The incident attracted a laureate on the staff of the *California Chronicle*, who, in Silas Wegg fashion, " dropped into verse : "

LOLA AND HER PET

One day when the season was drizzly,
And outside amusements were wet,
Fair Lola paid court to her Grizzly
And undertook petting her pet.

But, ah, it was not the Bavarian
  Who softened so under her hand,
No ermined King octogenarian,
  But Bruin, coarse cub of the land.

So, all her caresses combatting
  He crushed her white slender hand first,
Refusing his love to her patting,
  As she had refused hers to *Pat* !

Oh, had her pet been him whose glory
  And title were won on the field,
Less bloodless had ended this story,
  More easy her hand had been *Heald* !

This doggerel was signed " F.S.", initials which masked the identity of Frank Soule, the editor of the *Chronicle*.

V

Never without her dog-whip, Lola took it with her to her cottage in Grass Valley. There she soon found a use for it. A journalist, in a column account of her career, was ungallant enough to finish by enquiring " if she were the devil incarnate ? " As the simplest method of settling the problem, " Lola summoned the impertinent scribbler and gave him such a hiding that he had no doubts left at all."

Shortly afterwards, there was trouble with another representative of the press. This was with one Henley Shipley, the editor of the *Marysville Herald*, who, notwithstanding that they were " regularly attended by the *élite* of the camp," had described her " Wednesday soirées " as " disgraceful orgies, inimical to our fair repute." Thereupon, says a sympathiser, the aspersed hostess " took her whip to him, and handed out a number of stinging and well merited cuts."

The opportunity being too good to miss, the editor of the *Sacramento Union* set to work and rushed out a special edition, with a long description of the incident :

This forenoon our town was plunged into a state of ludicrous excitement by the spectacle of Madame Lola

Montez rushing through Mill Street, with a lady's delicate riding whip in one hand and a copy of the *Marysville Herald* in the other, vowing vengeance on "that scoundrel of an editor," etc. She met him at the Golden Gate Saloon, a crowd, on the *qui vive*, following in her footsteps. Having struck at him with her whip, she then applied woman's best weapon—her tongue. Meanwhile, her antagonist kept most insultingly cool. All her endeavours being powerless, the "Divine Lola" appealed to the miners, but the only response was a burst of laughter. Mr. Shipley, the editor, then retired in triumph, having, by his calmness, completely worn down his fair enemy.

The immediate cause of the fracas was the appearance of sundry articles, copied from the *New York Times*, referring to the "Lola Montez-like insolence, barefaced hypocrisy, and effrontery of Queen Christina of Spain." The entire scene was decidedly rich.

One can well imagine it.

Never prepared to accept hostile criticism without a protest, Lola sent her own version of the occurrence to a rival organ :

" This morning, November 21," she wrote, " the newspaper was handed me as usual. I scanned it over with little interest, saw a couple of abusive articles, not mentioning me by name, but, as I was afterwards told, had been prepared by the clever pen of this great statesman of the future, and present able writer, as a climax and extinguisher to all the past and future glories of Lola Montez. I wonder if he thought I should come down with a cool thousand or two, to stock up his fortune and cry ' Grace, Grace ! '

" This is the only attempt at blackmail I have been subjected to in California, and I hope it will be the last. On I read the paper till I saw my name in good round English, and the allusions to my ' bare-faced hypocrisy and insolence.' Europe, hear this ! Has not the ' hypocrisy ' been on the

Lola Montez in " Lola in Bavaria."   A " Play with a Purpose "

AUTOBIOGRAPHY

AND

LECTURES

OF

LOLA MONTEZ

COUNTESS OF LANDSFELD

Lola as a Lecturer. From stage to platform

other side ? What were you thinking of, Alexandre Dumas, Beringer, Méry, and all my friends when you told me my fault lay in my too great kindness ? Shipley has judged me at last to be a hypocrite. To avenge you, I, bonnet on head and whip in hand—that whip which was never used but on a horse— this time to be disgraced by falling on the back of an ASS . . . The spirit of my Irish ancestors (I being three-quarter Irish and Spanish and Scotch) took possession of my hand ; and, on the most approved Tom Sayers principles, I took his, on which—thanks to some rings I had—I made a cutting impression. This would-be great smiter ended the combat with a certain amount of abuse, of which—to do him justice—he is a perfect master. *Sic transit gloria* SHIPLEY ! Alas, poor Yorick ! "

The atmosphere of Grass Valley could scarcely be described as tranquil. Its surface was always being ruffled ; and it was not long before Lola was again embroiled in a collision with one of her neighbours. This time she had a passage at arms with a Methodist minister in the camp, the Rev. Mr. Wilson, who, with a sad lack of Christian charity, informed his flock that this new member among them was " a feminine devil devoid of shame, and that the ' Spider Dance ' in her repertoire was an outrage." There were limits to clerical criticism. This was clearly one of them. As she could not take her whip to a clergyman, she took herself. " Resolved to teach the Rev. Wilson a lesson, she called on him in her dancing dress, while he was conducting a confirmation class."

" Without," says a member of the gathering, " any preliminaries beyond saying ' Good afternoon,' she proceeded to execute the dance before the astonished gaze of the company. Then turning to the minister, she said, ' The next time you think fit to make me and this dance a subject for a pulpit discourse, perhaps you will know better what you are talking about.' She then took her departure, before the reverend gentleman could sufficiently collect his senses to say or do anything."

But, notwithstanding these breaks in its monotony, Lola felt that she was not really adapted to the routine of Grass Valley. Once more, the theatre called her. Answering the call, she went back to it. But on the return journey she did not take Patrick Hull. She also shed the name he had given her, and resumed that of Countess of Landsfeld.

" It looks better on the bills," she said, when she discussed plans for a prospective tour.

The *Grass Valley Telegraph* gave her a good " send off " in a fulsome column ; and the miners presented her with a " farewell gift " in the form of a nugget. " Rough, like ourselves," said their spokesman, " but the genuine article."

CHAPTER XV

"DOWN UNDER"

I

THIS time Lola was going further afield. A long way further. Two continents had already been exploited. Now she would discover what a fresh one held.

Her plan was to leave the Stars and Stripes for the Southern Cross. As an initial step, " she sold her jewels for 20,000 dollars to the madam of a fashionable brothel." Having thus secured adequate funds, she assembled a number of out-of-work actors and actresses and engaged them to accompany her on a twelve months' tour in Australia. Except for Josephine Fiddes (who was afterwards to understudy Adah Isaacs Menken, of *Mazeppa* renown) and, perhaps, her leading man, Charles Follard, they were of a distinctly inferior calibre.

The departure from California was duly notified in a paragraph sent round the press :

" We beg to inform our readers and the public generally that on June 6 the celebrated Lola Montez left San Francisco, at the head of a theatrical troupe of exceptional talent, bound for distant Australia. The public in the Antipodes may confidently look forward to a rare treat."

The voyage across the Pacific being in a sailing vessel, was a longish one and occupied nearly ten weeks from start to finish. However, anchor was dropped at last ; and on August 23, 1855, a " colossal attraction " was announced in " Lola Montez in Bavaria " at the Victoria Theatre, Sydney. There, thanks to the interest aroused by her exploits in other parts of the world, the newcomer was assured of a good reception.

But theatrical stars were always accorded a special measure of deference by the colonists. Thus, Miss Catherine Hayes, who was playing at an opposition house, was invited to luncheon by the Bishop of Sydney and to dinner by the Attorney-General; and a Scottish conjurer, " Professor " Anderson, was given an " address of welcome " by the Town Council.

While these particular honours were not enjoyed by Lola (who, for some reason best known to herself, had elected to be entered in the passenger-list as " Madam Landsfeld Heald "), she was none the less accorded considerable publicity. " The eccentric and much advertised Lola Montez," said the *Herald* on the morning after her New South Wales début, pounces upon us direct from California, and the excitement of her visit is emptying the opposition theatre. Last night the Countess looked positively charming and acted very archly. ... On the fall of the curtain, she presented Mr. Lambert (who played the King of Bavaria) with an elegant box of cigarettes."

Naturally enough, the star was interviewed by the journalists. " At the Victoria Theatre," says one of them, " I was privileged to have a talk with Madame Lola after the performance had concluded. I found her—much to my surprise —to be a very simple-mannered, well-behaved, cigar-loving young lady."

An odd picture of Sydney audiences is given by the author of *Southern Lights and Shadows*. " The young ladies of Australia," he says, " are in many respects remarkable. At thirteen they have more ribbons, jewels, and lovers than any other young ladies of the same age. They prattle insipidly from morning to night. The first time I visited a theatre I sat next one of them who had at least half a dozen rings worn over her gloves. . . . The affectation of *ton* among them is astonishing. They are special patrons of the drama, and, on the appearance of a star, they flock to the dress circle in hundreds. The pit is generally well filled with a display of shirt-sleeves, pewter pots, and babies. The upper boxes are usually given up to that division of the community partial to pink bonnets and cheeks to match ; and flirtations are carried on in the most flagrant and unblushing manner."

The author of this sketch also has something to say about Sydney as a town :

" One part of George Street is as much like Bond Street in London as it is possible for one place to resemble another. Like Bond Street, too, it is hourly paraded by the Bucks and Brummels of the Colony. The Café François is much frequented by the young swells and sprigs of the city. Files of *Punch, The Times*, sherry coblers, an entertaining hostess, and a big-bloused lubberly host are the special points left in my recollection. They serve 800 meals a day at this establishment, the rent of which is £2,400 a year."

II

During this Sydney engagement, Lola, ever interested in the cause of charity, organised a " Grand Sebastopol Matinée Performance," the proceeds being " for the benefit of our wounded heroes in the Crimea." As the cause had a popular appeal, the house was a bumper one. Possibly, it was the success of this *matinée* that led to an imaginative chronicler adding : " Our distinguished visitor, Madame Lola Montez, Countess of Landsfeld, is, with her full company of Thespians, on the point of leaving us for Balaclava. There, at the special request of Lord Raglan and Miss Florence Nightingale, she will inaugurate a theatre for the enjoyment of our gallant warriors and their Allies."

Another odd tit-bit was sent to England by the theatrical correspondent of a London paper. This declared that a masculine member of her company " jumped into the harbour, mortified at discovering that Madame Lola had turned a more friendly face on a younger brother of the Duke of Wellington who had followed her to Sydney from Calcutta." The artistic temperament.

At intervals, however, other and better established items of news were received from Australia and, as opportunity offered, found a niche in the London papers. From these it would appear that all was not going smoothly with Lola's plans, and that the start of the Antipodean venture was somewhat tempestuous.

" In Sydney," says a letter on the subject, " a regrettable fracas recently occurred at the theatre where Madame Montez has been playing. Stepping in front she endeavoured to quell the uproar by announcing that, while she herself ' rather liked a good row,' she would appeal to the gallantry of the *gentlemen* in the pit and gallery to respect the wishes of a lady and not interfere with the enjoyment of others by interrupting the performance. The request, however, fell on deaf ears. The uproar continued for some time, and was much increased by the actors and actresses squabbling among themselves on the stage."

There was a good deal of " squabbling " among the company. Its members were not a happy family. They had been engaged by their principal to support her. Instead, however, of rendering such support, a number of them did all they could to wreck the tour. Thereupon, Lola, adopting strong measures, discharged the malcontents and left for Melbourne by the next steamer. That she was justified in her action is clear from a letter which her solicitors sent to the Press :

" Our client, Madam Lola Montez, was unwise enough to engage, at enormous cost to herself, a very inferior company in California. Before starting, she made large advances to every one of them ; paid their passages from America (where they were nearly all heavily in debt) to Australia ; and trusted that, in return for her immense outlay, she would at least receive efficient assistance from them. But this band of obscure performers not only loaded her with insults while they continued to live on her, but on their arrival in Sydney they one and all refused to discharge their allotted tasks.

" When Madam Montez (not unnaturally irritated by such conduct) proposed, through us, to cancel their agreements on reasonable terms, they insisted on the fulfilment of the contract which they themselves had been the first to break, and made claims upon her amounting to about £12,000. This *moderate* demand being very properly refused by our client, they secured an order for her arrest in respect of a number of separate actions. Only one of these (a claim for £100) was lodged in time for a warrant to be issued. When, furnished with this, Mr. Brown, the sheriff's officer, appeared on board the steamer, Madam tendered him £500, which, however, he refused to accept, insisting that she should also settle the various other claims for which he did not have warrants. Our client refused to leave the vessel, for which refusal, we, as her solicitors, are quite willing to accept responsibility."

The fact that there was talk of instituting proceedings against the captain of the steamer and his subordinates led the solicitors to add a postscript :

" Those who governed the movements of the *Watarah* are ready to answer for their conduct. They saw a lady threatened with arrest at the last moment for a most unjust claim, tendering five times the amount demanded, and having that offer refused. Hence, they did not feel called upon to interfere."

Another account of the episode is a little different. This declares that, just before starting from Sydney, she "dismissed with a blessing " two members of the company. As they wanted something more easily negotiable, they issued a writ of attachment. When the sheriff's officer attempted to serve it : " Madame Lola, ever ready for the fray, retired to her cabin and sent word that she was quite naked, but that the sheriff could come and take her if he wanted to." An embarrassing predicament ; and, unprepared to grapple with it, " Poor Mr. Brown blushed and retired amid roars of laughter."

Having thus got the better of the Sydney lawyers, and filled up the vacancies in her company with fresh and more amenable recruits, Lola reached the Victorian capital without further adventure. A picture of the city, as it was when she landed there, is given by a contemporary author :

" Melbourne is splendid. Fine wide streets, finer and wider than almost any in London, stretch away for miles in every direction. At any hour of the day thousands of persons may be observed scurrying along them with true Cheapside bustle." The Melbourne youth, however, appears to have been precocious. " I was delighted," remarks this authority, " with the Colonial young stock. The average Australian boy is a slim, olive-complexioned young rascal, fond of Cavendish, cricket, and chuck-penny, and systematically insolent to girls, policemen, and new chums. . . . At twelve years of age, having passed through every phase of probationary shrewdness, he is qualified to act as a full-blown bus conductor. In the purlieus of the theatres are supper-rooms (lavish of gas and free-mannered waitresses), and bum-boat shops where they sell play-bills, whelks, oranges, cheroots, and fried fish."

But, notwithstanding the existence of these amenities, all was not well where Lola was concerned. The Sydney correspondent of the *Argus* had injured her chances of making a favourable impression by writing a somewhat imaginative account of her troubles there :

" I need not tell you that the Montez has gone to Melbourne, as she will have arrived before this letter, and is not the sort of woman to keep her arrival secret. It may not, however, be so generally known that she has made what is colonially termed a ' bolt ' from here. . . . Thinking, perhaps, that Australia was not yet a part of the civilised world, and that a company of players could not be secured here, Madame brought a set of comedians from San Franscisco. They were quite useless. More competent help could have been had on the spot."

Lola said nothing. Her leading man however, Mr. Follard, had something to say, and wrote a strong letter to the editor :

" Permit me to state, with all due deference to your correspondent's term ' bolt,' that Madame Lola Montez left quietly and unostentatiously. . . . The attempt to stop her leaving Sydney and prevent her engagement in Melbourne was an exhibition of meanness at which every honest heart must feel disgusted. Alone, in a strange land, without friends or protector, her position as a woman should in itself have saved her from the unmanly abuse heaped upon her and the contemptible attitude manifested by some of her company."

A second adverse factor against which Lola had to contend in Melbourne was that prices had been doubled for her engagement there. This was considered a grievance by the public. The difficulty, however, adjusted itself, for the programme she offered was one that proved specially attractive.

" The highest degree of excitement was," ran the *Herald* criticism, " produced upon visitors to the Theatre Royal by the actual presence of this extraordinary and gifted being, with the praises of whose beauty and *esprit* the whole civilised world has resounded. . . . After curtseying with inimitable grace to the audience, the fair *artiste* withdrew amidst a fresh volley of cheers."

But Lola, who never missed an opportunity of airing her opinions, aired them now :

" At the end of the performance," says a report, " Madame Lola Montez was vociferously called and addressed the audience in an animated speech, commenting upon some remarks that had been published in a certain journal. When a gentleman ventured to laugh while she was enumerating the political benefits she had conferred on Bavaria, the fair orator promptly informed him that such conduct was not usually considered to be courteous."

The Melbourne engagement finished up with a triple bill.

The principal item was a novelty she had, the " Spider Dance," which Lola had brought from America. In this she appeared with hundreds of wire spiders sewn on her attenuated ballet skirts ; and, when any of them fell off, she had to indulge in pronounced wriggles and contortions to put them back in position. The accompanying movements of her body were held to be by some standards " daring and suggestive." In fact, so much so that the representative of the *Argus* dubbed the number " the most libertinish and indelicate performance that could possibly be given on the public stage. We feel compelled," he continued solemnly, " to denounce in terms of unmeasured reprobation the performance in which Madame Montez here figures." Yet, Sir Charles Hotham, the Governor, together with Lady Hotham and their guests, had witnessed it without sustaining any serious damage. But perhaps they were made of tougher material.

The critic of the *Morning Herald* at this period (understood to be R. H. Horne, " the Jules Janin of Melbourne ") was either less thin-skinned or else more broad-minded than his *Argus* comrade. At any rate, he saw nothing much to call for these strictures. Thinking that the newcomer had not been given fair play, he endeavoured to counteract the adverse opinion that had been expressed by publishing a laudatory one of a column length, in which he declared : " Madame Montez went through the entire measure with marked elegance and precision, and the curtain fell amid salvoes of well merited applause."

Convinced that here was a critic who really knew his business, and a friend on whom she could rely to do her justice, Lola wrote to the editor :

GRAND IMPERIAL HOTEL,
September, 1855.

SIR,

A criticism of my performance of the "Spider Dance" at the Theatre Royal was published in this morning's *Argus*, couched in such language that I must positively answer it.

The piety and ultra-puritanism of the *Argus* might prevent the insertion of a letter bearing my signature. Therefore, I address myself to you.

The " Spider Dance " is a national one, and is witnessed with delight by all classes in Spain, and by both sexes from Queen to peasant.

I have always looked upon this dance as a work of high art ; and I reject with positive scorn the insinuation of your contemporary that I wish to pander to a morbid taste for what is improper or indelicate.

I shall be at my post to-morrow evening ; and will then adopt a course that will test the value of the opinion advanced by the *Argus*.

The promised " course " was merely to deliver a long speech from the stage, and ask the audience to decide whether she should give the vexed item, or not. The audience were emphatic that she should ; and, when she had finished, " expressed their views on the subject by uttering loud groans for the *Argus* and lusty cheers for the *Herald*."

Honours to Lola !

But the " Spider Dance " was still to prove a source of trouble. The next morning a certain Dr. Milton, who had constituted himself a champion of morals, appeared at the police-court and applied for a warrant for the arrest of Lola Montez, on the grounds that she had " outraged decency."

" I am in a position," he declared, " to produce unquestionable evidence of the indelicacy of her performance."

" You must take out a summons in the proper fashion," said the magistrate, who clearly had no sympathy with busybodies.

But, before he could do so, Dr. Milton found himself served with a writ for libel. As a result, nothing more was heard of the matter.

In addition to its Mawworms, of which it was afflicted with an appreciable number of specimens, the city of Melbourne would appear to have had other drawbacks at this period. According to R. H. Horne, local society was somewhat curiously constituted. " There is an attempt," he says, " at the nucleus of a ' court circle ' ; and if the Home Government think fit to make a few more Australian knights and baronets there may be good hopes for the enlargement of the enchanted hoop. The Melbourne ' Almack's ' is to be complimented on the moral courage with which its directors have resisted the claims for admission of some of the wealthy unwashed and other unsuitables. Money is not quite everything, even in Melbourne."

There were further strictures on the morals of Victoria, as compared with those of New South Wales :

" The haunts of villainy in Sydney are not surpassed by those in Melbourne ; but, with regard to drunkenness and prostitution, the latter place is far worse than Sydney. The Theatre Royal contains within itself four separate drinking-bars. The Café de Paris, in the same building, has two bars. In the theatre itself there is a drinking public every night, especially when the house is crowded. Between every act it is the custom of the audience to rush out for a nobbler of brandy. The only exceptions are the occupants of the dress-circle, more especially when the Governor is present."

By the way, the " List of Beverages " shows that, in proof of her popularity, a " Lola Montez Appetiser," consisting of " Old Tom, ginger, lemon and hot water," was offered to patrons.

Alcohol was not alone among the objects at which " Orion " Horne tilted. He also disapproved of cricket. " The mania," he says, " for bats and balls in the boiling sun during last summer exceeded all rational excitement. The newspapers caught the epidemic, and, while scarcely noticing other far more useful games, they devoted columns upon columns to minute accounts of the matches of a hundred different clubs. The very walls of Melbourne became infected. On the return of the Victorians from Sydney, a reporter for the *Herald*

designated them 'the laurelled warriors.' If there is no
great harm in this, the thing has been carried too far."

It is just as well, perhaps, for Horne's peace of mind that
the present day value attached to " Ashes " had not arisen,
and that an Australian XI did not visit England until
another twenty years had passed.

III

After Melbourne, the next step in Lola's itinerary was
Geelong. The programme she offered there was a generous
one, for it included a " Stirring drama, entitled, *Maidens,
Beware !* and the elegant and successful comedy, *The Eton
Boy*," to which were added a " sparkling comedietta " and a
" laughable farce." This was good value. The Geelong
critic, however, did not think very much of the principal item
in this bill. " It has," he observed solemnly, " an impossible
plot, with situations and sentiments quite beyond the understanding of us barbarians."

This supercilious attitude was not shared by the simple-
minded diggers, who found *Maidens, Beware !* very much to
their taste. But nothing else could have been expected, for it
offered good measure of all the elements that ensure success
every time they are employed. Thus, the hero is wrongfully
charged with a series of offences committed by the villain ;
a comic servant unravels the plot when it becomes intricate ;
and the heroine only avoids " something worse than death "
by proving that a baronet, " paying unwelcome addresses,"
(but nothing else) has forged a will.

Having a partiality for the society of diggers, with whom she
had always got on well, Lola next betook herself to Ballarat.
It was an unpropitious moment for a theatrical venture
in that part of the world. The atmosphere was somewhat
unsettled. The broad arrows and ticket-of-leave contingent
who made up a large section of the community were clamouring for a republic ; and there was a considerable amount of
rioting. A rebel flag had been run up by the mob ; and the

military had to be called out to suppress the activities of the
" Ballarat Reform League." Still, Lola was not the woman
to run away from danger. As she had told a Sydney audience,
she " rather liked a good row."

The coming of Lola Montez to Ballarat was heralded by a
preliminary paragraph :

" Our readers will be pleased to learn that the world-
renowned Lola, a lady who has had Kings at her beck, and
who has caused nearly as much upheaval in the world as Helen
of Troy, is about to appear among us. On leaving Melbourne
by coach, she presented the booking clerk with an autographed
copy of a work by the famous Mrs. Harriet Beecher Stowe.
Young gentlemen of Ballarat, look out for your hearts !
Havoc will assuredly be played among them."

Her colourful career attracted the laureates. One of them
found in it inspiration for a ballad, " Lola, of the rolling
black eye ! " which was sung at every music-hall in the
Colony. A second effort regarded the matter in its graver
aspects. The first verse ran as follows :

> She is more to be pitied than censured,
> She is more to be helped than despised.
> She is only a lassie who ventured
> On life's stormy path ill-advised.
> Do not scorn her with words fierce and bitter,
> Do not laugh at her shame and downfall,
> For a moment just stop to consider
> *That a man was the cause of it all!*

Ludwig of Bavaria had done better than this. A lot better.
Annoyed at the innuendo it contained, Lola flourished her
whip afresh and threatened the bard with an action for
damages.

The Victoria Theatre, Ballarat (where Lola Montez was to
give the diggers a sample of her quality), was a newly built
house, " reflecting," declared an impressed reporter, " every
modern elegance. In front of the boxes," he continued,
" are panels, chastely adorned with Corinthian festoons,

encircling a gilded eagle emblematic of liberty. Above the proscenium is an ellipse, exhibiting the Australian coat of arms. The ceiling is ornamented by a dome, round which are grouped the nine Muses, and the chandelier is the biggest in the Colony. From the dress-circle there is direct communication with the adjoining United States Hotel, so that first-class refreshments can be procured without the slightest inconvenience. There are six dressing-rooms ; and Madame Lola Montez has a private and sumptuously furnished apartment."

As the repertoire she offered was to include ("by special request") the "Spider Dance," she took the precaution of sending a description of it to the *Ballarat Star* :

> The characteristic and fascinating SPIDER DANCE has been performed by MADAME LOLA MONTEZ with the utmost success throughout the United States of America and before all the Crowned Heads of Europe.
>
> This dance, on which malice and envy have endeavoured to fix the stain of immorality, has been given in the other Colonies to houses crammed from floor to ceiling with rank and fashion and beauty. In Adelaide His Excellency the Governor-General, accompanied by Lady McDonnell and quite the most select ladies of the city, accorded it their patronage, while the Free and Accepted Masons did Madame Lola Montez the distinguished honour of attending in full regalia.

It was on February 16, 1856, that Lola Montez opened at Ballarat. A generous programme was offered, for it consisted of "the elegant and sparkling comedy, *A Morning Call*; the laughable farce, *The Spittalsfields Weaver*; the domestic drama, *Raffaelo, the Reprobate*; and the Shakespearean tragedy, *Antony and Cleopatra*; all with new and sumptuous scenery, dresses, and appointments."

In accordance with the fashion of the period, the star had to recite a prologue. An extract from it was as follows :

'Tis only right some hurried words to say
As to the name this theatre bears to-day,
For I would have you fully understand
I seek for patrons men of every land.
'Tis not alone through prejudice has been
Attached the name of Britain's virtuous Queen.
And may your gen'rous presence and applause
Mutual content and happy evenings cause !

But this was merely an introduction. There was more to
follow, for the " personal " touch had yet to be delivered.

As for *myself*, you'll find in Lola Montez
The study how to please my constant wont is !
Yet I am vain that I'm the first star here
To shine upon this Thespian hemisphere.
And only hope that when I say " Adieu ! "
You'll grant the same I wish to you—
May rich success reward your daily toil,
Nor men nor measures present peace despoil,
And may I nightly see your pleasant faces
With these fair ladies, your attendant Graces !

IV

But, despite this auspicious start, all was not set fair at
Ballarat. As had happened in other places, Lola was to fall
foul of a critic who had disparaged her. Furiously indignant,
and horsewhip in hand, she rushed into the editor's office and
executed summary vengeance upon him.

" A full account of this remarkable business," announced
the opposition journal, " will be given by us to-morrow. Our
readers may anticipate a perfect treat." They got it, too, if one
can trust the report of a "few choice observations" delivered by
Lola to her audience on the second night of her engagement:

" Ladies and Gentlemen : I am very sure that all of you in
this house are my very good friends ; and I much regret that
I now have a most unpleasant duty to perform. I had
imagined that, after all the kindness I have experienced from
the miners in California, I should never have had anything painful to say to you. Now, however, I am compelled to do so.

" I speak to the ladies, as members of my own sex, and to the gentlemen, as my natural protectors. Well, what I have to tell you is that there is a certain gentleman in this town called Seekamp. Just take out the E's, and what is left of his name becomes *Skamp*. Listen to my story, and then judge between us. This Mr. Seekamp, who is the editor of the *Ballarat Times*, actually told me, in the hearing of another lady and two quite respectable gentlemen, that the miners here were a set of——. No, I really cannot sully my lips with the shocking word he used—and that I was not to believe them.

" Mr. Seekamp called on me, with a certain proposition, and accepted my hospitality. You all know he is just a little fond of drinking. Well, while he was at my house the sherry, the port, the champagne, and the brandy were never off the table. He ate with me, and he drank with me. In fact, he drank so freely that it was only my self-respect that prevented me having him removed. But I said to myself, ' After all, he is an editor ; perhaps this is his little way.'

" Well, I did as Mr. Seekamp wanted, and as a result, I was a ten pound note out of pocket by it. I was green, but I was anxious to avoid making enemies among editors. Yet, when his paper next appears, I am referred to in it as being notorious for my immorality. Notorious, indeed ! Why, I defy everybody here, or anywhere else, to say that I am, or ever was, immoral. It's not likely that, if I wanted to be immoral, I should be slaving away and earning my bread by hard work. What do you think ?

" Ladies and Gentlemen, I appeal to you. Is it fair or generous of this Seekamp person to behave to me like this ? The truth is, my manager, knowing that he was a good-for-nothing fellow, gave my printing orders to another editor. In revenge, the angry Seekamp says he will hound me from this town. Ladies and Gentlemen, I appeal to you for protection."

" And here," adds the report, " the intrepid Lola retired amid deafening applause. Three hearty cheers were given for Madame and three lusty groans for her cowardly traducer."

On the following night there was more speech-making.
This time, Lola complained to the audience that she had been
freshly aspersed by the objectionable Seekamp. " I offered,"
she said, " though merely a woman, to meet him with pistols,
but the cur who attacks a lady's character runs away from
my challenge. He says he will drive me from the Diggings.
Well, I intend to turn the tables, and to make Seekamp
de-camp. I very much regret," she added, " having been
compelled to assert myself at the expense of Mr. Seekamp,
but, really it was not my fault. His attacks on my art were
most ungentlemanly. I challenged him to fight a duel, but
the poltroon would not accept."

In the best tradition of the *Eatanswill Gazette*, the *Ballarat
Star* referred to the *Ballarat Times* as " our veracious contemporary and doughty opponent," and alluded to the
" unblushing profligacy of its editorial columns." The
proprietor of the United States Hotel and the solicitor for
Lola Montez also sailed into the controversy and challenged
Mr. Seekamp to " eat his words." That individual, however,
not caring about such a diet, refused to do anything of the
sort.

The matter did not end there, and a number of correspondents took up the cudgels on behalf of Lola Montez.

" Is it possible," wrote one of them to the editor of the
Star, " that Mr. Seekamp can, in his endeavour to blacken
the fair fame of a woman, insinuate that he is also guilty of
the most shocking immorality ? I blush to think it." There
was also a letter in a similar strain from " John Bull," and
another from " An Eton Boy," animadverting upon Mr.
Seekamp's grammar.

Feeling herself damaged in reputation, Lola's next step was
to instruct her solicitor to bring an action for libel against
Seekamp. The magistrate remitted the case to the superior
court at Geelong. But, as an apology was offered and
accepted, nothing more was heard of it.

This, however, was not the end of her troubles at Ballarat,

for horse-whips were again to whistle in the air. But, this time Lola got more than she bargained for. She was using her whip on one Mr. Crosby, the manager of the theatre there, when that individual's spouse—a strong-minded and muscular woman—wrested the weapon from her and laid it across her own back.

The account given by an eye-witness is a little different. " At Ballarat," he says, " Lola pitched into and cross-buttocked a stalwart Amazon who had omitted to show her proper respect."

" Cross-buttocked " would appear to be an expression which, so far, has eluded the dictionary-makers.

In other parts of the Colony, however, Lola's reception more than made up for any little unpleasantnesses at Ballarat. " Her popularity," says William Kelly, an Australian squatter, " was not limited to the stage. She was welcomed with rapture on the gold fields, and all the more for the liberal fashion in which she ' shouted ' when returning the hospitality of the diggers. Her pluck, too, delighted them, for she would descend the deepest shafts with as much nonchalance as if she were entering a boudoir."

From Sandhurst Lola Montez travelled to Bendigo, where the tour finished. There, says a pressman, " she lived on terms of the most cordial amity with the entire populace, and without a single disturbing incident to ruffle the serenity of the intercourse."

V

Having completed her tour in Australia, with considerable profit to herself, Lola Montez disbanded her company, and, in the autumn of 1856, returned to Europe. She had several offers from London ; but, feeling that a rest was well earned, she left the ship at Marseilles and took a villa at St. Jean de Luz. While there, she appears to have occupied a certain amount of public attention. At any rate, Émile de Girardin, thinking it good " copy," reprinted in *La Presse* a letter she had written to the *Estafette* :

St. Jean de Luz,
September 3, 1856.

Sir : The French and Belgian papers are announcing as a positive fact that the suicide of Monsieur Mauclerc (who deliberately precipitated himself from the top of the Pic du Midi cliff) was caused by various troubles I had occasioned him. If he were still living, Monsieur Mauclerc would himself, I feel certain, contradict this calumny.

It is true that we were married ; but, finding, after eight days, that our union was not likely to turn out a happy one, we parted by mutual consent. The story of my responsibility for the Pic du Midi business only exists in the imaginative brain of some journalist who revels in supplying tragic details. Anyhow, Mr. Editor, I count upon your sympathy to exculpate me from any share in the melancholy event.—Yours, LOLA MONTEZ.

Mauclerc, however, so far from being dead, was still very much alive, and was sunning himself just then at Bayonne. Having read this letter, he answered it in the next issue :

I have just seen in the columns of *La Presse* a letter from Lola Montez. This gives an account of a deliberate jump from the top of a cliff and of a marriage with myself as the chief actor in each catastrophe. All I have to say about them is that I know nothing of these important occurrences. I assure you, sir, I have never felt any desire to " precipitate " myself, either from the Pic du Midi or from anywhere else ; nor have I ever had the distinction of being the husband of the famous Countess of Landsfeld for a matter of even eight days.—MAUCLERC. Artist dramatique.

September 9, 1856.

Lola ignored this *démenti*. Possibly, however, she did not read it, for she was just then arranging another trip to America.

CHAPTER XVI

FAREWELL TO THE FOOTLIGHTS

I

HAVING booked a number of engagements there, in December, 1857, Lola landed in New York for the second time. Directly she stepped off the ship, she was surrounded by a throng of reporters. Never losing the chance of making a speech, she gave them just what they wanted.

" America," she said, as they pulled out their note-books, " is the last refuge left the victims of tyranny and oppression in the old world. It is the finest monument to liberty ever erected beneath the canopy of heaven."

For her reappearance she offered the public *Lola Montez in Bavaria*, which had already done good service. By this time, however, it was a little frayed.

" The drama represents her as a coquettish and reckless woman," was the considered opinion of one critic. " We assure our readers she is nothing of the sort."

This testimonial was a help. Still, it could not infuse fresh life into a piece that had obviously outlived its popularity. Hence, she soon changed the bill for a double one, *The Eton Boy* and *Follies of a Night*. But the cash results were not much better ; and when she left New York and tried her luck in Boston the week's receipts were scarcely two hundred dollars. This, in theatrical parlance, was " not playing to the gas."

Realising that she was losing her grip, she cast about for some fresh method of attracting the public. It was not long before she hit on one. As she was in a democratic country, she would make capital out of her " title." A plan was soon matured. This was to hold " receptions," where anybody would be welcome who was prepared to pay a dollar.

A dollar for ten minutes' chat with a genuine countess, and, for another 50 cents, the privilege of shaking her hand. A bargain. The tariff appealed to thousands. Among them Charles Sumner, the distinguished jurist, who declared of Lola Montez that, " She was by far the most graceful and delightful woman I ever met."

Her next scheme for raising the financial wind was to employ her pen. It was true that her " memoirs," strung together in Paris, had fallen flat—owing to the pusillanimity of the editor of *Le Pays*—but a full length " autobiography " would, she thought, stand a better prospect. Apart, too, from other considerations, there was now more material on which to draw. An embarrassing amount of it. She could say some-thing—a lot—about the happenings in Bavaria, in France, in California, and in Australia. All good stuff, and a field hitherto untouched.

The pen, however, being still an unaccustomed weapon, she availed herself of outside help ; and practically the whole of the *Autobiography of Lola Montez* was written for her (on a profit-sharing agreement) by a clerical collaborator, the Rev. Chauncey Burr.

The tale of the Odyssey—as set forth in this joint pro-duction—established contact with glittering circles and the breathing of perfumed air. Within its chapters emperors and kings and princes jostle one another ; scenes shift continually from capital to capital ; and plots follow counter-plots in breathless fashion. Yet those who purchased the volume in the fond belief that it would turn out to be the analysis of a modern Aspasia were disappointed. As a matter of fact, there was next to nothing in it that would have upset a Band of Hope committee-meeting. This, however, was largely because, an adept at skating over thin ice, the Rev. Mr. Burr ignored, or

Lola Montez in Middle Life. A characteristic pose

" Lectures and Life."   From stage to platform

coloured, such happenings as did not redound to the credit
of his subject.

The " Autobiography " (alleged) finishes on a high note :

" Ten years have elapsed since the events with which Lola
Montez was connected in Bavaria ; and yet the malice of the
diffusive and ever vigilant Jesuits is as fresh and as active as it
was at the first hour it assailed her. It is not too much to say
that few artists of her profession ever escaped with so little
censure ; and certainly none ever had the doors of the highest
social respectability so universally open to them as she had,
up to the time she went to Bavaria. And she denies that
there was anything in her conduct there which ought to have
compromised her before the world. Her enemies assailed her,
not because her deeds were bad, but because they knew of no
other means to destroy her influence."

Although too modest to acknowledge it, this passage is
obviously the Rev. Chauncey Burr verbatim.

An offer to serialise part of the " autobiography " in the
columns of Le Figaro was accepted. In correcting the proofs,
Lola still clung to the earlier account that had already done
service in the " memoirs " contributed to Le Pays. But she
embellished it with fresh embroideries. Thus, to keep up the
Spanish connection, she now claimed as her aunts the Marquise
de Pavestra and the Marquise de Villa-Palana, together
with an equally imaginary Uncle Juan ; and she also, for the
first time, gave her schoolgirl friend, Fanny Nicholls, a sister
Valerie.

The " autobiography " had originally been accepted for
Le Pays by Anténon Joly. When, however, shortly afterwards, MM. de la Guéronnière and de Lamartine acquired the
journal, they repudiated the contract. Hence, its transfer to
Le Figaro. But this organ also developed a sudden queasiness,
and, after the first few instalments had appeared, declined to
print the remainder, on the grounds that they were " too
scandalous." Some time afterwards, Eugéne de Mirecourt,
thinking he had a bargain, secured the interrupted portions

and made them the basis of a chapter on Lola Montez in his *Les Contemporains*. This chapter is marked throughout by severe disapproval. Thus, it begins :

" The woman who revives in the nineteenth century the scandals of Jeanne Vaubernier belongs to our gallery, and the abject materialism accompanying her misconduct will be revealed in the pages that follow."

De Mirecourt was not too happy in his self-appointed task. Like everything else from his pen, the entire section is distinctly imaginative. Thus, he declares that Lola, while living in Madrid, was " supported by five or six great English lords " ; and, among other amorous incidents, says that a Brahmin priest fell in love with her ; that she conducted a "scandalous intrigue" with a young French diplomat who was carrying despatches to the Emperor of China ; and that her husband, Lieutenant James, once intercepted a tender passage between herself and a rajah. Further embroideries assert that Lola's father was the son of a Lady Gilbert, and that her mother was the daughter of a " Moorish warrior who abjured paganism." To this rigmarole he adds that she was sent to a boarding-school at Bath, kept by a Mrs. Olridge, where she had an early *liaison* with the drawing-master.

It was perhaps as well for de Mirecourt, and others of his kidney, that libel actions had not then been added to the perils of authorship. Still, if they had, Lola would not have troubled to bring one. To take proceedings in America against a man living in France was difficult. Also, by this time she was so accustomed to studied misrepresentation and deliberate falsehoods that she refused to interfere.

" It doesn't matter what people choose to say about me," she remarked contemptuously, when she was informed by a friend in Paris of the liberties being taken with her name.

Although (except when she took it into her own hands) she liked to keep clear of the law, this was not always possible. Such an instance occurred in March, 1858, when a Mr. Jobson of New York brought an action against her in respect of an alleged debt. The proceedings would appear to have been conducted in a fashion that must have been peculiar to the time and place ; and, in an effort to discredit her, she was subjected to a cross-examination that would now be described as " third degree."

" Were you not," began the plaintiff's counsel, " born in Montrose, the daughter of one Molly Watson ? "

When this was denied, he put his next question.

" How many intrigues have you had during your career ? "

" None," was the answer.

" We'll see about that, Madam," returned the other, consulting his brief. " To begin with, were you not the mistress of King Ludwig ? "

" You are a vulgar villain," exclaimed Lola indignantly. " I can swear on the Bible, which I read every night, but you don't, that I never had what you call an ' intrigue ' with him. As a matter of fact, I did him a lot of good."

" In what way ? " enquired the judge, looking interested.

" Well, I moulded his mind to the love of freedom."

" Before you ran off with your first husband," continued counsel, " were you not employed as a chambermaid ? "

" Never," was the emphatic response. " And, let me tell you, Mr. Attorney, it is not at all a shameful thing to be a chambermaid. If I had been born one, I should consider myself a much more distinguished woman than I am."

When her own counsel, coming to the rescue, dubbed Mr. Jobson a " fellow," there followed, in the words of a reporter, " an unseemly fracas." From abuse of one another, the rival attorneys took to fisticuffs ; the spectators and officials joined in the struggle ; and an ink pot was hurled by the furious Jobson at the occupants of the jury-box. This being considered contempt of court, he was arrested, and the judge, gathering up his papers, left the Bench, announcing that the further hearing would be adjourned.

II

After this experience, Lola developed a fresh activity. Like a modern Joan of Arc, she suddenly announced that she heard " Voices," and that, on their instructions, she was giving up the stage for the platform. Her plans were soon completed ; and, on February 3, 1858, she mounted the rostrum and made her début as a lecturer, at the Hope Chapel, New York.

There were beery chuckles from the reporters who were " covering " this effort. " Lola Montez in the chapel pulpit is good fun," was the conclusion at which one of them arrived ; and another headed his column, " A Desperado in Dimity."

Judging from his account of this initial sample (a lecture on " Beautiful Women "), the *Tribune* representative did not regard it very seriously :

" Temperance, exercise, and cleanliness, preached Lola the plucky ; light suppers and reasonable hours ; jolly long walks in thick boots and snug wrappers for the benefit of the complexion. From these, said Lola, come good digestion, good humour, and good sense. And that's the way, my dear Flora, to be healthy and wealthy—speaking crinolinely and red-petticoatedly—and wise."

Lola was before her time. Nowadays she would have set up as a " beauty specialist." Had she done so, she would have secured a big income from the sale of creams and perfumes, powders and paints, and dyes and unguents, and all the other nostrums with which women endeavour to recover their vanished charms. But, instead of becoming a practitioner, she became an author and compiled a handbook, *The Arts of Beauty, or Secrets of a Lady's Toilet*. This went very fully into the subject, and had helpful hints on " Complexion Treatment," " Hair Culture," " Removal of Wrinkles," and what was then coyly termed " Bust Development." Importance was also attached to " Intellect," as a sovereign specific for repairing the ravages of advancing years. "A beautiful mind," announced the author, "is the first thing required for a beautiful face."

Lola's light was not hidden under any bushel. An American firm of publishers, convinced that there was money in this sort of thing, made an acceptable offer and issued the work with a prefatory inscription :

> TO
>
> ALL MEN AND WOMEN
>
> OF EVERY LAND
>
> WHO ARE NOT AFRAID OF THEMSELVES
>
> WHO TRUST SO MUCH TO THEIR OWN SOULS THAT THEY DARE TO
>
> STAND UP
>
> IN THE MIGHT OF THEIR
>
> OWN INDIVIDUALITY
>
> TO MEET THE TIDAL CURRENTS OF THE WORLD, THIS BOOK IS
>
> RESPECTFULLY DEDICATED BY
>
> THE AUTHOR

The title-page of this effort ran as follows :

> THE
> ## ARTS OF BEAUTY
> OR
> ## SECRETS OF A LADY'S TOILET
> WITH HINTS TO GENTLEMEN
> ON THE
> ART OF FASCINATION
> BY MADAME LOLA MONTEZ
> COUNTESS OF LANDSFELD
> NEW YORK
> DICK AND FITZGERALD, PUBLISHERS
> 18 ANN STREET

A Canadian publisher, John Lovell, on the look-out for a novelty, read this effort and suggested that a friend of his, Émile Chevalier, of Paris, should sponsor an edition of Lola's *Arts of Beauty* for consumption on the boulevards. " I am too much an admirer of the gifted author," was M. Chevalier's response, " to undertake the work without consulting her." Accordingly, he got into touch with Lola, offering to have a translation made. " Thank you," she replied, " but I wish to do it myself. You, however, can put in any corrections you think necessary. I have not written anything in French since the death of poor Bon-Bon [Dujarier], and I want to see if I still remember the language." Apparently she did so, for, shortly afterwards, the manuscript was sent across the Atlantic and delivered to M. Chevalier. Within another month it was on the bookstalls. " I have retouched it very little," says the editor in his preface, " as I was anxious to preserve Madame Lola's distinctly original style. Her pen is as mordant as her dog-whip."

M. Chevalier was charmed with the fashion in which Lola had acquitted herself, and wrote florid letters of thanks to her in New York. With a supplementary lecture on " Instructions for Gentlemen in the Art of Fascination," which was added to fill up the book, he declared himself much impressed. " This," he says, " exhibits a profound knowledge of the human heart, and is altogether one of the finest and most piquant criticisms on American manners with which I am familiar." " Who," he continues, warming to his work, " is more thoroughly qualified to discuss the development and preservation of natural beauty than the Countess of Landsfeld ? ; and in an introductory puff he adds : " These observations are very judicious, and as applicable in Europe as in America. They should, I feel, be indelibly engraved on the minds of all sensible women."

Perhaps they were. At any rate, the result of M. Chevalier's enterprise was a distinct success, and the Paris bookshops soon got rid of 50,000 copies. In fact, Lola was very nearly a best-seller.

In addition to her expert views on " Beautiful Women,"
Lola had plenty of other subjects up her sleeve, to be incor-
porated in a series of lectures. The list covered a wide range,
for it included such diverse headings as " Ladies with Pasts,"
" Heroines of History," " Romanism," " Wits and Women
of Paris," " Comic Aspects of Love," and " Gallantry." On
all of these matters she had plenty to say. On some of them
quite a lot, for they ran to an average of a dozen closely
printed pages, and, when delivered in public, took up three
hours. In the one on " Beautiful Women " precise details
were given as to the adventitious causes contributing to her
own sylph-like figure, glossy hair and pearly teeth, etc., and a
number of prescriptions were also offered. These, she
recommended, should be manufactured at home. " For a
few shillings and a little trouble," she pointed out, " any lady
can secure an adequate supply of all such things, composed of
materials far superior to the expensive compounds bought
from druggists ; " and the recipes, she insisted, " had been
translated by herself from the original French, Spanish,
German, and Italian." Among these were *Beaume à
l'Antique*, *Unction de Maintenon*, and *Pommade de Seville* ;
and " a retired actress at Gibraltar " was responsible for a
specific for " warding off baldness." Lola put it in two
words—" avoid nightcaps." But she was sympathetic about
scalp troubles. " Without a fine head of hair, no woman can
be really beautiful. . . . The dogs would bark at and run away
from her in the street." To be well covered on top was, she
held, " quite as important for the opposite sex." " How like a
fool or a ruffian," she remarked, " do the noblest masculine
features appear if the hair of the head is bad. Many a dandy
who has scarcely brains or courage enough to catch a sheep
has enslaved the hearts of a hundred girls with his Hyperion
locks ! "

Although nominally the author of them, these lectures were,
like her previous flight, really strung together by that clerical
" ghost," the Rev. Chauncey Burr, with whom she had

collaborated in her " memoirs." Wielding a ready pen, he gave good value, for the chapters were well sprinkled with choice classical quotations and elegant extracts from the poets, together with allusions to Aristotle and Theophrastus, to Madame de Staël and Washington Irving.

In the lecture on " Gallantry," Lola had a warm encomium for King Ludwig.

" His Majesty," she informed her audience, " is one of the most refined and high-toned gentlemen of the old school of manners. Hs is also one of the most learned men of genius in all Europe. To him art is more indebted than to any other monarch who has ever lived. King Ludwig is the author of several volumes of poems, which are evidence of his natural genius and elaborately cultivated taste. . . . He worships beauty like one of the old troubadours ; and his gallantry is caused by his love of art. He was the greatest and best King Bavaria ever had."

In another passage she had a smack at the Catholic Church :

" An evil hour brought into Ludwig's counsels the most despotic and illiberal of the Jesuits. Through the influence of his ministers the natural liberality of the King was perpetually thwarted ; and the Government degenerated into a petty tyranny, where priestly influence was sucking out the very lifeblood of the people."

More than something of a doctrinaire, her observations on " Romanism " (which she dubbed " an abyss of superstition and moral pollution ") might have fallen from the lips of a hot-gospeller of to-day. " Who," she asked her hearers, " shall compute the stupefying and brutalizing effects of such religion ? Who will dare tell me that this terrible Church does not lie upon the bosom of the present time like a vast, unwieldy, and offensive corpse ? America does not yet recognise how much she owes to the Protestant principle. It is that principle which has given the world the four greatest facts of modern times—steamboats, railroads, telegraphs, and the American Republic."

This somewhat novel definition of " the four greatest facts of modern times " was received with rapture by its hearers.

Despite certain jeers from some of the reviewers, the lectures continued to attract the public. The novelty of Lola Montez at the rostrum drew large audiences everywhere ; and she had no difficulty in arranging a long tour. Feeling, when it came to an end, that a similar measure of success might be secured on the other side of the Atlantic, she resolved to visit England.

Just before leaving America for this purpose, she wrote to a one-time Munich acquaintance, who was then editing a New York magazine :

YORKVILLE,
August 20, 1858.

MY DEAR MR. LELAND,

I wish to thank you for the very kind notice you gave in your interesting magazine of my first book, and I have requested Messrs. Dick and Fitzgerald, my publishers, to send to your private address a copy of my *Arts of Beauty*. I hope, as a *critique*, it will be found " not wanting " (I do not mean not wanted).

Will you give my best and kindest regards to our friend Caxton ; and, with the hope of hearing from you before I leave for Europe, which will be in a couple of months, I remain, far or near, your friend,

LOLA MONTEZ.

Of course, there was a postscript :

" The subject of my lectures in Europe will be on America. This should prove attractive."

Another letter suggests that an appointment with Leland had not been kept :

I should have much liked to have seen you before my departure for Ireland on Tuesday by Pacific, but I cannot control circumstances, you know ; and therefore all I ask you until my return next July is a " place in your memory." Maybe, I shall write to you, or, maybe, not. But, whatever is, be sure that *You* will not be forgotten by Yrs.

LOLA MONTEZ.

Again the inevitable postscript :

" Give my best and kindest regards to *our friend*. Tell him I shall certainly manage to fill his columns with plenty more newspaper lectures."

According to himself, Lola looked upon the young American with something more than mere friendship. " Once," he says, in his reminiscences, " she proposed to make a bolt with me to Europe, which I declined. The secret of my influence," he adds smugly, " was that I always treated her with respect, and never made love."

III

It was at the end of November, 1858, that Lola landed once more in the United Kingdom. She began her campaign there in Dublin, where, twenty-four years earlier, she had lived as a young bride, danced at the Castle, and flirted with the Viceroy's aides-de-camp. During the interval a crowded chapter, and one full of colour and life and movement, had been written.

All being in readiness, the public were duly informed of her plans by an advertisement :

> MADAME LOLA MONTEZ, COUNTESS OF LANDSFELD, will give a Lecture on " America and its People," at the Round Room, Rotundo, on Wednesday evening, December 8. Reserved seats, 3s. ; unreserved, 2s. 6d.

The début would appear to have been highly successful. " The announcement of the lecture," said a report the next morning, " created a degree of interest almost unparalleled among the Dublin public. The platform was regularly carried by a throng of admirers, giving Madame Lola Montez barely space to reach her desk. She was listened to with enraptured attention and warm manifestations of approval "; and "very properly, an ill-bred fellow, who exclaimed, ' hee-haw ' at regular intervals, was loudly hissed."

For some reason or other, Lola was constantly embroiled with journalists. Thus, during this Dublin visit she had a passage at arms with one of them, who had published some damaging criticisms about her life in Paris. Thereupon, she wrote an angry letter to the editor of the *Daily Express*. As, however, she was alluding to events that had taken place nearly fifteen years earlier, her memory was somewhat at fault. Thus, she insisted that, when Dujarier met his death, she was living in the house of a Dr. and Mrs. Azan ; and also that " the good Queen of Bavaria wept bitterly when she left Munich."

But, if Lola Montez was not very reliable, the editor of the *Dublin Daily Express* was similarly slipshod in his comments. " It is now," he declared, " well established that Lola Montez was born in 1824, her father being the son of a baronet."

Crossing from Ireland to England, Lola, prior to appearing in London, undertook a tour in the provinces. On January 8, 1859, she appeared at the Free Trade Hall, Manchester, where her subject was "Portraits of English and American Character." This went down very well, although, to her disappointment, John Bright declined to take the chair. At Liverpool, however, "the public went almost wild with excitement"; and, as a result, her share of the box-office receipts was £250. But, although she attracted the mob, she managed to upset the suscepti- bilities of the critics. " Some of Madam's allusions," declared a shocked hearer, " were in questionable taste, and, as she delivered her address, the epithet ' coarse ' fell from several members of the audience."

A visit to Chester, which followed the Liverpool one, was marked by an unfortunate incident :

" We learn with sorrow," said an eye-witness, " that on Thursday last the lady introduced, if not American, certainly not English, manners into one of our most venerable cathedrals. When, accompanied by a masculine escort, she entered the sacred edifice, the gentleman (?) demurred to removing his hat. While in dispute on this point of etiquette, Madam's pet dog attempted to join her. On being informed by the sexton that such canine companionship was inadmissible, her anger was aroused and she withdrew in considerable dudgeon."

The provincial tour was an extensive one ; and, during it, she encountered a certain amount of competition. Thus, at Bristol she was sandwiched in between Barnum and a quarterly meeting of the Bible Society. None the less, " the fair Lola had a very cordial reception from a number of respectable citizens." But she was to have a set-back in one town that must have held many memories of her girlhood. This was Bath, where she appeared in the Assembly Rooms. The attitude of the press was distinctly inimical. " We must say," was one acid comment, " that a greater *sell* we have not met with for a very long time. All the audience got for their money were some remarks of the most commonplace and twaddling description. They lasted about an hour, and even this was an hour too much." Still, Brighton, where the tour finished, more than made up for Bath ; and she was so successful there that " the Pavilion was crammed to the doors, and additional lectures had to be given." Thus, all was well that ended well.

A provincial triumph was worth having. Lola, however, had set her heart on conquering London. With this end in view, accordingly, she despatched an emissary ahead to make the preliminary arrangements. Offers of theatres were showered upon her. One was from that remarkable figure, Edward Tyrell Smith. She would probably have done well under his management, for nobody understood showmanship better than this British Barnum. In this direction he had nothing to learn from anybody. Beginning his career as a sailor, he had soon tired of a life on the ocean wave, and, abandoning the prospect of becoming another Nelson, had joined the police force as a humble constable. But he did not remain one long ; and became in turn a Fleet Street publican, the proprietor of a Haymarket night-house, an auctioneer, a picture dealer, a bill discounter (with a side line in usury), and the editor of a Sunday organ. Next, the theatre attracted his energies ; and in 1852 he secured a lease of Drury Lane at the moderate rental of £70 a week. On Boxing-night he offered his first programme there. This consisted of *Uncle Tom's Cabin* (with " fierce bloodhounds complete "), followed by a full length pantomime and a " roaring farce." Value for money in those palmy days. But, as an entrepreneur, Mr. Smith was always ahead of his period. Thus, he abolished the customary charge for booking ; and, instead of increasing them, he lowered his prices when he had a success ; and it is also to his credit that he introduced matinées.

Such a manager deserved to go far. This one did go far. Having discovered his niche, the pushful Smith soon had his fingers in several other pies. Thus, from Drury Lane he went to the Alhambra, and from the Alhambra to Astley's, with intervening spells at the Lyceum and the Elephant and Castle. He also took in his stride Her Majesty's and Cremorne. All was fish that he swept into his net. Some, of course, were minnows, but others were Tritons. Charles Mathews and the two Keans, together with Giuglini and Titiens, served under his banner, as did also acrobats, conjurers, and pugilists. He " ran " opera, circuses, gambling hells, and " moral waxworks " simultaneously ; and, these fields of endeavour not being enough for him, he added to them by standing for Parliament (opposing Samuel Whitbread) and editing the *Sunday Times*. Always a man of resource, when he was conducting a tavern he put his barmaids into " bloomers." This daring stroke had its reward ; and, by swelling the consumption of beer, perceptibly increased his bank balance. Hence, it is not perhaps unnatural that such widely spread activities should have inspired a lyrical apostrophe :

Awake, my Muse, with fervour and with pith,
To sing the praise of Lessee Edward Smith !

Yet, shrewd as he was, Mr. Smith was himself once bitten. During his money-lending interval, he happened to discount (at what he considered a " business " rate) some bills for £600 out of which Prince Louis Napoleon, then sheltering in London, had been swindled by some card-sharpers at the notorious Judge and Jury Club. The next morning, the victim, coming to his senses, went to the police, and the police went to the sharpers. As a result, the members of the gang were arrested and the bills were cancelled. Feeling that he had a genuine grievance, since he was out of pocket by the transaction, the acceptor waited until a turn of Fortune's wheel had established Louis Napoleon at the Tuileries. He then wrote to him for permission to open some pleasure gardens in Paris on the lines of those he had conducted at Cremorne. The desired permission, however, was withheld.

" No gratitude," said the disappointed applicant.

IV

Tempting as were the prospects he offered, Lola, after some discussion, felt that she could do better, from a financial point of view, without the help of Mr. E. T. Smith. Accordingly, making her own arrangements, she hired the St. James's Hall, where, on April 7, 1859, she delivered the first of a series of four lectures.

Although a considerable interval had elapsed since she was last in London, the public had not forgotten the dramatic circumstances under which she had then appeared at Marlborough Street police court. This fact, combined with the lure of her subject, " Beautiful Women," was sufficient to cram every portion of the building with an interested and expectant audience. They came from all parts. Clapham and Highgate were no less anxious for guidance than Kensington and Belgravia. If an entertainment-tax had been levied at that period the revenue would have benefited substantially. " The appearance on the platform of the fair lecturer," said one account, " was responsible for the most extensive display of opera glasses that has been seen in London since the Empress Eugénie visited the Opera."

By an unfortunate coincidence, the St. James's Hall *première* clashed with another attraction elsewhere. This was the confirmation that evening of the dusky King of Bonny by the Bishop of London. Still, a considerable number managed to attend both items ; and, of the two, the lecture proved the greater draw.

Striking a note of warning at the outset, Lola began by telling her hearers that, " It is the penalty of Nature that young girls must fade and become as wizened as their grand-mothers." But she had a message of hope to offer, for, she said, " wrinkles can be warded off and autumn tresses made to preserve their pristine freshness." The cure was merely careful dieting and the " abolition of injurious cosmetics and the health-destroying bodice." Taking the measure of her audience, she laid on flattery with a trowel. " You have," she assured them, " only to look into the ranks of the upper classes to see around you the most beautiful women in Europe ; and where this is concerned, I must give the preference to the nobility of England." Among the examples held up for admiration by her were the Duchess of Sutherland—" the paragon and type of Britain's aristocracy "—and " the very voluptuous Lady Blessington." Approval for the Duchess of Wellington, however, was less pronounced, since, while admitting her physical charms, Lola declared her to be " of little intellect, and as cold as a piece of sculpture."

Claiming to have visited Turkey (but omitting to say when), Lola offered an item unrecorded in the archives of the British Embassy there :

" In Turkey I saw very few beautiful women. The lords

of creation in that part of the world treat the opposite sex as you would geese—stuff them to make them fat. Through the politeness of Sir Stratford Canning, English Ambassador at Constantinople, I was kindly permitted to visit the Sultan's harem as often as I pleased and there look upon the ' lights of the world.' These ' lights of the world ' consisted of five hundred bodies of unwieldy avoirdupois. The ladies of the harem gazed upon my leanness with commiserating wonder."

The lecture finished up on a high note :

" It has been my privilege to see some of the most celebrated beauties that shine in the gilded courts of fashion throughout the world—from St. James's to St. Petersburg, from Paris to India—and yet I am unaware of any quality that can atone for the absence of an unpolished mind and an unlovely heart. A charming activity of soul is the real source of woman's beauty. It is that which gives the sweetest expression to her face and lights up her *personnel.*"

In the matter of publicity Lola had nothing of which to complain ; and the next morning descriptive columns were published by the dozen.

The début of Madame Lola Montez (announced the *Star*), in the presence of a large and fashionable gathering, was a decided success. Every portion of the spacious and elegant building was completely filled. Madame presented herself in that black velvet costume which seems to be the only alternative to white muslin for ladies who aspire to be considered historic. Not Marie Stuart herself could have become it better than Lola Montez. Her face, air, attitude, and elocution are thoroughly and bewilderingly feminine. Perhaps her smartest and happiest remark was the one in which, with a pretty affectation, she says, " If I were a gentleman, I should like an American young lady to flirt with, but a typical English girl for a wife." This dictum was received with much applause.

One can well believe it.

An anonymous leader, but which, from its florid touches, was evidently penned by George Augustus Sala, dwelt on Lola's personality :

> Some disappointment may have been caused by the appearance of the fair lecturer. A Semiramis, a Zenobia, a Cleopatra, in marvellous robes of gold and silver tissue, might have been looked for ; but, in reality, the rostrum was occupied by a very handsome lady, with a very charming voice and a very winning smile. . . . Madame Lola Montez lectures very well and very naturally. Some will go to hear the accomplished elocutionist ; others will be envious to see the wife of Captain James and silly Mr. Heald ; the friend of Dujarier and Beauvalon ; the *cara sposa* of King Ludwig. Phryne went to the bath as Venus—and Madame Lola Montez lectures at St. James's Hall.

Taking a professional interest in everything connected, however remotely, with the drama (and having more time in which to do it) the *Era* offered its readers a considered opinion at greater length :

> If any amongst the full and fashionable auditory that attended her first appearance fancied (with a lively recollection of certain scandalous chronicles in the newspapers touching upon her antecedents) that they were about to behold a formidable-looking woman, of Amazonian audacity and palpably strong-wristed as well as strong-minded, their disappointment must have been grievous ; greater if they anticipated the legendary bulldog at her side, and the traditionary pistols in her girdle, and the horse-whip in her hand. The Lola Montez who made a graceful and impressive obeisance to those who gave her on Thursday night so cordial and encouraging a reception appeared simply as a good-looking lady in

the bloom of womanhood, attired in a plain black dress, with easy unrestrained manners. . . . The lecture might have been a newspaper article, the first chapter of a book of travels, or the speech of a long-winded American Ambassador at a Mansion House dinner. All was exceedingly decorous and diplomatic, slightly gilded here and there with those commonplace laudations that stir a British public into the utterance of patriotic plaudits. A more inoffensive entertainment could hardly be imagined ; and when the six sections into which the lady had divided her discourse, were exhausted, and her final bow elicited a renewal of the applause that had accompanied her entrance, the impression on the departing visitors must have been that of having spent an hour in company with a well-informed lady who had gone to America, had seen much to admire there, and, coming back, had had over the tea-table the talk of the evening to herself. Whatever the future disquisitions of the Countess of Landsfeld may be, there is little doubt that many will go to hear them for the sake of the peculiar celebrity of the lecturer.

To this, the *Era* reporter naïvely added : " Her foreign accent might belong to any language from Irish to Bavarian." Lola did not have the field entirely to herself. While she was telling the St. James's Hall public how to improve their appearance at very small cost, a rival practitioner, with a *salon* in Bond Street, was, in the advertisement columns of the morning papers, announcing her readiness to furnish the necessary requisites at a very high figure. This was a " Madame Rachel," some of whose dupes parted with as much as five hundred guineas, on the understanding that she would make then " Beautiful for ever ! "

Like Lola Montez, " Madame Rachel " brought out a puff pamphlet, directing attention to her specifics. This production beat the effort of the Rev. Chauncey Burr, for it bristled with references, to the Bible and Shakespeare, to Grace Darling and Florence Nightingale. Among her nostrums was a bottle of " Jordan Water," which she sold at the modest figure of £15 15s. a flask. Chemical analysis, however, revealed it to have come, not from Palestine, but from the River Thames. She also supplied, on extortionate terms, various drugs and " medical treatment " of a description upon which the Law frowns heavily. As a result, " Madame Rachel " left Bond Street for the dock of the Old Bailey, where she was sent to penal servitude for swindling.

In the lecture on " Wits and Women of Paris," Lola did not forget her old friends. She had a good word for Dumas :

" Of the literary lights during my residence in Paris, Alexandre Dumas was the first, as he would be in any city anywhere. He was not only the boon companion of princes, but he was the prince of boon companions. He is now about fifty-five years old, a tall, fine-looking man, with intellect stamped on his brow. Of all the men I ever met he is the most brilliant in conversation. He is always sought for at convivial suppers, and is always sure to attend them."

Discretion, perhaps, prevented her saying anything about Dujarier and the tragedy of his death. Still, she had something to say about Roger de Beauvoir, whom she declared to be " one of the three men that kept Paris alive when I was there." Her recollection of Jules Janin rankled. " He was," she said, " a malicious and caustic critic. Everybody feared him, and everybody was civil to him through fear. I do not know anyone (even his wife) who loves him in Paris." But Eugéne Sue was in another category. " He was an honest, sincere, truth-loving man ; and it will be long before Paris can fill the place which his death has made vacant."

In the " Heroines of History " lecture the audience were told that " All history is full of startling examples of female heroism, proving that woman's heart is made of as stout a stuff and of as brave a metal as that which beats within the ribs of the coarser sex." But, feminist as she was, Lola had no sympathy with any suggestion to grant them the franchise. " Women who get together in conventions for the purpose of ousting men will never," she declared, " accomplish anything. They can effect legislation only by quiet and judicious counsel. These convention women are very poor politicians."

The last lectures in the series dealt with " Comic Aspects of Love," and " Strong-minded Women." Among the typical specimens offered for consideration were such diverse personalities as Semiramis, Queen Elizabeth, the Countess of Derby, George Sand, and Mrs. Bloomer. In the discourse on " The Comic Aspects of Love " the range swept from Aristotle and Plato to Mahomet and the Mormons. If the B.B.C. had been in existence, Lola would undoubtedly have been booked for a " talk." As it was, two of the lectures were reprinted in *The Welcome Guest*, " a magazine of recreative reading for all," with Robert Browning, Charles Kingsley and Monckton Milnes among its contributors. Thinking they had a market, an enterprising publisher rushed out a volume, *The Lectures of Lola Montez*. When a copy reached the editor, it was reviewed in characteristically elephantine fashion by the *Athenæum* :

" We can imagine the untravelled dames of Fifth Avenue listening with wonder to a female lecturer who seems to have lived hand in glove with all the crowned heads of Europe ; and who can tell them, not only Who's-Who, but also repeat their conversations, criticise their personal appearances, and describe the secret arts by which the men preserve their powers and the women their beauty."

CHAPTER XVII

THE CURTAIN FALLS

I

AT the end of the year 1859, Lola, once more a bird of passage, was on the way back to America, taking with her some fresh material for another lecture campaign. This, entitled " John Bull at Home," fell very flat ; and instead of, as hitherto, addressing crowded halls, she now found scanty gatherings wherever she was booked. Even when the charge of admission was reduced from the original figure of a dollar to one of 25 cents, " business " did not improve. Uncle Sam made it obvious that he took no sort of interest in John Bull, either at home or elsewhere.

America, however, was, as it happened, taking a very lively interest in something else just then that did happen to be connected with John Bull's country. This was the visit of the Prince of Wales. It had been announced by an imaginative journalist that H.R.H. was to be " piloted " during his tour by John Camel Heenan, otherwise the " Benicia Boy." It was, however, under the more rigid tutelage of General Bruce that the distinguished guest landed on American shores. Mere prose not being adequate to record the historic incident a laureate set to work :

> He came ! A slender youth and fair !
> A courtly, gentlemanly grace—the Grace of God !
> The tenure of his mother's Throne, and great men's fame
>   Sat like a sparkling jewel on his brow.
> Ah, Albert Edward ! When you homeward sail
> Take back with you, and treasure in your soul
>   A wholesome lesson which you here may learn !

251

While he was in New York a ball in honour of the Prince was given at the Opera House by the " Committee of Welcome." This inspired a second laureate, Edmund Clarence Stedman :

> But as ALBERT EDWARD, young and fair,
> Stood on the canopied dais-chair,
> And looked from the circle crowding there
> To the length and breadth of the outer scene,
> Perhaps he thought of his mother, the QUEEN :
> (Long may her empery be serene !
> Long may the Heir of England prove
> Loyal and tender ; may he pay
> No less allegiance to her love
> Than to the sceptre of her sway !)

The visit of the Prince of Wales was not the only attraction challenging the popularity of Lola Montez at this period. There was another rival, and one in more direct competition with herself. This was Sam Cowell, a music-hall " star " from England. A comedian of genuine talent, he took America by storm with a couple of ballads, " The Rat-Catcher's Daughter " and " Villikins and his Dinah." The public flocked to hear him in their thousands. Lola's lectures fell very flat. Even fresh material and reduced prices failed to serve as a lure. The position was becoming serious.

But, while her manager looked glum when he examined the box-office figures, Lola was not upset, for she had suddenly developed another activity, and one to which she was giving all her attention. This was the occult. The " Voices " at whose bidding she had abandoned the stage a couple of years earlier were now insistent that she should drop the platform ; and, casting in her lot with the " Spirits," get into touch with a mysterious region vaguely referred to as " the Beyond."

It was a time when spiritualism was flourishing like a green bay tree. Mrs. Hayden ("the wife of a respectable journalist ") and the Fox Sisters had been playing their pranks for years and collecting dollars from dupes all over the country ; and their rivals, the Davenport Brothers, with Daniel Dunglas Home (Browning's " Sludge, the Medium ") were hum-

Countess of Landsfeld.   A favourite portrait
(*Harvard Theatre Collection*)

Grave of Lola Montez, in Green-wood Cemetery, New York
(Photo by Miss Ida M. Mellen, New York)

bugging Harvard professors, financial magnates, and Supreme Court judges ; and, not to be behindhand, other experts were (for a cash consideration) calling up Columbus and Shakespeare and Napoleon, who talked to them at séances as readily as if they were at the end of a telephone, but with pronounced American accents.

Lola's first reaction was all that could be desired. There never was a more promising recruit or a more receptive one. Quite prepared to take the " Voices " on trust, and to contribute liberally to the " cause," she attended a number of psychic circles, arranged by Stephen Andrews and other charlatans ; listened to mysterious rappings and tappings coming out of the darkness ; felt inanimate objects being lifted across the room ; heard tambourines rattled by invisible hands ; and unquestionably swallowed all the traditional tomfoolery that appears to be part and parcel of such " phenomena."

This state of things might have continued indefinitely. By, however, an unfortunate mischance, a " medium," from whom much was expected, went, in his endeavour to give satisfaction, a little too far. Not keeping a vigilant eye on European happenings, he announced at one such gathering that the " spirit " addressing the assembly was that of Ludwig of Bavaria. As, however, Ludwig was still in the land of the living (where, by the way, he remained for several years to come) it was a bad slip. The result was, Lola felt her faith shaken, and, convinced that she was being exploited, shut up her purse, and withdrew from the promised " guidance."

II

Under stress of emotion, some women take to the bottle ; others to the Bible. With Lola Montez, however, it was a case of from Bunkum to Boanerges, from the circle to the conventicle. Spiritualism had been tried and found wanting. Casting about for something with which to fill the empty niche and adjust her equilibrium, she turned to religion for consolation. The brand she selected was that favoured by the Methodists. One would scarcely imagine that Little Bethel would have had much appeal to her. But perhaps its very drabness and remoteness from the world of the footlights proved a welcome relief.

Having " got religion," Lola fastened upon it with characteristic fervour. It occupied all her thoughts ; and in the process she soon developed what would now be dubbed a marked inferiority-complex.

" Lord," she wrote at this period, " Thy mercies are great to me. Oh ! how little are they deserved, filthy worm that I am ! Oh ! that the Holy Spirit may fill my soul with prayer ! Lord, have mercy on Thy weary wanderer, and grant me all I beseech of Thee ! Oh ! give me a meek and lowly heart. Amen."

A doctor, had she consulted one just then, would probably have prescribed a blue pill.

There is a theory that the " Light " had been vouchsafed as the result of a chance visit to Spurgeon's Tabernacle when she was last in England. Although Spurgeon himself never put forward any such claim, a diary that Lola kept at the time has a significant entry :

LONDON,
September 10, 1859.

How many, many years of my life have been sacrificed to Satan and my own love of sin ! What have I not been guilty of in thought or deed during these years of wretchedness ! Oh ! I dare not think of the past. What have I not been ! I only lived for my own passions ; and what is there of good even in the best natural human being ! What would I not give to have my terrible and fearful experience given as an awful warning to such natures as my own !

A week later, things not having improved during the interval, she took stock of her position in greater detail :

I am afraid sometimes that I think too well of myself. But let me only look back to the past. Oh ! how I am humbled. . . . How manifold are my sins, and how long in years have I lived a life of evil passions without a check ! To-morrow (the Lord's Day) is the day of peace and happiness. Once it seemed to me anything but a happy day. But now all is wonderfully changed in my heart. . . . This week I have principally sinned through hastiness of temper and uncharitableness of feeling towards my neighbour. Oh ! that I could have only love for others and hatred of myself !

Another passage ran :

To-morrow is Sunday, and I shall go into the poor little humble chapel, and there will I mingle my prayers with the fervent pastor, and with the good and true. There is no pomp or ceremony among these. All is simple. No fine dresses, no worldly display, but the honest Methodist breathes forth a sincere prayer, and I feel much unity of souls.

The " conversion " of Lola Montez was no flash in the pan, or the result of a sudden impulse. It was a real one, deep and sincere and lasting. Her former triumphs on the stage and in the boudoir had become as dust and ashes. Compared with her new-found joy in religion, all else was vanity and emptiness. " I can forget my French and German, and everything else I have valued," she is declared to have said to a pressman, who, scenting a " news story," followed hot-foot on her track, " but I cannot forget my Christ."

She had been " Montez the Magnificent." Now she was " Montez the Magdalen." The woman whose voluptuous beauty and unbridled passion had upset thrones and fired the hearts of men was now concerned with the saving of souls. As such, she resolved to spread " the Word " among others less happily circumstanced. To this end, she preached in conventicles and visited hospitals, asylums, and prisons, offering a helping hand to all who would accept one, and especially to " unfortunates " of her own sex. She had her disappointments. But neither snubs nor setbacks, nor sneers nor jeers could turn her from the path she had elected to tread.

" In the course of a long experience as a Christian minister," says a clergyman whom she encountered at this period, " I do not think I ever saw deeper penitence and humility, more real contrition of soul, and more bitter self-reproach than in this poor woman."

" With," he adds, in an oleaginous little tract on the subject, " a heart full of generous sympathy for the poor outcasts of her own sex, she devoted the last few months of her life to visiting them at the Magdalen Asylum, near New York. . . . She strove to impress upon them not only the awful guilt of breaking the divine law, but the inevitable earthly sorrow which those who persisted with thoughtless desperation in sinful courses were assuredly treasuring up for themselves."

But, except those who encountered her charity and self-sacrifice, there were few who had a good word for Lola Montez in her character as a Magdalen. People who had fawned upon her in the days of her success now jeered and sneered and affected to doubt the reality of her penitence. " Once a sinner, always a sinner," they declared ; and " Lola in the pulpit is rich ! " was another barbed shaft.

In thus abandoning the buskin for the Bible, Lola Montez was following one example and setting another. The example she followed was that of Mlle Gautier, of the Comédie Française, who, after flashing across the horizon of Maurice de Saxe (and several others), left the footlights and retired to a convent. " It is true," she says in her memoirs, " that I have encountered during my theatrical career a number of people whose morals have been as irreproachable as their talents, but I myself was not among them." This was putting it—well—mildly, for, according to Le d'Hoefer, " her stage career was marked by a freedom of manner pushed to the extremity of licence."

In the sisterhood that she joined the new name of Mlle Gautier was Sister Augustine. As such, she lived a Carmelite nun for thirty-two years. But time did not hang heavy on her hands, for, in addition to religious exercises and domestic tasks, she occupied herself with painting miniatures and composing verses. " I am so happy here," she wrote from her cell, " that I much regret having delayed too long entering this holy place. The real calm and peace I have now discovered have made me imagine all my previous life an evil dream."

The example that Lola Montez was setting was to be followed, fifty years later, by another member of her calling. This was Eve Lavalliére, who, after a distinctly hectic career, cut herself adrift from the footlights of Paris and entered the mission-field of North Africa. " Here at your feet," she says in one of her letters, " lies the vilest, lowest, and most contemptible object on earth, a worm from the dung-heap, the most infamous, the most soiled of all creatures. Lord, I am but a poor sheep in your flock ! "

There is also something of a parallel between the career of Lola Montez and that of Theodora, who, once in the circus ring, and, at the start, a lady of decidedly easy virtue, afterwards became the consort of the Emperor Justinian and shared his throne. Like Lola, too, Theodora endeavoured to make amends for her early slips by voluntarily abandoning the pomp and power she had once enjoyed and giving herself up to the redemption of " fallen women."

III

Perhaps the " Spirits " resented being abandoned by her in summary fashion ; perhaps she had overtaxed her energies addressing outdoor meetings in all weathers. At any rate, and whatever the cause, while she was travelling in the country during the winter of 1860, Lola Montez was suddenly stricken down by a mysterious illness. As it baffled the hospital doctors, she had to be taken back to New York. There, instead of getting better, she gradually got worse, developing consumption, followed by partial paralysis.

" What a study for the thoughtless ; what a sermon on the inevitable result of human vanity ! " was the ghoulish comment of a scribbler.

Rufus Blake, an entrepreneur, under whose banner she had once starred, has some reminiscences of her at this period, " She lived," he says, " in strict retirement, reading religious books, and steadily, calmly, hopefully preparing for death, fully convinced that consumption had snapped the pillars of her life and that she was soon to make her final exit."

After an interval, word of Lola's collapse reached England by means of a cutting in a theatrical paper. There it appears to have touched a long slumbering maternal chord. " Mrs. Craigie," says a paragraphist, " suddenly arrived in America, anxious, as next of kin, to secure her daughter's property. On discovering, however, that none existed, she hurried back again, leaving behind her a sum of three pounds for medicine and other necessities."

Cast off by her fair-weather friends, bereft of her looks, poverty-stricken, and ravaged by an insidious illness, the situation of Lola Montez was, during that winter of 1860, one to excite pity among the most severe of judges. Under duress, even her new found trust in Providence began to falter. Was prayer, she wondered forlornly, to fail her like everything else ? Suddenly, however, and when things were at their darkest, a helping hand was offered. One bitter evening, as she sat brooding in the miserable lodging where she had secured temporary shelter, she was visited by a Mrs. Buchanan, claiming her as a friend of the long distant past. The years fell back ; and, with an effort, Lola recognised in the visitor a girl, now a mature matron, whom she had last met in Montrose.

The sympathy of Mrs. Buchanan, shared to the full by her husband, a prosperous merchant, was of a practical description.

Although familiar with the many lapses in Lola's career, they counted for nothing beside the fact that she was in sore need. Bygones were bygones. Insisting that the stricken woman should leave her wretched surroundings, Mrs. Buchanan took her into her own well-appointed house, provided doctors and nurses, and did all that was possible to smooth her path. Deeply religious herself, she soon won back her faltering faith, and summoned a clergyman, the Rev. Dr. Hawks, to prepare her for the inevitable and rapidly approaching end.

A smug little booklet, *The Story of a Penitent : Lola Montez*, published under the auspices of the " Protestant Society for the Promotion of Evangelical Knowledge," was afterwards written by this shepherd. Since his name did not appear on the title page, he was able to make several unctuous references to himself.

" Most acceptable," he says in one characteristic passage, " were his ministrations. Refreshing, too, to his own spirit were his interviews with her."

" It was," he continues, " in the latter part of 1860 that I received a message from the unhappy woman so well known to the public under the name of Lola Montez, earnestly requesting me to visit her and minister to her spiritual wants. She had been stricken down by a paralysis of her left side. For some days she was unconscious, and her death seemed to be at hand. She had, however, rallied, and a most benevolent Christian female, who had been her schoolmate in Scotland in the days of her girlhood, and knew her well, had stepped forward and provided for the temporal comfort of the afflicted companion of her childhood. The real name of Lola Montez was Eliza G., and she was of respectable family in Ireland, where she was born."

But neither the Rev. Mr. Hawks, with his oiliness and smug piety, nor Mrs. Buchanan, with her true womanly sympathy and understanding, could bring Lola Montez back to health, any more than—for all their pills and purges—could the doctors and nurses round her bed. She lay there, day after day, aware of their presence, but unable to move or speak. Yet, able to think. Thoughts crowded upon her in a series of flashing pictures ; a bewildering phantasmagoria, coming out of the shadows, and beckoning to her. Childhood's memories of India ; hot suns, marching men, palanquins and elephants ; Montrose and a dour Calvinism ; Bath and Sir Jasper Nicolls ; love's young dream ; Lieutenant James and the runaway marriage in Dublin ; another experience of India's coral strand ; kind-hearted Captain Craigie and hard-hearted George Lennox ; the Consistory Court proceedings ; fiasco at Her Majesty's Theatre ; Ranelagh and Lumley ; *wanderjahre* and odyssey ; Paris and Dujarier ; Ludwig and the steps of a throne ; passion and poetry ; intrigues and liaisons ; Cornet Heald and Patrick Hull ; voyages from the old world to the new ; mining camps and backwoods ; palaces and conventicles ; glittering triumphs and abject failures. And now, gasping and struggling for breath, the end.

The sands were running out. The days slipped away, and, with them, the last vitality of the woman who had once been so full of life and the joy of living.

The doctors did what they could. But it was very little, for Lola Montez was beyond their help. The end was fast at hand. It came with merciful swiftness. On January 17, 1861, she turned her face to the wall and drew a last shuddering breath.

" I am very tired," she whispered.

The funeral took place two days later. " Accompanied by some of our most respected citizens and their families," says an eye-witness, " the cortège left the house of Mrs. Buchanan for Green-Wood cemetery."

" The Rev. Dr. Hawks," adds a second account, " was constantly at the bedside of Lola Montez, and gave her the benefit of his pastoral care as freely as if she had been a member of his own flock. He conducted her obsequies in an impressive fashion ; and Mr. Brown, his assistant, who had himself attended so many funerals and weddings in his day, was seen to wipe the tears from his eyes, as he heard the reverend gentleman remark to Mrs. Buchanan that he had never met with an example of more genuine penitence."

" Is not this a brand plucked from the burning ? " enquired the Rev. Mr. Hawks, as he stood addressing the company assembled round the grave. He himself was assured that the description was thoroughly applicable to the woman lying there. " I never saw," he declared, " a more humble penitent. When I prayed with her, nothing could exceed the fervour of her devotion ; and never have I had a more watchful and attentive hearer when I read the Scriptures. . . . If ever a repentant soul loathed past sin, I believe hers did."

Possibly, since it could scarcely have been Mrs. Buchanan, it was this clerical busybody who was responsible for the inscription on Lola's headstone :

MRS. ELIZA GILBERT
DIED
JANUARY 17, 1861.

An odd mask under which to shelter the identity of the gifted woman who, given in baptism the names Marie Dolores Eliza Rosanna, had flashed across three continents as Lola Montez, Countess of Landsfeld.

IV

Misrepresented as she had been in her life, Lola Montez was even more misrepresented after her death. The breath was scarcely out of her body, when a flood of cowardly scurrilities was poured from the gutter press. Her good deeds were forgotten ; only her derelictions were remembered.

One such obituary notice began :

" A woman who, in the full light of the nineteenth century,

renewed all the scandals that disgraced the Middle Ages, and, with an audacity that is almost unparalleled, seated herself upon the steps of a throne, is worthy of mention ; if only to show to what extent vice can sometimes triumph, and to what a fall it can eventually come."

An editorial, which was published in one of the New York papers, contained some odd passages :

" Among the most ardent admirers of Lola Montez was a young Scotsman, a member of the illustrious house of Lennox, who was with difficulty restrained by his family from offering her his hand. In London the deceased led a gay life, being courted by the Earl of Malmesbury and other distinguished noblemen. Wherever she went, she was the observed of all observers, conquering the hearts of men of all countries by her beauty and blandishments, and their admiration by her unflinching independence of character and superior intellectual endowments."

The death of Lola Montez did not pass without comment in England. The *Athenæum* necrologist accorded her half a column of obituary, in which she was described as " this pretty, picaroon woman, whose name can never be omitted from any chronicle of Bavaria."

A Grub Street hack, employed by the curiously named *Gentleman's Magazine*, slung together a column of abuse and lies, founded on tap-room gossip :

" When not yet sixteen, she ran away from a school near Cork with a young officer of the Bengal Army, Lieutenant Gilbert (*sic*), who married her and took her to India. In consequence of her bad conduct there, he was soon obliged to send her back to Europe. She first tried the stage as a profession, but, failing at it, she eventually adopted a career of infamy."

A writer in *Temple Bar* has endeavoured, and, on the whole, with fair measure of success, to preserve the balance :

" With more of the good and more of the evil in her composition than in that of most of her sisters, Lola Montez made a wreck of her life by giving reins to the latter ; and she stands out as a prominent example of the impossibility of a woman breaking away from the responsibilities of her sex with any permanent gain, either to herself or to society. Her passionate, enthusiastic and loving nature was her strength which, by fascinating all who came into contact with her, was also her weakness."

Cameron Rogers, writing on " Gay and Gallant Ladies," sums up the career of Lola Montez in deft fashion :

" Thus passed one who has been called the Cleopatra and the Aspasia of the nineteenth century. A very gallant and courageous lady, certainly ; and, though she used her beauty and her mind not in accordance with the Decalogue, yet worthy to be remembered as much for the excellent vigour of the latter as for the perfection of the former. Individual damnation or salvation in such a case as hers are matters of strict opinion ; but for Lola's brief to the last judgment there is an ancient tag that might never be more aptly appended. Like the moral of her life, it is exceedingly trite—*Quia multum amavit*."

This is well put.

V

Even after she was in it, and might, one would think, have been left there in peace, the dead woman was not allowed to rest quietly in her grave. Some years later her mantle was impudently assumed by an alleged actress, who, dubbing herself " Countess of Landsfeld," undertook a lecture tour in America. If she had no other gift, this one certainly had that of imagination. " I was born," she said to a reporter, " in Florence, and my mother, Lola Montez, was really married to the King Ludwig of Bavaria. This marriage was strictly valid, and my mother's title of countess was afterwards conferred on myself. The earliest recollections I have are of being brought up by some nuns in a convent in the Black Forest. But for the help of the good Dr. Döllinger, who assisted me to escape, I should still have been kept there, a victim of political interests."

This nonsense was eagerly swallowed ; and for some time the pseudo-" Countess " attracted a following and reaped a rich harvest. It was not until diplomatic representations were made that her career was checked.

On Christmas Day, 1898, a New York obituary announced the death of a woman, Alice Devereux, the wife of a carpenter in poor circumstances. It further declared that she was the " daughter of the notorious Lola Montez, and may well have been the grand-daughter of Lord Byron." To this it added : " Society has maintained a studious and charitable reserve as to the parentage of Lola Montez. All that is definitely known on the subject is that a fox-hunting Irish squire, Sir Edward Gilbert, was the husband of her mother." Thus is " history " written.

Nor would the " Spirits " leave poor Lola in peace. In the year 1888 a woman " medium," calling herself Madam Anna O'Delia Diss DeBar (but, under pressure, admitting to several *aliases*) claimed to be a daughter of Lola Montez. As such, she conducted a number of séances, and, in return for cash down, evoked the spirit of her alleged mother. Some of the cash was extracted from the pocket of a credulous lawyer, one Luther Marsh. Thinking he had not had fair value for his dollars, he eventually prosecuted Madam for fraud, and had her sent to prison.

She was not disturbed again until the winter of 1929, when an Austrian " medium," Rudi Schneider, with, to adopt the jargon of his craft, a " trance-personality " called Olga (who professed to be an incarnation of Lola Montez), gave some séances in London. The extinguishing of the lights and the wheezing of a gramophone were followed by the usual " manifestations." Thus, curtains flapped, books fell off chairs, tambourines rattled in locked cupboards, and bells jangled, etc. But Lola Montez herself was too bashful to appear. None the less, a number of " scientists " (all un-named) afterwards announced that " everything was very satisfactory."

Thinking that these claims to get into touch with the dead should be subjected to a more adequate test, Mr. Harry Price, director of the National Laboratory of Psychical

Research, arranged for Rudi Schneider to give a sample of his powers to a committee of experts. As a convincing test, Major Hervey de Montmorency (a nephew of the Mr. Francis Leigh with whom Lola had once lived in Paris) suggested that the accomplished " Olga " should be asked the name of his uncle (which was different from his own) and the circumstances under which they had parted. This was done, and " Olga " promised to give full details at the next sitting. But the promise was not kept. " She conveniently shelved every question," says the official report. Altogether, Rudi Schneider's stock fell.

VI

The body of Lola Montez, Countess of Landsfeld, and Canoness of the Order of St. Thérèse, has now been crumbling in the dust of a distant grave, far from her own kith and kindred, for upwards of seventy years. Her name, however, will still be remembered when that of other women who have filled a niche in history will have been forgotten.

Lola Montez was no common adventuress. By her beauty and intelligence and magnetism she weaved a spell on well nigh all who came within her radius. Never any member of her sex quite like this one. Had she been born in the Middle Ages, superstition would have had it that Venus herself was revisiting the haunts of men in fresh guise. But she would then probably have perished at the stake, accused of witchcraft by her political opponents. As it was, even in the year 1848 a sovereign demanded that a professional exorcist should " drive the devil out of her."

To present Lola Montez at her true worth, to adjust the balance between her merits and her demerits, is a difficult task. A woman of a hundred opposing facets ; of rare culture and charm, and of whims and fancies and strange enthusiasms each battling with the other. Thus, by turns tender and callous, hot-tempered and soft-hearted ; childishly simple in some things, and amazingly shrewd in others ; trusting and suspicious ; arrogant and humble, yet supremely indifferent to public opinion ; grateful for kindness and loyal to her friends, but neither forgetting nor forgiving an injury. Men had treated her worse than she had treated them.

For the rest, a flashing, vivid personality, full of resource and high courage, and always meeting hard knocks and buffets with equanimity. Lola Montez had lived every moment of her life. In the course of their career, few women could have cut a wider swath, or one more colourful and glamorous. She had beauty and intelligence much above the average. All the world had been her stage ; and she had played many parts on it. Some of them she had played better than others ; but all of them she had played with distinction. She had boxed the compass as no woman had ever yet boxed it. From adventuress to evangelist ; coryphée, courtesan, and convert, each in turn. At the start a mixture of Cleopatra and Aspasia ; and at the finish a feminine Pelagian. Equally at home in the company of princes and poets and diplomats and demireps, during the twenty years she was before the public she had scaled heights and sunk to depths. Thus, she had queened it in palaces and in camps ; danced in opera houses and acted in booths ; she had bent monarchs and politicians to her will ; she had stood on the steps of a throne, and in the curb of a gutter ; she had known pomp and power, riches and poverty, dazzling successes and abject failures ; she had conducted amours and liaisons and intrigues by the dozen ; she had made history in two hemispheres ; a king had given up his crown for her ; men had lived for her ; and men had died for her.

As with the rest of us, Lola Montez had her faults. Full measure of them. But she also had her virtues. She was gallant and generous and charitable. At the worst, her heart ruled her head ; and if she did many a foolish thing, she never did a mean one.

In the final analysis, when the last balance is struck, this will surely be placed to her credit.

APPENDIX I

EXTRACTS FROM "ARTS OF BEAUTY"
By Madame Lola Montez,
COUNTESS OF LANDSFELD

A Beautiful Face

IF it be true "that the face is the index of the mind," the recipe for a beautiful face must be something that reaches the soul. What can be done for a human face that has a sluggish, sullen, arrogant, angry mind looking out of every feature ? An habitually ill-natured, discontented mind ploughs the face with inevitable marks of its own vice. However well shaped, or however bright its complexion, no such face can ever become really beautiful. If a woman's soul is without cultivation, without taste, without refinement, without the sweetness of a happy mind, not all the mysteries of art can ever make her face beautiful. And, on the other hand, it is impossible to dim the brightness of an elegant and polished intellect. The radiance of a charming mind strikes through all deformity of features, and still asserts its sway over the world of the affections. It has been my privilege to see the most celebrated beauties that shine in all the gilded courts of fashion throughout the world, from St. James's to St. Petersburgh, from Paris to Hindostan, and yet I have found no art which can atone for an unpolished mind, and an unlovely heart. That chastened and delightful activity of soul, that spiritual energy which gives animation, grace, and living light to the animal frame, is, after all, the real source of beauty in a woman. It is *that* which gives eloquence to the language of her eyes, which sends the sweetest vermilion mantling to the cheek, and lights up the whole *personnel* as if her very body thought. That, ladies, is the ensign of beauty, and the herald of charms, which are sure to fill the beholder with answering emotion and irrepressible delight.

Paints and Powders

If Satan has ever had any direct agency in inducing woman to spoil or deform her own beauty, it must have been in tempting her to use *paints* and *enamelling*. Nothing so effectually writes *memento mori !* on the cheek of beauty as this ridiculous and culpable practice. Ladies ought to know that it is a sure spoiler of the skin, and good taste ought to teach them that it is a frightful distorter and deformer of the natural beauty of the " human face divine." The greatest charm of beauty is in the *expression* of a lovely face ; in those divine flashes of joy, and good-nature, and love, which beam in the human countenance. But what expression can there be in a face bedaubed with white paint and enamelled ? No flush of pleasure, no thrill of hope, no light of love can shine through the incrusted mould. Her face is as expressionless as that of a painted mummy. And let no woman imagine that the men do not readily detect this poisonous mask upon the skin. Many a time have I seen a gentleman shrink from saluting a brilliant lady, as though it was a death's head he were compelled to kiss. The secret was that her face and lips were bedaubed with paints.

A violently rouged woman is a disgusting sight. The excessive red on the face gives a coarseness to every feature, and a general fierceness to the countenance, which transforms the elegant lady of fashion into a vulgar harridan. But, in no case, can even *rouge* be used by ladies who have passed the age of life when roses are natural to the cheek. A *rouged* old woman is a horrible sight—a distortion of nature's harmony !

Paints are not only destructive to the skin, but they are ruinous to the health. I have known paralytic affections and premature death to be traced to their use. But alas ! I am afraid that there never was a time when many of the gay and fashionable of my sex did not make themselves both contemptible and ridiculous by this disgusting trick.

Let every woman at once understand that paint can do nothing for the mouth and lips. The advantage gained by the artificial red is a thousand times more than lost by the sure destruction of that delicate charm associated with the idea of " nature's dewy lip." There can be no *dew* on a painted lip. And there is no man who does not shrink back with disgust from the idea of kissing a pair of painted lips. Nor let any woman deceive herself with the idea that the men do not instantly detect paint on the lips.

A Beautiful Bosom

I am aware that this is a subject which must be handled with great delicacy ; but my book would be incomplete without some notice of this " greatest claim of lovely woman." And, besides, it is undoubtedly true that a proper discussion of this subject will seem *peculiar* only to the most vulgar minded of both sexes. If it be true, as the old poet sung, that

" Heaven rests on those two heaving hills of snow,"

why should not a woman be suitably instructed in the right management of such extraordinary charms ?

The first thing to be impressed upon the mind of a lady is that very low-necked dresses are in exceeding bad taste, and are quite sure to leave upon the mind of a gentleman an equivocal idea, to say the least.

A word to the wise on this subject is sufficient. If a young lady has no father, or brother, or husband to direct her taste in this matter, she will do well to sit down and commit the above statement to memory. It is a charm which a woman, who understands herself, will leave not to the public eye of man, but to his imagination. She knows that *modesty* is the divine spell that binds the heart of man to her forever. But my observation has taught me that few women are well informed as to the physical management of this part of their bodies. The bosom, which nature has formed with exquisite symmetry in itself, and admirable adaptation to the parts of the figure to which it is united, is often transformed into a shape, and transplanted to a place which deprives it of its original beauty and harmony with the rest of the person. This deforming metamorphosis is effected by means of stiff stays, or corsets, which force the part out of its natural position, and destroy the natural tension and firmness in which so much of its beauty consists. A young lady should be instructed that she is not to allow even her own hand to press it too roughly. But, above all things, to avoid, especially when young, the constant pressure of such hard substances as whalebone and steel ; for, besides the destruction to beauty, they are liable to produce all the terrible consequences of abscesses and cancers. Even the padding which ladies use to give a full appearance, where there is a deficient bosom, is sure in a little time to entirely destroy all the natural beauty of the parts. As soon as it becomes apparent that the bosom lacks the rounded fullness due to the rest of her form, instead of trying to repair the deficiency with artificial padding, it should be clothed as loosely as possible, so as to avoid the least artificial pressure. Not only its growth is stopped, but its complexion is spoiled by these tricks. Let the growth of this beautiful part be left as unconfined as the young cedar, or as the lily of the field.

BEAUTY OF DEPORTMENT

It is essential that every lady should understand that the most beautiful and well-dressed woman will fail to be *charming* unless all her other attractions are set off with a graceful and fascinating deportment. A pretty face may be seen everywhere, beautiful and gorgeous dresses are common enough, but how seldom do we meet with a really beautiful and enchanting demeanour ! It was this charm of deportment which suggested to the French cardinal the expression of " the native paradise of angels." The first thing to be said on the art of deportment is that what is becoming at one age would be most improper and ridiculous at another. For a young girl, for instance, to sit as grave and stiff as " her grandmother cut in alabaster " would be ridiculous enough, but not so much so, as for an old woman to assume the romping merriment of girlhood. She would deservedly draw only contempt and laughter upon herself.

Indeed a modest mien always makes a woman charming. Modesty is to woman what the mantle of green is to nature—its ornament and highest beauty. What a miracle-working charm there is in a blush—what softness and majesty in natural *simplicity*, without which pomp is contemptible, and elegance itself ungraceful.

There can be no doubt that the highest incitement to love is in modesty. So well do wise women of the world know this, that they take infinite pains to learn to wear the semblance of it, with the same tact, and with the same motive that they array themselves in attractive apparel. They have taken a lesson from Sir Joshua Reynolds, who says : " men are like certain animals who will feed only when there is but little provender, and that got at with difficulty through the bars of a rack ; but refuse to touch it when there is an abundance before them." It is certainly important that all women should understand this ; and it is no more than fair that they should practise upon it, since men always treat them with disingenuous untruthfulness in this matter. Men may amuse themselves with a noisy, loud-laughing, loquacious girl ; it is the quiet, subdued, modest, and seeming bashful deportment which is the one that stands the fairest chance of carrying off their hearts.

APPENDIX II

EXTRACTS FROM "LOLA MONTEZ' LECTURES"

BEAUTIFUL WOMEN

THE last and most difficult office imposed on Psyche was to descend to the lower regions and bring back a portion of Proserpine's beauty in a box. The too inquisitive goddess, impelled by curiosity or perhaps by a desire to add to her own charms, raised the lid, and behold there issued forth—a vapour ! which was all there was of that wondrous beauty.

In attempting to give a definition of beauty, I have painfully felt the force of this classic parable. If I settle upon a standard of beauty in Paris, I find it will not do when I get to Constantinople. Personal qualities, the most opposite imaginable, are each looked upon as beautiful in different countries, and even by different people of the same country. That which is deformity in New York may be beauty in Pekin. At one place the sighing lover sees " Helen " in an Egyptian brow. In China, black teeth, painted eyelids, and plucked eyebrows are beautiful ; and should a woman's feet be large enough to walk upon, their owners are looked upon as monsters of ugliness.

With the modern Greeks and other nations on the shores of the Mediterranean, corpulency is the perfection of form in a woman ; the very attributes which disgust the western European form the highest attractions of an Oriental fair. It was from the common and admired shape of his countrywomen that Reubens, in his pictures, delights in a vulgar and almost odious plumpness. He seems to have no idea of beauty under two hundred pounds. His very Graces are all fat.

Hair is a beautiful ornament of woman, but it has always been a disputed point as to what colour it shall be. I believe that most people nowadays look upon a red head with disfavour—but in the times of Queen Elizabeth it was in fashion. Mary of Scotland, though she had exquisite hair of her own, wore red fronts out of compliment to fashion and the red-headed Queen of England.

That famous beauty, Cleopatra, was red-haired also ; and the Venetian ladies to this day counterfeit yellow hair.

Yellow hair has a higher authority still. The ORDER OF THE GOLDEN FLEECE, instituted by Philip, Duke of Burgundy, was in honour of a frail beauty whose hair was yellow.

So, ladies and gentlemen, this thing of beauty which I come to talk about, has a somewhat migratory and fickle standard of its own. All the lovers of the world will have their own idea of the thing in spite of me.

But where are we to detect this especial source of power ? Often forsooth in a dimple, sometimes beneath the shade of an eyelid or perhaps among the tresses of a little fantastic curl !

I once knew a nobleman who used to try to make himself wise, and to emancipate his heart from its thraldom to a celebrated beauty of the court, by continually repeating to himself : " But it is short-lived," " It won't last—it won't last ! "

Ah, me ! that is too true—it won't last. Beauty has its date, and it is the penalty of nature that girls must fade and become wizened as their grandmothers have done before them.

In teaching a young lady to dress elegantly we must first impress upon her mind that symmetry of figure ought ever to be accompanied by harmony of dress, and that there is a certain propriety in habiliment, adapted to form, complexion, and age. To preserve the health of the human form is the first object of consideration, for without that you can neither maintain its symmetry nor improve its beauty. But the foundation of a just proportion must be laid in infancy. " As the twig is bent the tree's inclined." A light dress, which gives freedom to the functions of life, is indispensable to an unobstructed growth. If the young fibres are uninterrupted by obstacles of art, they will shoot harmoniously into the form which nature drew. The garb of childhood should in all respects be easy—not to impede its movements by ligatures on the chest, the loins, the legs, or the arms. By this liberty we shall see the muscles of the limbs gradually assume the fine swell and insertion which only unconstrained exercise can produce. The chest will sway gracefully on the firmly poised waist, swelling in noble and healthy expanse, and the whole figure will start forward at the blooming age of youth, and early ripen to the maturity of beauty.

The lovely form of women, thus educated, or rather thus left to its natural growth, assumes a variety of charming characters. In one youthful figure, we see the lineaments of a wood nymph, a form slight and elastic in all its parts. The shape :

> " Small by degrees, and beautifully less,
> From the soft bosom to the slender waist ! "

A foot as light as that of her whose flying step scarcely brushed the " unbending corn," and limbs whose agile grace moved in harmony with the curves of her swan-like neck, and the beams of her sparkling eyes.

To repair these ravages, comes the aid of padding to give shape where there is none, stays to compress into form the swelling chaos of flesh, and paints of all hues to rectify the dingy complexion ; but useless are these attempts—for, if dissipation, late hours, immoderation, and carelessness have wrecked the loveliness of female charms, it is not in the power of Esculapius himself to refit the shattered bark, or of the Syrens, with all their songs and wiles, to save its battered sides from the rocks, and make it ride the sea in gallant trim again. The fair lady who cannot so moderate her pursuit of pleasure that the feast, the midnight hour, the dance, shall not recur too frequently, must relinquish the hope of preserving her charms till the time of nature's own decay. After this moderation in the indulgence of pleasure, the next specific for the preservation of beauty which I shall give, is that of gentle and daily exercise in the open air. Nature teaches us, in the gambols and sportiveness of the lower animals, that bodily exertion is necessary for the growth, vigour, and symmetry of the animal frame ; while the too studious scholar and the indolent man of luxury exhibit in themselves the pernicious consequences of the want of exercise.

Many a rich lady would give thousands of dollars for that full rounded arm, and that peach bloom on the cheek, possessed by her kitchen-maid. Well, might she not have had both, by the same amount of exercise and simple living ?

But I weary of this subject of cosmetics, as every woman of sense will at last weary of the use of them. It is a lesson which is sure to come ; but, in the lives of most fashionable ladies, it has small chance of being needed until that unmentionable time, when men shall cease to make baubles and playthings of them. It takes most women two-thirds of their lifetime to discover that men may be amused by, without respecting, them ; and every woman may make up her mind that to be really respected she must possess merit ; she must have accomplishments of mind and heart, and there can be no real beauty without these. If the soul is without cultivation, without refinement, without taste, without the sweetness of affection, not all the mysteries of art can make the face beautiful ; and, on the other hand, it is impossible to dim the brightness of an elegant and polished mind ; its radiance strikes through the encasements of deformity, and asserts its sway over the world of the affections.

GALLANTRY

A history of the beginning of the reign of gallantry would carry us back to the creation of the world ; for I believe that about the first thing that man began to do after he was created, was to make love to woman.

There was no discussion, then, about " woman's rights," or "woman's influence "—woman had whatever her soul desired, and her will was the watchword for battle or peace. Love was as marked a feature in the chivalric character as valour ; and he who understood how to break a lance, and did not understand how to win a lady, was held to be but half a man. He fought to gain her smiles—he lived to be worthy of her love.

In those days, to be " a servant of the ladies " was no mere figure of the imagination—and to be in love was no idle pastime ; but to be profoundly, furiously, almost ridiculously in earnest. In the mind of the cavalier, woman was a being of mystic power. As in the old forests of Germany, she had been listened to like a spirit of the woods, melodious, solemn and oracular. So when chivalry became an institution, the same idea of something supernaturally beautiful in her character threw a shadow over her life, and she was not only loved but revered. And never were men more constant to their fair ladies than in the proudest days of chivalry.

There is no such thing as genuine gallantry either in France or England. In France the relation between the sexes is too fickle, variable, and insincere, for any nearer approach to gallantry than flirtation ; while in England the aristocracy, which is the only class in that country that could have the genuine feeling of gallantry, are turned shop-owners and tradesmen. The Smiths and the Joneses who figure on the signboards have the nobility standing behind them as silent partners. The business habits of the United States and the examples of rapid fortunes in this country have quite turned the head of John Bull, and he is very fast becoming a sharp, thrifty, money-getting Yankee. A business and commercial people have no leisure for the cultivation of that feeling and romance which is the foundation of gallantry. The activities of human nature seek other more practical and more useful channels of excitement. Instead of devoting a life to the worship and service of the fair ladies, they are building telegraphs, railroads, steamboats, constructing schemes of finance, and enlarging the area of practical civilization.

HEROINES OF HISTORY

In attempting to give a definition of strong-minded women, I find it necessary to distinguish between just ideas of strength and what is so considered by the modern woman's rights' movement.

A very estimable woman by the name of Mrs. Bloomer obtained the reputation of being strong-minded by curtailing her skirts six inches, a compliment which certainly excites no envious feeling in my heart ; for I am philosophically puzzled to know how cutting six inches off a woman's dress can possibly add anything to the height of her head.

One or two hundred women getting together in convention and resolving that they are an abused community, and that all the men are great tyrants and rascals, proves plainly enough that they—the women —are somehow discontented, and that they have, perhaps, a certain amount of courage, but I cannot see that it proves them to have any remarkable strength of mind.

Really strong-minded women are not women of words, but of deeds ; not of resolutions, but of actions. History does not teach me that they have ever consumed much time in conventions and in passing resolutions about their rights ; but they have been very prompt to assert their rights, and to defend them too, and to take the consequences of defeat.

Thus all history is full of startling examples of female heroism, which prove that woman's heart is made of as stout a stuff and of as brave a mettle as that which beats within the ribs of the coarser sex. And if we were permitted to descend from this high plane of public history into the private homes of the world, in which sex, think you, should we there find the purest spirit of heroism ? Who suffers sorrow and pain with the most heroism of heart ? Who, in the midst of poverty, neglect and crushing despair, holds on most bravely through the terrible struggle, and never yields even to the fearful demands of necessity until death wrests the last weapon of defence from her hands ? Ah, if all this unwritten heroism of woman could be brought to the light, even man himself would cast his proud wreath of fame at her feet !

Rousseau asserts that " all great revolutions were owing to women." The French Revolution, the last great and stirring event upon which the world looks back, arose, as Burke ill-naturedly expresses it, " amidst the yells and violence of women." We accept the compliment which Burke here pays to the power of woman, and attribute the coarseness of his language to the bitter repugnance which every Englishman of that day had to everything that was French. No, Mr. Burke, it was not by " yells and violence " that the great women of France helped on that mighty revolution—it was by the combined power of intellect and beauty. Nor will women who get together in conventions for the purpose of berating men, ever accomplish anything. They can effect legislation only by quiet and judicious counsel, with such means as control the judgment and the heart of legislators. And the experience of the world has pretty well proved that a man's judgment is pretty easily controlled when his heart is once persuaded.

COMIC ASPECT OF LOVE

My subject to-night is the comic aspect of love. No doubt most of you have had some little experience, at least in the sentimental and sighing side of the tender passion ; and what I propose to do is to give you the humorous or comic side. Perhaps I ought to begin by begging pardon of the ladies for treating so sacred a thing as love in a comic way, or for turning the ludicrous side of so charming a thing as they find love to be, to the gaze of men—but I wish to premise that I shall not so treat sensible or rational love. Of that beautiful feeling, less warm than passion, yet more tender than friendship, I shall not for a moment speak irreverently ; of that pure disinterested affection—as charming as it is reasonable, which one sex feels for the other, I cannot speak lightly. But there is a certain romantic senseless kind of love, such as poets sometimes celebrate, and men and women feign, which is a legitimate target for ridicule. This kind of love is fanciful and foolish; it is not the offspring of the heart, but of the imagination. I know that generous deeds and contempt of death have sometimes covered this folly with a veil. The arts have twined for it a fantastic wreath, and the Muses have decked it with the sweetest flowers: but this makes it none the less ridiculous nor dangerous. Love of this romantic sort is an abstraction much too light and subtle to sustain a tangible existence in the midst of the jostling relations of this busy world. It is a mere bubble thrown to the surface by the passions and fancies of men, and soon breaks by contact with the hard facts of daily life. It is a thing which bears but little handling. The German Wieland, who was a great disciple of love, was of opinion that "its metaphysical effects began with the first sigh, and ended with the first kiss!" Plato was not far out of the way when he called it " a great devil "; and the man or woman who is really possessed of it will find it a very hard one to cast out.

Of the refinements of love the great mass of men can know nothing. The truth is that sentimental love is so much a matter of the imagination that the uncultivated have no natural field for its display. In America you can hardly realise the full force of this truth, because the distinctions of class are happily nearly obliterated. Here intellectual culture seems to be about equally divided among all classes. I suppose it is not singular in this country to find the poorest cobbler, whose little shanty is next to the proud mansion of some millionaire, a man of really more mental attainments than his rich and haughty neighbour; in which case the millionaire will do well to look to it that the cobbler does not make love to his wife; and if he does, nobody need care much, for the millionaire will be quite sure to reciprocate.

The great statute, "tit-for-tat," is, I believe, equally the law of all nations; besides, love is a great leveller of distinction, and it is in this levelling mission that it performs some of its most ridiculous antics. When a rich man's daughter runs off with her father's coachman, as occasionally happens, the whole country is in a roar of laughter about it. There is an innate, popular perception of the ridiculous, but everybody sees and feels that in such cases it is misplaced and grotesque. Everyone perceives that the woman's heart has taken the bit in its mouth, and run away with her brains. But, as comedy is often nearly allied to tragedy, so sorrow is sure to come as soon as the little honeymoon is over. This romantic love cannot flourish in the soil of poverty and want. Indeed, all the stimulants which pride and luxury can administer to it can hardly keep it alive. The rich miss who runs away with a man far beneath her in education and refinement must inevitably awake, after a brief dream, to a state of things which have made her unfortunate for life; and he, poor man, will not be less wretched, unless she has brought him sufficient money to give him leisure and opportunity to indulge his fancies with that society which is on a level with his own tastes and education.

WITS AND WOMEN OF PARIS

The French wits tell a laughable story of an untravelled Englishman who, on landing at Calais, was received by a sulky red-haired hostess, when he instantly wrote down in his note-book : " All French women are sulky and red-haired."

We never heard whether this Englishman afterwards corrected his first impressions of French women, but quite likely he never did, for there is nothing so difficult on earth as for an Englishman to get over first impressions, and especially is this the case in relation to everything in France. An aristocratic Englishman may live years in Paris without really knowing anything about it. In the first place, he goes there with letters of introduction to the Faubourg St. Germain, where he finds only the fossil remains of the old *noblesse*, intermixed with a slight proportion of the actual intelligence of the country, and here he moves round in the stagnant circles of historical France, and it is a wonder if he gets so much as a glimpse of the living progressive Paris. There is nothing on earth, unless it be a three-thousand-year-old mummy, that is so grim and stiff and shrivelled, as the pure old French nobility. France is at present the possessor of three separate and opposing nobilities. First, there is the nobility of the Empire, the Napoleonic nobility, which is based on military and civil genius ; second, there is the Orleans nobility, the family of the late Louis-Philippe, represented in the person of the young Comte de Paris ; third, the Legitimists, or the old aristocracy of the Bourbon stock, represented in the person of Henry V, Duc de Bordeaux, now some fifty years old, and laid snugly away in exile in Italy.

No description which I can give can convey a just idea of the fascination of society among such wits as Dejazet ; and nowhere do you find that kind of society so complete as in Paris. Nowhere else do you find so many women of wit and genius mingling in the assemblies and festive occasions of literary men ; and I may add that in no part of the world is literary society so refined, so brilliant, and charmingly intellectual as in Paris. It is a great contrast to literary society in London or America. Listen to the following confession of Lord Byron : " I have left an assembly filled with all the great names of *haut-ton* in London, and where little but names were to be found, to seek relief from the *ennui* that overpowered me, in a cider cellar ! and have found there more food for speculation than in the vapid circles of glittering dullness I had left."

One of the most remarkable and the most noted persons to be met with in Paris is Madame Dudevant, commonly known as Georges Sand. She is now about fifty years of age (it is no crime to speak of the age of a woman of her genius), a large, masculine, coarse-featured woman, but with fine eyes, and open, easy, frank, and hearty in her manner to friends. To a discerning mind her writings will convey a correct idea of the woman. You meet her everywhere dressed in men's clothes—a custom which she adopts from no mere caprice or waywardness of character, but for the reason that in this garb she is enabled to go where she pleases without exciting curiosity, and seeing and hearing what is most useful and essential for her in writing her books. She is undoubtedly the most masculine mind of France at the present day. Through the folly of her relations she was early married to a fool, but she soon left him in disgust, and afterwards formed a friendship with Jules Sandeau, a novelist and clever critic. It was he who discovered her genius, and first caused her to write. It was the name of this author, Jules Sandeau, that she altered into Georges Sand—a name which she has made immortal.

Georges Sand in company is silent, and except when the conversation touches a sympathetic chord in her nature, little given to demonstration. Then she will talk earnestly on great matters, generally on philosophy or theology, but in vain will you seek to draw her into conversation on the little matters of ordinary chit-chat. She lives in a small circle of friends, where she can say and do as she pleases. Her son is a poor, weak-brained creature, perpetually annoying the whole neighbourhood by beating on a huge drum night and day. She has a daughter married to Chlessindur, the celebrated sculptor, but who resembles but little her talented mother. Madame Georges Sand has had a life of wild storms, with few rays of sunshine to brighten her pathway ; and like most of the reformers of the present day, especially if it is her misfortune to be a woman, is a target to be placed in a conspicuous position, to be shot at by all dark, unenlightened human beings who may have peculiar motives for restraining the progress of mind ; but it is as absurd in this glorious nineteenth century to attempt to destroy freedom of thought and the sovereignty of the individual, as it is to stop the falls of Niagara.

There was a gifted and fashionable lady (the Countess of Agoult), herself an accomplished authoress, concerning whom and Georges Sand a curious story is told. They were great friends, and the celebrated pianist Liszt was the admirer of both. Things went on smoothly for some time, all *couleur de rose*, when one fine day Lizst and Georges Sand disappeared suddenly from Paris, having taken it into their heads to make the tour of Switzerland for the summer together. Great was the indignation of the fair countess at this double desertion ; and when they returned to Paris, Madame d'Agoult went to Georges Sand, and immediately challenged the great writer to a duel, the weapons to be finger-nails, etc. Poor Lizst ran out of the room, and locked himself up in a dark closet till the deadly affray was ended, and then made his body over in charge to a friend, to be preserved, as he said, for the remaining assailant. Madame d'Agoult was married to an old man, a book-worm, who cared for nought else but his library ; he did not know even the number of children he possessed, and so little the old philosopher cared about the matter that when a stranger came to the house, he invariably, at the appearance of the family, said : "Allow me to present to you my wife's children " ; all this with the blandest smile and most contented air.

ROMANISM

I know not that history has anything more wonderful to show than the part which the Catholic Church has borne in the various civilizations of the world.

What a marvellous structure it is, with its hierarchy ranging through long centuries almost from apostolic days to our own ; living side by side with forms of civilisation and uncivilisation, the most diverse and the most contradictory, through all the fifteen hundred years and more of its existence ; asserting an effective control over opinions and institutions ; with its pontificate (as is claimed) dating from the fisherman of Galilee, and still reigning there in the city that heard Saint Peter preach, and whom it saw martyred ; impiously pretending to sit in his chair and to bear his keys ; shaken, exiled, broken again and again by schism, by Lutheran revolts and French revolutions ; yet always righting itself and reasserting a vitality that neither force nor opinion has yet been able to extinguish. Once with its foot on the neck of kings, and having the fate of empires in its hands, and even yet superintending the grandest ecclesiastical mechanism that man ever saw ; ordering fast days and feast days, and regulating with omnipotent fiat the very diet of millions of people ; having countless bands of religious soldiery trained, organized, and officered as such a soldiery never was before nor since ; and backed by an infallibility that defies reason, an inquisition to bend or break the will, and a confessional to unlock all hearts and master the profoundest secrets of all consciences. Such has been the mighty Church of Rome, and there it is still, cast down, to be sure, from what it once was, but not yet destroyed ; perplexed by the variousness and freedom of an intellectual civilisation, which it hates and vainly tries to crush ; laboriously trying to adapt itself to the Europe of the nineteenth century, as it once did to the Europe of the twelfth ; lengthening its cords and strengthening its stakes, enlarging the place of its tent, and stretching forth the curtains of its habitations, even to this Republic of the New World.

The only wonder is that such a church should be able to push its fortunes so far into the centre of modern civilization, with which it can feel no sympathy, and which it only embraces to destroy. I confess I find it difficult to believe that a total lie could administer comfort and aid to so many millions of souls ; and the explanation is. no doubt, that it is all not a total lie ; for even its worse doctrines are founded on certain great truths which are accepted by the common heart of humanity.

There is such a thing as universal truth, and there is such a thing as apostolic succession, made not by edicts, bulls, and church canons, but by an interior life divine and true. But all these Rome has perverted, by hardening the diffusive spirit of truth into so much mechanism cast into a mould in which it has been forcibly kept ; and by getting progressively falser and falser as the world has got older and wiser, till the universality became only another name for a narrow and intolerant sectism, while the infallibility committed itself to absurdity, and which reason turns giddy, and faith has no resource but to shut her eyes ; and the apostolic succession became narrowed down into a mere dynasty of priests and pontiffs. A hierarchy of magicians, saving souls by machinery, opening and shutting the kingdom of heaven by a " sesame " of incantations which it would have been the labour of a lifetime to make so much as intelligible to St. Peter or St. Paul.

Now who shall compute the stupefying and brutalising effects of such a religion ? Who will dare say that a principle which so debases reason is not like bands of iron around the expanding heart and struggling limbs of modern freedom ?

Who will dare tell me that this terrible Church does not lie upon the bosom of the present time like a vast unwieldy and offensive corpse, crushing the life-blood out of the body of modern civilization ? It is not as a religious creed that we are looking at this thing ; it is not for its theological sins that we are here to condemn it ; but it is its effect upon political and social freedom that we are discussing. What must be the ultimate political and social freedom that we are discussing ? What must be the ultimate political night that settles upon a people who are without individuality of opinions and independence of will, and whose brains are made tools of in the hands of a clan or an order ? Look out there into that sad Europe, and see it all ! See, there, how the Catholic element everywhere marks itself with night, and drags the soul, and energies, and freedom of the people backwards and downwards into political and social inaction—into unfathomable quagmires of death !

INDEX